T0381170

Design Thinking

Design Thinking is a set of strategic and creative processes and principles used in the planning and creation of products and solutions to human-centered design problems.

With design and innovation being two key driving principles, this series focuses on, but is not limited to, the following areas and topics:

- User Interface (UI) and User Experience (UX) Design
- Psychology of Design
- Human-Computer Interaction (HCI)
- Ergonomic Design
- Product Development and Management
- Virtual and Mixed Reality (VR/XR)
- User-Centered Built Environments and Smart Homes
- Accessibility, Sustainability and Environmental Design
- Learning and Instructional Design
- Strategy and best practices

This series publishes books aimed at designers, developers, storytellers and problem-solvers in industry to help them understand current developments and best practices at the cutting edge of creativity, to invent new paradigms and solutions, and challenge Creatives to push boundaries to design bigger and better than before.

More information about this series at https://www.apress.com/series/15933

Regenerating Learning

Transforming How You Learn with Generative AI

Patrick Parra Pennefather

Apress®

Regenerating Learning: Transforming How You Learn with Generative AI

Patrick Parra Pennefather
University of British Columbia
Vancouver, Canada

ISBN-13 (pbk): 979-8-8688-1060-2   ISBN-13 (electronic): 979-8-8688-1061-9
https://doi.org/10.1007/979-8-8688-1061-9

Managing Director, Apress Media LLC: Welmoed Spahr
Acquisitions Editor: James Robinson-Prior
Development Editor: Jim Markham
Coordinating Editor: Gryffin Winkler

Cover image designed by eStudioCalamar

Distributed to the book trade worldwide by Springer Science+Business Media New York, 233 Spring Street, 6th Floor, New York, NY 10013. Phone 1-800-SPRINGER, fax (201) 348-4505, e-mail orders-ny@springer-sbm.com, or visit www.springeronline.com. Apress Media, LLC is a California LLC and the sole member (owner) is Springer Science + Business Media Finance Inc (SSBM Finance Inc). SSBM Finance Inc is a **Delaware** corporation.

For information on translations, please e-mail booktranslations@springernature.com; for reprint, paperback, or audio rights, please e-mail bookpermissions@springernature.com.

Apress titles may be purchased in bulk for academic, corporate, or promotional use. eBook versions and licenses are also available for most titles. For more information, reference our Print and eBook Bulk Sales web page at http://www.apress.com/bulk-sales.

Any source code or other supplementary material referenced by the author in this book can be found here: https://www.apress.com/gp/services/source-code.

If disposing of this product, please recycle the paper

Table of Contents

About the Author

Patrick Parra Pennefather is an Associate Professor and Researcher at the University of British Columbia within the Faculty of Arts and the Emerging Media Lab. His research is focused on collaborative learning practices, emerging technology development, research creations, and GraphRAG research and development within the field of machine learning. Patrick also works with learning organizations and technology companies around the world to adopt generative AI strategically within complex and interdependent team environments and designs learning courses that meet the needs of diverse communities to aid the development of the next generation of technology designers and developers.

About the Technical Reviewer

 **Souki Mansoor** is a dynamic force at the intersection of AI, creative direction, and social impact.

As founder of the consultancy Bell & Whistle, she guides leaders and creatives in leveraging generative technology for positive change, working to reshape how we perceive AI in society and our daily lives.

Coming from a rich decade-long background in nonfiction filmmaking, Souki's work has graced Sundance, Tribeca, and TED and can be seen today on Netflix, HBO, and Showtime, with her directorial debut "Firelei Baez" garnering critical acclaim and a Best Director award. A growing voice in the AI community, she's spoken at Cannes Lions on AI in Creativity and DEI, UTA's AI Symposium, USC's School for Cinematic Arts, Runway's AI Film Festival, Hollywood's AI On The Lot, and RealScreen West.

When not playing a friendly neighborhood tech sherpa or falling into generative vortexes, she finds delight in nibbling spoonfuls of cashew butter, learning to pull the perfect espresso shot, and life with her husband Axel and their 63 houseplants.

Acknowledgments

To Dr. Sheinagh Anderson who listened deeply to the content in the book way more often than I expected, added her own thoughts, and provoked me to go deeper on pretty much everything. An accomplished researcher, artist, educator, and spiritual director, Anderson brought up stories that at first did not seem to relate to the content, but later I realized that many of her stories about learning allowed her and I to relate to the idea of all there is to learn interacting with, reading about, and investigating this ecosystem we call generative artificial intelligence. Together and through the writing of this book, we persistently questioned the nature of knowledge, knowing and intelligence, the limits of human knowledge and knowing, what constitutes being creative, historical patterns humanity seems destined to repeat, and how we as humans can free ourselves of patterned behaviors and inherited ways of being.

To my colleagues who are embracing generative AI and wrestling with unknown unknowns when it comes to its use in the work they do every day. Those colleagues are part of intersecting circles of explorers and experimenters. They include instructors, professors, researchers, creatives, community leaders and herders, business professionals, not-for-profit developers and starters, and individuals wrestling with this new technology and as a result radically transforming who they are and what they do.

To Michael Hicks, Souki Mansoor, Darren DeCoursey, Dan Jackson, Walker Rout, and Kris Krüg contributing their voices to this text. They are each mentioned throughout the book, and their voices represent a wide cross-section of industries, each adapting, reconciling, and iterating how they are using generative AI for their own creative workflows. Special thanks to Souki for daring to read this text in an earlier form and providing helpful feedback.

ACKNOWLEDGMENTS

To James Rout, principal consultant at Cognitive Analytics and AI, who has pushed me to develop content, workshops, and recorded videos, making that content palatable and understandable to everyone. This is not an easy task as those deeply involved in developing machine learning tools know well. Hours of conversations, brainstorms, and research have led us to persistently transform what it is that our organization offers, in order to benefit organizations wanting to integrate this technology but not knowing where to begin. Those conversations inspired the book into being what it is now.

To my students past and present who have dared to explore different generative AI tools in the courses I teach and have bravely pushed certain systems to their limits. All of my students have inspired me over the past 20 years to teach differently, iterate on my teaching methods and approaches, and embrace the value of continuous improvement.

Finally, to the humans that have contributed to all the corpora that are out there (including myself). While the authorship of this book assigned to a single human is the convention, in reality it would be more accurate to have et al. beneath my name.

About the Images in This Book

Figure 1. *AI systems deal with obsolescence as much as ink has had to. AI-generated image*

The human-machined images in this book have been extensively edited, using a variety of techniques and workflows, all of which were iteratively denoised by hand-me-down machine learning models on a private computer, not accessing the Internet, and by the time of this printing are likely obsolete. The workflows for the images have been as follows.

First versions of images were all generated using a customized and private machine learning model using OpenClip via ComfyUI on a PC, trained on an LAION-5B dataset.[1] All generated images were birthed from a text prompt and image owned by the author. In addition, some public domain images that were not part of the dataset were sourced and uploaded into the ML model from various repositories[2] focusing on the Xie Yi style of hand brush painting exemplified by Ming Dynasty (1368–1644) artist, Xu Wei—best known for his Xie Yi, or freestyle flower-and-bird paintings. Grapes (1521), by Xu Wei, was accessed via the Palace Museum, Beijing China. Other images that had stylistic features, which inspired the images in this book, were accessed via the Art Institute of Chicago,[3] and all images included a CCO Public Domain Assignation. These include

- Kano Motonobu, "Ink Landscape," hanging scroll, ink on paper, dated roughly 1499–1599 AD

- Xugu, Black Birds, hanging scroll, ink and colors on paper, 1824–1896

- Zhao Mengfu, Horse and Groom in the Wind, in James Cahill, Ge jiang shan se – Hills Beyond A River: Chinese Painting of the Yuan Dynasty, 1279–1368

Source and Accessibility: LAION collects a significant portion of its data from public domain sources and freely available web content. Public domain images are images that are free from copyright restrictions, allowing anyone to use, modify, and distribute them without legal repercussions.

---

[1] https://github.com/mlfoundations/open_clip
[2] https://jenikirbyhistory.getarchive.net/topics/ancient+chinese+art
[3] https://www.artic.edu/collection?is_public_domain=1&page=7

Use of Datasets: Public domain images are often included in LAION's datasets because they can be legally used to train AI models without the need for specific permissions. This accessibility is important for creating large datasets necessary for training models to understand and generate visual content.

Contribution and Permissions: LAION also encourages users to submit images to their datasets. When users submit images, they typically grant LAION permission to include these images in their datasets. These contributions help expand the diversity and quality of the datasets, which is necessary for training AI models that need to understand a wide range of visual concepts.

Ethical Considerations: LAION takes care to ensure that user-submitted images are used ethically. This includes obtaining explicit consent from contributors and making sure that the images do not violate any privacy or copyright laws.

Quality Control: LAION's datasets are curated and often annotated with metadata that helps AI models learn from the images more effectively. This might include labels describing the content of the images, which are needed for supervised learning.

Open Source Ethos: LAION's datasets are generally made available under open source licenses, meaning that they can be freely accessed, used, and modified by researchers, developers, and organizations. This openness is a key part of LAION's mission to democratize AI research and development.

As mentioned in the book, many companies and organizations training generative AI go through various iterations after releasing their prototypes to the public. This is no different than those organizations dedicated to providing a corpus of public domain works for some of those machine learning models to train with. While no not-safe-for-work (NSFW) images were generated using LAION 5B in my own generated image sets, their recent update and the announcement inspired me to run all image prompts through their new downloadable corpus which cleaned their current set of links going to any suspected Child Sexual Abuse Material (CSAM) content.

All images were then highly edited in Affinity, removing backgrounds and unwanted figures, converting to black and white, adding single colors to some images as additional layers, and adding paint splattering effects ("ink and splatter" brushes) to strive for a visual consistency throughout the images used. Some parts of each image were also removed in the process, and over a hundred black and white ink splatter content was generated and added as additional layers to all images. Screenshots of interactions with LLMs and visual models were all created by the author using a combination of Miro, Claude 3.5, Napkin AI, and ChatGPT4o.

Prompt Constraints

The following were eliminated from all prompts:

- Use of the phrase "In the style of," followed by any living artist's name or the name of any artist whose work is copyrighted

- Use of the name of any living artist

- Use of any artist who published work that is not in the public domain

- Any reference to art from the 20th and 21st centuries

- Any art created in the last 100 years; any photos of any art that were taken by living photographers for the past 100 years and/or not deemed public domain

Reverse Image Checking and Generative AI Image Identifiers

Despite the guarantees of "no copyrighted works" that LAION or any other generative AI system claims, to ensure all images were not sourcing from any living artist or copyrighted work, a number of approaches were taken. First, reverse image checks were implemented for all images using Google as it has the largest dataset of images. None of the final images used in the book were discovered using Google image checker. In addition, a total of 250 images that had any degree of likeness (according to Google) were scanned and cross-checked for each image used in the book. Images or parts of an image that resembled a copywritten work were not included in the book and deleted from my hard drive.

All of the images were run through a minimum of two public generative AI image detector machine learning models. To be transparent, they were first tested with a real photo taken by the author to gauge the accuracy of their algorithms. Detectors also rely on a corpus of data but also use proprietary algorithms to detect if an image has been created with generative AI. It's good to test these systems as you would test any other generative AI platform.

Figure 2. *Original photo by author proved to be 91% human using Hugging Face's AI Image Detector*[4]

---

[4] https://huggingface.co/spaces/umm-maybe/AI-image-detector

Images in the book were tested with a minimum of two of the top-rated detectors currently available. This was done to better understand whether or not different machine learning models could detect if the images uploaded were AI generated.

Some provide more detailed analytics like FotoForensics and AI or Not (with paid-for advanced features), including the ability to predict if it's a Midjourney, Stable Diffusion, GAN, or Dall-E 3 image.[5] Because of the level of post-generated editing, scores in Figures 2 and 3 were common, even though some images were drastically altered by me.

Figure 3. *Bull in a China Shop tested with Illuminarty revealed a low probability of 13.8%. AI-generated image*

Figure 4. *The same image tested with Hugging Face's AI Image Detector is likely more accurate with a 75% made with AI probability. AI-generated image*

Human vs AI Probability

Human: 26%   AI: 74%

Figure 5. *The same image used with Content at Scale AI Image Detection revealed a close similarity to Hugging Face's detector at 74% human created*

Preface

Welcome to the brand-new wake-up call that is generative AI. For some, the technology is right by their bedside jolting them from peaceful sleep at 5am, provoking them to take action, learn about it, and unravel the mystery of how to integrate it within the work that they do. For others, it is a faint alarm sound heard at a distance, not even in their home, like a car alarm audible from two blocks away. Some more established AI researchers, developers, creatives, and companies are not aware of any alarm as they have been working creatively with the technology for a long time. Early developers of the technology, however, are sounding the alarm now in Oppenheimeresque tones and rhythms. No matter what you hear or the headline that captures your attention for about 12 seconds of your busy day, the annoying sound is persistent and is not really going away anytime soon no matter how much you may try and ignore it, take a break from it, or block it out. In the hurricane of alarm and adoption, this technology is inadvertently proposing a perfect storm of learning around its edges. In the eye of the hurricane, development teams of all sizes and value are busy in the labs crafting tools that they believe might solve human problems of all kinds. Extending the metaphor, as we move outward, we have creatives and organizations rethinking how this technology might solve a human problem, challenge established ways of learning and working, or provoke new forms of creation and artistic expression. As the hurricane hits our situational contexts, our work, and our homes, the tech blows around the messy and very human phenomena, like bias and lies, that we already know exist. That's OK because we are protected from it, in an underground shelter we have made for the big day. The perfect storm of learning provoked by generative AI is not just about learning how to use the technology to change human patterns of work and life. The technologies are reorienting how we think we learn, what we learn, what we need to learn, when and where we learn about knowledge production, how humans communicate with each other, and the economic, social, political, creative, ethical, and technological factors that inform how we navigate human-influenced existence on this planet.

Narrow AI

In case you don't already know, generative AI is not that new of a technology, but it is an evolution of the development of machine learning models or systems that have been developed for over 60 years. Its development is also tied to the development of the computer. Generative AI that you might have played with, like ChatGPT or Midjourney, are considered narrow AI which have been designed for specific tasks like generating text or images. These dominantly open source systems have recently received neural steroids and a GAN facelift and are increasingly being developed privately for investors and more public consumption. Generative AI platforms have experienced increased investment to make the tech more accessible and profitable, with global use estimates of 250 million users in 2023, doubling from its use in 2020 and continuing to be adopted.[6] For some sobering context to balance the hype or fear, that's less than 5% of a global population of about 8 billion estimated back in 2020.

That doesn't mean we are not affected by other narrow AI. As of 2024, there are approximately 5.16 billion active social media users worldwide, making up about 59% of the global population. Facebook remains the largest social media platform with over 3.15 billion monthly active users, representing approximately 39% of the global population. YouTube is

---

[6] https://www.statista.com/forecasts/1449844/ai-tool-users-worldwide #statisticContainer

the second most popular platform with over 2.5 billion active users, accounting for about 31% of the global population. Instagram is the fourth largest platform with more than 2 billion users, which is roughly 25% of the world's population. TikTok has rapidly grown to surpass 1 billion active users, representing around 13% of the global population.

While your mind has likely drifted with all the stats, this is important information to know. Why? All of these platforms leverage AI algorithms to make recommendations of other consumable content based on your interactions within each platform and with other humans (or cats) on those platforms. At times, user patterns are also analyzed to inform development teams as to what new features they might develop, and in what has become the norm, to target users with specific advertising content that the companies can profit from. The excellent book *How to Build Your Social Media Policy*[7] (translated from the French) is worth a read for those who want to go deeper. As will be discussed in Chapter 12, many humans are also susceptible to algorithmic collusion, a new era of price fixing indirectly facilitated by third-party companies with industries like real estate and gasoline. Poetically, and in homage to David Bowie, algorithms are putting out the fire with gasoline.

Like other technologies before it, some humans in privileged contexts with sufficient means to access generative AI platforms are being asked to integrate it in our work, teaching and learning, reconcile its use individually based on many ethical dilemmas that surface from that use, and magically make our work more "efficient." Is this technology a little bit different than other technologies that have promised to make human work easier, better, or automated? Who should be worried about being replaced in the work we currently do, when you have CEOs, wannabe thought leaders, futurists, and social media influencers constantly posting

---

[7] Pelletier, E., Dubois, D., & Poirier, K. (2011). Comment bâtir votre politique d'utilisation des médias sociaux. Éditions Y. Blais.

about the coming of even "smarter" and more "human" AI (AGI)? What do we need to know in case of its adoption in our work environments? Do we need to pay closer attention to that faint alarm sound? What do we do with all these statistics meant to forecast adoption while selling promises?

What have you learned about AI and where has that knowledge come from?

Artificial Puffery

You've heard the hype. AI is going to replace jobs. AI is revolutionizing how we work, making everything more efficient. It is surpassing human "intelligence" and will eventually have the capacity to act independently from a human operator. In case you didn't know, narrow AI systems have been spying on you for a while now. Not in the traditional surveillance tracking methods already established in certain city centers internationally, but in a more inconspicuous and annoying way, observing your search engine patterns and targeting you with ads accordingly. Public perception influenced by media portals has, over time, and thanks to box office hits like *Terminator* and others, persuaded many humans that AI is a technology that will also become sentient, control us, and take over all human work because all our tasks, creativity, and efforts can be automated. Beware of the large language models. They'll take your job. Beware of generative AI, as it plunders and extracts all knowledge, with or without permission or compensation. Worse is the seemingly incessant puffery, those promotional statements and exaggerations that make broad, boastful, or subjective claims about a sentient AI without providing factual evidence. Puffery is often used in advertising and marketing, but can appear in various forms of communication as hyperbole, propaganda, and sensationalism. Vague predictions are difficult to prove or disprove. Vague predictions are the lifeblood of spreading the use of generative AI. Let's see how an LLM deals with that last statement when prompted (or in the case below, provoked) to be vague in its own description.

VagueBot: Vague predictions sort of serve as a kind of cornerstone of AI because they perchance allow for a wide range of interpretations and polyphonic adaptability in various contexts. By not being overly unambiguous, these predictions can accommodate a multitude of unpredictable outcomes, making AI systems appear sort of more flexible and maybe even insightful. This broad applicability helps AI maintain a suspect amount of relevance across diverse scenarios, more or less guaranteeing that its outputs can be seen as somewhat useful or occasionally accurate, regardless of the specifics. Consequently, the inherent ambiguity in such predictions contributes to the perception of AI as kind of a powerful and versatile tool, capable of maybe providing randomly valuable insights in an array of situations. So, in the future, AI might kind of continue to sort of evolve in ways that could be seen as pretty significant or maybe just kind of interesting or at the very least not trivial.

Misnomers, Context, and Semantics

For some more tangible background, the term machine learning emerged in the 1950s. It was introduced by Arthur Samuel, an American developer in computer gaming and artificial intelligence. Samuel is credited with defining machine learning in 1959 as a field of study that enables computers to learn without being explicitly programmed. On the surface, we can make sense as to what that means. We might translate Samuel's thoughts and likely summarize him incompletely by concluding that a computer learns without being programmed. If you start to repeat that sentence over and over, then go research if that's possible, and deepen your understanding of code, you will realize the irrationality of that statement. More specifically, a developer might say, "the software application is programmed to complete tasks and use logic to complete some other tasks without having to be always prompted to take on those tasks." You might even rip a coder away from their computer screen for 60 seconds and ask how they might actually say it: "the software is provided a means through which to determine (and replicate) patterns provided in the input, without explicit logic operating over the input domain (patterns often completely incomprehensible for humans to model)."[8] If the very idea of intelligence regarding AI makes you feel stupid, you're not alone; at least you don't have to pass the Turing Test. Wrapping our heads around the language of how this technology actually works is an important step toward its broader acceptance and usefulness. Tasking our LLM VagueBot to define intelligence when it comes to AI leads us to an interesting proclamation to take to heart.

VagueBot: The thing about intelligence in AI is that it's not entirely clear-cut; it sort of varies depending on the context and the specific applications. Sometimes, it's about being able to kind of solve problems or maybe recognize patterns, while other times it might be about sort of interacting with humans in a way that feels kind of natural or intuitive, I guess. So, overall, intelligence in AI is this nebulous concept that can mean different things in different situations, and it's all sort of about how we perceive the capabilities and behaviors of these systems in a kind of broad and maybe ever-evolving way.

AI or the debatable misnomer, artificial intelligence, is an umbrella term under which LLMs like ChatGPT and other probabilistic automated machines fall under. Machine learning models have been called intelligent because of their ability to perform complex tasks that would typically require human-like analysis and decision-making. The nuance is in how different people with different worldviews define "human-like." The word intelligence is also a very human-centric one that places its intelligence above any other sentient being's intelligence. AI has the word "intelligence" embedded within it, because of the correlation that

---

[8] Walker Rout. Discord exchange, 2024.

it mimics human cognitive processes by analyzing large amounts of data, identifies patterns using statistical methods like probability (estimating the likelihood of events) and regression (finding relationships between different pieces of information), and creates new content or making guesses about future trends, behaviors, or outcomes based on those patterns. This ability to "learn" from data and generate results that appear to be based on understanding is why it's often referred to as "intelligent."

The seeming simplicity espoused by Alan Turing's seminal paper, "Computing Machinery and Intelligence"[9] (1950), a foundational text in the field of artificial intelligence, will trigger your inner semiotician. Turing's approach to defining intelligence is referred to as pragmatic, emphasizing that instead of attempting to pin down a precise definition of intelligence, we should consider whether a machine can perform tasks or exhibit behaviors that would be considered intelligent if performed by a human. This operational definition sidesteps philosophical debates about the nature of intelligence and focuses on practical criteria that can be tested and observed. Why the sidestep shuffle? Turing was not interested in philosophizing about the nature of intelligence likely to avoid controversy, in an attempt to advance the field, to establish testable criterion for machine intelligence, to avoid highly abstract debates, and likely to not slow down the progress of his work. Historically, the many debates on what constitutes machine intelligence have continued to this day.

"Can machines think?", asked Turing. What is your question?

Despite the logic that AI is difficult to equate to human intelligence, as AI does not possess consciousness, non-simulated self-awareness, human creativity, emotional or spiritual intelligence, to combat the misunderstanding that gets communicated about the technology by

---

[9] Turing, A.M. (1950). Computing Machinery and Intelligence. Mind, 59, 433–460. https://doi.org/10.1093/mind/LIX.236.433

tech companies with intentions that cannot be separated from capitalist structures, we need to come up with our own definitions of intelligence. Doing so will help counter the sensationalism around AI "replacing," "outperforming," and making decisions better than humans can.[10] Disregarding the artificial part of the acronym, which has become more of a habit than you might think, is another risk in falsely comparing machine intelligence to be the equivalent of human intelligence. Can some narrow AI outperform humans in data analysis? Yes, foundational machine learning models can identify patterns in unstructured data very quickly if they are in a specific readable format and therefore will compute faster than the median human can. Capturing outliers or data that doesn't fit a pattern the AI looks for, however, is a very human task. Reasoning what the implications of the data that we analyze are, and having that inform what actions to take based on that analysis, is also dependent on the features that define us differently, and less precisely, as differently human.

The Habit of Anthropomorphizing

Humans are fantastic at anthropomorphizing though. The tendency to anthropomorphize AI, or imbue it with human characteristics, stems from several factors. Research shows that when machines behave in ways that resemble human behavior, users feel more comfortable and connected. Assigning human characteristics to AI makes complex technology easier to understand. Anthropomorphizing AI can create an emotional bond between the user and the machine, enhancing user experience and satisfaction. This is especially evident in AI companions or virtual assistants, where human-like traits might engender trust and empathy.[11]

---

[10] Souki Mansoor, interview, 2024.

[11] Inie, N., Druga, S., Zukerman, P., & Bender, E. M. (2024). From "AI" to Probabilistic Automation: How Does Anthropomorphization of Technical Systems Descriptions Influence Trust?. arXiv preprint arXiv:2404.16047.

Popular culture, through science fiction and media, has long portrayed AI as human-like entities. All these narratives, myths, memes, and tropes shape public perception and expectations, making it almost presumptive to attribute human characteristics to AI. Designers and researchers who imbue human traits onto AI have inherited old misnomers. Researchers often use terms typically associated with human skills and capacities when referring to AIs, emphasizing the supposed similarities between humans and machines. In the witty repartee that is "Artificial Intelligence Meets Natural Stupidity," McDermott points out the misuse of words, even labeling them "wishful mnemonics" by researchers and programmers. Words now taken for granted, like "learning" and "intelligence," were established in 1976, where AI emerged as a more robust field of practice.[12]

How do we explain the tendency to humanize AI among experts who should be well aware of AI's non-human nature?

Arleen Salles and others attempt to answer that exact question in their more recent article.[13] The research and design of machine learning models has evolved, fragmented, and spun off into hundreds of different directions and applications, so it's easy to get confused by the language of learning and intelligence the inventors themselves persistently proclaim their systems to have.

Does it really matter if we anthropomorphize our chatbots? Does it help some humans learn new skills or knowledge?

---

[12] McDermott, D. 1976. Artificial intelligence meets natural stupidity. Acm Sigart Bulletin 57: 4. doi:10.1145/1045339.1045340.

[13] Salles, A., Evers, K., & Farisco, M. (2020). Anthropomorphism in AI. AJOB neuroscience, 11(2), 88–95.

Layered Cake of Learning

The story that is less told about the influence that generative AI has is its potential impact on anybody learning anything, anywhere. We are not talking about learning in a formal context like a school or university, although snail-pace integration, exhaustive debates, hundreds of guidelines, and outright resistances are all evolving in those environments as well. When we hear stories about education being disrupted by generative AI, they tend to be about how LLMs will support, augment, transform, or disrupt formal places of learning and established ways of teaching. The narrative seems to be less driven by learning outside of school, which all of us do for some of the time that we spend on the planet. This is why the technology is different than previous technologies that have come before. Generative AI, AI, and machine learning's impact on learning is a layered phenomenon. While we learn how to use it, we also have the potential to learn the social, cultural, creative, economic, and techno-centric realities that form its ecosystem.

Ever since we have been confronted with one of Frankenstein's monsters (GPT) with a difficult-to-understand acronym, inundated by news media portals, techno-linguists, and glib CEO marketeers, we have a number of responses, all of them valid. No matter what the response is, there's rich learning to be had. Let's say you completely resist the technology and have no interest in using it for whatever reason. Feeling that way or by making social comments about it to that end, you are still teaching and learning about resistance. You might have even dug in your heels as a researcher to validate those reasons and wish to share them. With resistance, there is great learning. Understanding why you resist might be applicable to just artificial intelligence, or it might be more broadly interesting for you to conduct inquiry upon the nature of technological resistance.

You might also be feeling like many companies and individuals out there that you're missing out on something special if you don't jump on the wave of adoption. Why is that? What is the root of your fear of missing out? Where's that come from? Why do you have it?

What exactly do you think you're missing?

Whom the Book Is For

We have been well behaved and dominantly passive learning bots overall in the historical patterning of our learning. We have followed the ten commandments of teachers past and adhered to what we have been told is the right way to learn and even what we should learn to be able to function in some type of idealized society. Each of us has reconciled this in our own way, quit, struggled, succeeded, and survived with our own scars to show for it. The focus of this book is to propose how generative AI might be influencing how, what, when, where, and why we learn while at work. In this way, the book is for anyone who learns, who can access generative AI technologies, and who is driven to rethink how they learn. It isn't just for those who call themselves students enrolled in academic programs nor for the teachers who instruct them. The book is more than learning about how to use generative AI. There are plenty of online tutorials and how-to books and blog posts for that. Instead, the book proposes a method of learning that is not as established, where you explore and interact with the technology to discover how you learn and explore new ways of learning. We leverage the inherent features and implied interactions that occur with generative AI in order to provoke you to dive deeper into how you've been programmed to learn. Learning with generative AI, you equally discover and learn about how you operate. That includes the choice to unlearn and how to change the patterns of learning you find yourself embedded within. The technology empowers you to reimagine and reinvent how you learn while doing your work. Just like you can regenerate content persistently using generative AI systems, so too can you regenerate what and how you learn.

Transforming Society and Learning with AI Is a Historical Pattern

Proclamations about technology's revolutionary power by people like Thomas Edison, have been made about previous technological innovations and their role in society and learning. Edison's 1922 quote, "the motion picture is destined to revolutionize our educational system and that in a few years it will supplant largely, if not entirely, the use of textbooks,"[14] has been cited hundreds of times across the educational technology literature. It is worth overusing. The predominant use of this quote is to reveal what many new generations of technology "evangelists" proclaim—that a new technological development like [insert technology here] will "revolutionize," "save," "alter," and "radicalize" education. Think of any technology and chances are a proclamation about its potential to radically transform education and society has been made. As Cuban (1986),[15] professor of education at Stanford, argued, the cycle of adoption begins with a number of broad promises that tend to be supported by company-sponsored research. This time, though, it is wild west different and much more direct. Assertions about the value of integrating generative

---

[14] Oppenheimer, T. (2007). The flickering mind: Saving education from the false promise of technology. Random House.

[15] Cuban, L. (1986). Teachers and machines: The classroom use of technology since 1920. Teachers college press.

AI in life and work are not always backed by research. Those that are tend to make assertions on small populations. Many assertions are survey based and engage in that sidestep shuffle when it comes to encouraging philosophical debates around those assertions. Other replacement theories are presented to us as evangelical certainties by CEOs with heartstrings wrenched by rapacious investors and shareholders.

> *Not now, we are assured, but Terminator's coming for you and your job soon.*

False Equivalencies and the Importance of Suspicious Curiosity

Embedded in the evangelizing and fearmongering of this technology is the persistent false equivalence that you will often encounter when people say AI intelligence outperforms human intelligence. The argument that artificial intelligence outperforms human intelligence is a type of sophism, or fallacious argument, misleadingly equating two different forms of intelligence.

The false equivalence has already led us down the path of reasoning that not only will AI replace us, it will also get rid of us. The result of these proclamations is fuel for each of us and the organizations we are a part of to learn about the technology and do so quickly. Only then can we accurately weigh the pros and cons of adopting or resisting it and/or understanding how it can be truly useful. Being like the suspiciously curious raccoon is a more helpful anthropomorphization to help navigate the pandemic of puffery that comes with the territory of AI, to help us distinguish between genuine advancements and exaggerated hype in how we understand, speak of, and use the technology. An open curiosity to integrating generative AI and being critical and discerning as to what we learn when interacting with it is an approach that will help us decipher how it might actually benefit each of us.

The Gap This Book Fills

This book fills a large gap that is ever widening. Content in the book addresses the need for workers in any industry to take responsibility for learning how to best use generative AI systems in their unique contexts. Some chapters will at the very least prepare you to inform and guide the small team you are a part of or influence leadership to navigate the territory of leveraging generative AI systems responsibly. Other chapters that follow provide you, employee, creative, and knowledge worker, who are currently working on a team or work independently within your own company or a larger organization, with the necessary information, knowledge, and processes for you to prepare for a generative AI–integrated workplace. There are different approaches we all have toward learning something new at work. It takes a combination of curiosity and good mentors to guide us through that process and, as much as they can, help us to understand if we have the capacity to learn whatever subject and apply it to everyday work.

Figure 6. *Suspiciously curious raccoon weighing the pros and cons of using generative AI at work. AI-generated image*

If not, then maybe we weren't wired for it. The same applies to using AI responsibly. Many of us are not programmed to learn all there is to know about it in order to use it in our work environments. At the same time, we don't need to understand all of the mechanics of how generative AI systems function in order to use one for our own purposes, especially if we regard it as a tool in our toolbox that might be able to solve some creative challenges or problems we might be having.

Besides pointing to all the more obvious benefits of learning how to use generative AI systems more effectively, the content in this book provides use cases, research, and educational theory to propose that interacting with the technology leads to a number of unanticipated learning outcomes. These outcomes challenge the very way in which we have come to learn, what we have learned, and what we may need to unlearn.

As generative AI becomes increasingly integrated within workplace environments at some point or other, we will each reach a critical point of having to decide if we are going to use the technology and how. Many of us, however, will not have a choice. Similar to what Richard Baldwin, an economist and professor at the Geneva Graduate Institute in Switzerland, stated during a panel at the 2023 World Economic Forum's Growth Summit, AI will not replace your job, but someone who knows how to use the technology and provide value to an organization just might one day.[16] At the time of publication, the quote seems antiquated, as some jobs are being replaced and creatives are facing the reality of having to integrate generative AI within what they do to remain competitive.

While perhaps more concentrated learning has been historically associated with an institution, the roots of teaching and learning are always fundamentally grounded in each of us and the world we interact with daily. The increasing number of accessible public generative AI tools creates an opportunity to learn anytime and anyplace, reinforcing that the center of learning is wherever you are, and whatever you need in the moment to learn to solve problems, pick up a new skill, to augment your own working process and the tasks you need to accomplish what you need.

Your capacity to improve how you learn with generative AI is dependent on whether or not you see its value. For those of you who wish to extend your knowledge of how you learn, it takes a little effort. Once

---

[16] https://www.weforum.org/agenda/2023/05/growth-summit-2023-heres-a-recap-of-what-just-happened/

you start the process, however, you will be able to take advantage of all the generative AI tools out there in order to support your transformed and iterative learning process and, with persistent effort and attention, your potential influence on transforming your workplace.

Figure 7. *Office workers in a tug of war with an AI represented as a small robot. Hundreds of iterations. Prompting challenges with the term "tug of war." AI-generated image*

A Critical Tug of War with Narrow AI

As we begin to understand what these powerful machine learning models can do, we also engage in reflective activities that make us critically question the nature of intelligence, creativity, value, work, artistic processes, data, power, ownership, knowledge, copyright, bias, untruths, energy, and more. Beyond what we can learn by using any generative AI in our work, perhaps unintentionally, we also learn about what it means to be a human engaged in human-guided technologically augmented processes by machines that might be better regarded without human attributes. The use of anthropomorphizing language significantly contributes to the hype and fear associated with AI. Authors of a recent thought-provoking paper argue that this practice is problematic because it obscures the negative consequences associated with AI use. When we employ personified language to describe AI systems, we inadvertently attribute human-like qualities to these technologies. This not only makes AI appear more powerful and capable than it actually is but also distracts from and minimizes the potential adverse effects of its deployment.

Consequently, this linguistic approach can lead to a skewed perception of AI, manifesting unrealistic expectations and overlooking critical ethical and practical issues.[17] Building on Inie et al.'s reference to AI as probabilistic automation systems, I extend that definition to generative AI as probabilistic automated compute machines (PacMacs). With these powerful systems, we learn about our own worldview and how that informs our use of the technology. We learn in many cases to relearn, and in other cases we have no choice but to take this technology on due to extrinsic motivators. We come to a new definition of what it means to be human in light of the technology that we might reluctantly accept to

---

[17] Inie, N., Druga, S., Zukerman, P., & Bender, E. M. (2024). From "AI" to Probabilistic Automation: How Does Anthropomorphization of Technical Systems Descriptions Influence Trust?. arXiv preprint arXiv:2404.16047.

learn how to use or litigiously reject. For those daring math, acronyms, and deeper learning, we also have the opportunity to learn about how the technology works under the hood and how we can customize our own private, open source machine learning models to retain control over our creations, content, and data.

Humans have constantly wrestled with the value of technologies in their lives, including those that may or may not support how we learn. Technologies interject. They interrupt the patterns of teaching and learning we've accepted are right for us. AI is pressing us to look at how we learn…anything. It is making us rethink what we know and also what we think we know about how we learn and how others learn.

However biased, however untrue some of the content might be that they generate, we can still learn something from any generative AI. One advantage that they have is how they might actually be able to support us in some of the work we undertake. Our workflows or the methods and processes we are used to in getting work done always involve some element of learning.

What emerging role will generative AI play in that process?

Figure 8. *PacMac spewing out content from its corpus with an occasional gem. AI-generated image*

In coming to grips with how public generative AI fits into our own unique learning process, we have the opportunity to leverage the technology anytime, anywhere. They might not help with certain tasks at all. On the other hand, they might be extremely useful with other tasks. The story of the Zen master Hakuin whose student was challenged to make a choice is worth reflecting on.

In ancient Japan, there was a Zen master named Hakuin who was revered for his teachings. One day, a student came to him with a dilemma. The student said, "Master, I stand at a crossroads in my life. One road is familiar and comfortable, while the other is unknown and daunting. How do I choose the right path?"

Master Hakuin took the student to a nearby river where two boats were tied to the shore. One boat was old and rickety but still afloat, while the other was new and sturdy. He said, "These boats represent the paths you speak of. The old boat may seem like a safer choice because it is familiar, but it may not take you far. The new boat, though untested, holds the potential for a longer journey."

The student looked at the boats and then at the master. "But Master, what if the new boat sinks?"

Hakuin smiled and replied, "In life, there are no guarantees. The unknown path may present challenges, but it also offers opportunities for growth and discovery. The familiar path, while safe, may limit your potential. To grow, you must be willing to embrace uncertainty and trust in your ability to navigate it."

When it comes to using generative AI at work, in addition to learning from interacting with the technology, we have an opportunity to position ourselves on a spectrum of full acceptance or full rejection of the technology.

How can we know where we stand unless we try the technology out?

What happens to the world of work around us if we do not?

What happens to the world of work around us if we do?

Chapter Breakdown and Overview

There's so much to learn about generative AI and how the way that it works is impacting all of us. There's no tangible order to the content needed to support the theme of learning. Instead, we can use visual metaphors to support our learning journey.

Breaking Down the Book with Visual Metaphors

There have been dozens of visual metaphors to describe how we learn and especially with different technologies. According to educational theorists Lakoff and Johnson,[18] metaphors are not just linguistic expressions but fundamental to human thought. They help us understand and communicate abstract ideas by relating them to more familiar, concrete experiences. Metaphors shape our perceptions and influence educational practices, policies, and how we come to think how people learn.

---

[18] Lakoff, G., & Johnson, M. (1980). Metaphors We Live By. University of Chicago Press.

An Iceberg of Learning

A good image that comes to mind to explain all the learning possible with generative AI and simultaneously provide a structure for the book is an iceberg. Think of the parts of an iceberg seen and unseen that make for a good metaphor, rather than AI being like the familiar iceberg that sinks the innocent passengers of a luxury liner. Traditionally, the iceberg model has been used in psychology, organizational behavior, business, and design thinking. Inspired by its more positive interpretation in the field of design thinking, the visible part of the iceberg reveals the more obvious learning that occurs with generative AI systems. You learn about how to use a tool incrementally deepening your knowledge. As you do so, you realize that maybe the best way to learn is to use a number of them in sequence and even automating part of that process. You most likely can figure out pretty quickly how the tech can help you because you are somewhat aware of your own working process. You learn quickly that in order to use generative AI at work you have to understand the guidelines or policies that your organization has in place. If they don't have any, then you realize that you cannot use the tool to generate content or share company content until that is resolved. You may further understand that you will need to learn how to integrate the technology securely, and finally you may come to the conclusion that the company will need some type of road map on how it will be used over time.

Getting Under the Water

Once you go beneath the surface of the iceberg, an entire ecosystem of learning awaits you that is triggered the moment you begin your interactions with it. Relearning how to learn is what you will begin to understand is necessary in order to not only take advantage of the technology but learn how that technology can transform your organization into a learning ecosystem. The chapters that follow assume that you are your best teacher. That means you can start reading the book in whatever order you see fit. For some readers, much of the knowledge contained in some chapters may already affirm their own beliefs, or epistemologies, around how people learn. Other research is drawn from a rich history of how different technologies have transformed learning and also what scholars have thought about the role of any technological media in different historical times. Accompanying every chapter is at least one resource: a research paper, web article, or book that expands on some of the ideas that are introduced.

Chapter Overviews

Positioning generative AI as part of a continuum of learning with technology, the Introduction first challenges the way we think about learning, rescuing it from our patterned past. It then discusses experiential learning and proposes that there is an ecosystem of learning offered to us when we interact with any generative AI. What we learn from AI is layered and meaningful in today's world.

Figure 9. *An iceberg model describes what you learn with generative AI on the surface and how the technology can let you go deeper to transform how you and your organization learns. AI-generated image*

Chapter 1: Ready Yourself to Learn from AI

This chapter emphasizes that to maximize learning with generative AI, you must "empty your cup" and let go of your preconceptions about learning. Embracing the unknown territory of AI involves relearning and unlearning past learning methods. Being ready to learn from AI means understanding its technology, history, and impact and weighing its pros and cons. That includes coming to the learning with no expectations and retelling your own learning stories to position learning from AI as a point of transformation.

Chapter 2: Reprogram Your Learning Patterns

This chapter proposes that to benefit from generative AI, you first need to look at and transform established patterns of teaching and learning and the roles teachers and learners play within them. You inevitably reprogram how you learn by questioning how you came to learn in the first place. Your attitudes about learning have shaped how you learn, so you need to better understand yourself, if you are going to shift the way you learn. Do you look down on school based on your experience of it? Has that affected your interest or desire to learn? Have you been called stupid? Have you, like most of us, failed at something and made fun of for it or felt lesser than somebody else? AI won't transform how you learn or what you learn on its own. When you interact with any generative AI system, your entire learning experience is navigated by you. Your tolerance, your patience, your curiosity, your persistence in getting the content and the knowledge out of any generative AI, while understanding its limitations, is how you will get the most out of the technology.

Chapter 3: Regulate Your Own Learning

This chapter challenges you to look to your own established methods of learning, challenging ideas of the "sage," "expert," and singular source of knowledge. The chapter details different types of teaching and learning interactions and draws from research to discuss their effectiveness. Generative AI is proposed as a solution to disrupt normative patterns of teaching and learning and how you come to think of intelligence. You are encouraged to identify your own patterns of teaching and critically evaluate them with a proposed design thinking tool.

Chapter 4: Relearn While Working

This chapter discusses the concept of "interruptive learning" in modern work environments, where interruptions are reframed as opportunities for staying knowledgeable and adaptable and improving your craft. It highlights the role of generative AI tools in supporting task completion and integrating learning during work. The chapter emphasizes the need for sufficient training time to effectively use these tools and the potential shift in organizational expectations for self-directed learning. It also explores mapping learning moments within workflows and differentiating between AI that accelerates interruptions and AI that replaces parts of the workflow.

Chapter 5: Design What You Need to Learn

The chapter introduces the concept of the "researcher/designer" persona, which helps set objectives and plot out the overall learning experience. It highlights the importance of human-centered design, considering personal learning environments, motivations, goals, and the impact on the surrounding environment and others involved in the learning process. You will be given tools that learning designers use in order to help guide you to design learning for yourself and others.

Chapter 6: Reenergize Doing

This chapter explores the potential of generative AI to facilitate learning and the practical application of knowledge. It underscores the necessity of active engagement and experimentation when using these tools, acknowledging that generative AI, such as LLMs, cannot replace the nuanced understanding required for task completion. The chapter emphasizes that while LLMs can serve as valuable starting points for generating knowledge, they lack the contextual awareness and specific insights necessary for fully personalized tasks. It empowers people at work to focus on applying generative AI tools while working on projects and proposes that organizations support workers in connecting individual and teamwork through documentation of that process.

Chapter 7: Reassess with Gen AI

This chapter proposes that it is premature to make generalizations about the efficiency of generative AI, including LLMs, in workplace environments. Current assessments rely on personal, contextual, and task-specific stories rather than comprehensive surveys. There are many unknowns regarding how AI will improve work, what that improvement means, and how it will be measured. While assessment tools can evaluate learning specific generative AI technologies, true insights come from applying these technologies to workflows. Each individual must develop their own criteria for assessing the effectiveness of AI tools by asking relevant questions about their application to their work processes. The development of assessment criteria and testing knowledge can be supported by an LLM.

Chapter 8: Adapt with AI

This chapter discusses how generative AI supports your need to adapt what you do and how you learn. The evolution of generative AI, from text-based systems to multimodal models capable of generating text, images, code, and soon video, shows how the technology has grown in response to user demands. Established software environments have integrated generative AI, transforming workflows. Creative professionals adept at adapting to new technologies can leverage AI to explore new possibilities and innovate. The chapter emphasizes viewing work as a continuous process, embracing failure, disrupting patterns, allowing for spontaneous adaptation, finding rest, and learning from AI's unexpected outputs.

Chapter 9: Prototype Learning

This chapter focuses on the craft of prototyping when engaging with generative AI. Prototyping involves evolving an initial idea through various stages into a developed prototype, a process that mirrors interactions with generative AI. Generative AI never reaches a final version, continually adapting based on user feedback. Engaging with AI teaches you about the prototyping process and how to manage and refine generated content, positioning you as curator and knowledge creator. Each interaction with AI creates a unique prototypical relationship, where generated content serves as raw material for experimentation and refinement. This ongoing, co-creative process highlights the value of generative AI in providing rough drafts and variations that you can develop further.

Chapter 10: Reiterate Your Learning

This chapter emphasizes the importance of iterative learning when using generative AI tools. To integrate AI effectively into learning processes, you will benefit from investing time in understanding how to use the tools, including mastering prompts, altering parameters, and leveraging different AI systems multimodally. Developing a relationship with AI through testing and experimentation helps identify what works best for your needs. Generative AI offers a path to personalize your learning by invoking a more critical connection with the technology. This iterative process not only supports learning outcomes but also cultivates critical thinking and discernment by understanding the limitations and potential of AI tools.

Chapter 11: Reconcile Using Generative AI

This chapter is split into three interconnected sections. Each explores the need to reconcile various factors when using generative AI. Adopting a stance of "suspicious curiosity" allows you to explore AI's potential benefits while remaining aware of its implications. Despite the mixed perceptions and ethical concerns surrounding AI, it is important to see the value of the technology for your specific use cases and weigh its pros and cons. This helps you address challenges and resistances that may arise, especially in professional settings. The chapter also highlights the significance of understanding and possibly adopting ethically developed and open source AI models, encouraging investigation into future-use technologies even if they are not immediately being used.

Chapter 12: Remember the Algorithms

This chapter emphasizes the importance of understanding algorithms when interacting with any AI. By learning about algorithms, you can better comprehend how they impact your work and daily life. This knowledge allows you to rethink what algorithms are, their purposes within AI, and how they drive the development and competitive applications that influence anyone contributing to the Internet or consuming its content. Algorithms embedded in machine learning models identify patterns and make predictions, affecting human activities and how knowledge is analyzed and used, regardless of prediction accuracy.

Chapter 13: Continuously Learn with AI

This chapter emphasizes the importance of continuous learning when interacting with AI systems, including generative AI models. It highlights how these interactions can activate an ecosystem of learning that activate your roles as a teacher, researcher, and learner. The chapter underscores that knowledge is infinite and that AI introduces new tools and strategies into your work, requiring you to relearn how to work rather than simply making tasks more efficient. It discusses the iterative process of learning, implementation, and feedback, where you refine and edit AI-generated content and test methods for efficiency. This continuous cycle of learning and adaptation ensures that generative AI becomes a valuable tool for ongoing professional development.

Chapter 14: Build Your Teaching Bots

This chapter highlights the increasing control users have over customizing chatbots powered by advanced generative AI models. These chatbots, now more responsive and capable of nuanced conversations, can be customized to specific knowledge domains through uploaded documents. Users can guide a bot's responses and even influence their emotional tone, making interactions feel more human-like. The evolution of generative AI allows users to build and personalize their own teaching bots to meet specific learning needs, enhancing the ability to complete tasks or expand knowledge. The key to this customization lies in understanding the personas users want their bots to embody.

Chapter 15: Reinvent Reinforcement

This chapter introduces reinforcement learning in education, focusing on the concept of reinforcement as a process of creating a strong foundation for embodied learning. The chapter illustrates how true learning involves fully supporting and practicing skills until they become second nature. Generative AI can extend cognitive abilities by providing vast, instant knowledge that complements what you already know. While AI can offer foundational knowledge, true mastery still requires practically applying the technology to solve your particular challenges. The chapter underscores the importance of building on the knowledge provided by AI to achieve deep, embodied learning, as a starting point.

Chapter 16: Learn with Other Bots

This chapter highlights the importance of learning with and from others, emphasizing that collaborative knowledge building expands both personal and organizational growth. In the context of AI, this collaborative learning is important due to the technology's rapid evolution. Learning generative AI alongside others creates the possibility for an exchange of knowledge, accelerating both the learning process and the practical application of skills newly acquired. Engaging in a community of practice allows individuals to benefit from each other's experiences and innovations, making the learning journey more effective and enriching.

Chapter 17: Transform Your Organization

This chapter emphasizes the importance of organizational learning and the need for companies to rethink the value of learning in the context of integrating generative AI. While previous chapters focused on individual creative activities, this chapter highlights the steep learning curve leaders face when implementing AI to transform processes. Leads will need to understand their internal workings, policies, and the varying levels of acceptance and resistance among employees. Key strategies include clarifying AI policies, providing comprehensive onboarding and support, and ensuring ongoing research to keep up with rapidly changing platforms. Teams must align on security, privacy, biases, data sovereignty, and the implications of using public vs. private machine learning models. Effective integration of generative AI requires persistent support, feedback milestones, and a clear understanding of emerging third-party services and frameworks.

Chapter 18: Reclaim Your Creative Content

This chapter emphasizes the importance of taking control over the narrative of the content you create when interacting with generative AI. It highlights the distinct value of human-created content, exemplified by the need for human creativity in comedic scripts and performances. The creative process, honed over years of training and iterative work, holds intrinsic value beyond the final product. In a future corpus-driven economy, rethinking and organizing your content as valuable data is urgent. This perspective doesn't diminish your own artistic essence, but acknowledges the commodification of content-hungry machine learning models. By claiming and valuing your content and the creative process, you safeguard your work's authenticity and significance in a capitalist-driven market.

Chapter 19: Disentangle the Hype

This chapter is dedicated to different forms of puffery, that rhetorical habit of making exaggerated, boastful claims without substantial evidence. It reveals some common themes in order to unravel what we tend to hear about AI. Hyperbole, sensationalism, and other forms of rhetoric are amplified by key figures in the generative AI space, as if their status and success with their company means we should really listen to them as futurist prophets. By disentangling the hype, you can make more grounded decisions regarding how you will come to use it.

Chapter 20: Inconclusive Intelligence

This chapter explores the profound questions of intelligence and creativity when interacting with generative AI. As we engage with AI, we are prompted to reconsider what it means to be intelligent, a concept historically reserved for humans. An LLM simulates intelligence, challenging our definitions and perceptions of how we come to define it. The anthropomorphic tendency to attribute human-like intelligence to AI is not new, predating computers. The development of cognitive science has long been intertwined with computer technology, using the brain-computer metaphor to understand human cognition. This analogy has shaped both theoretical and practical advancements in AI, emphasizing the ongoing dialogue between understanding the brain and attempts to simulate brain functions through the logic machines that are deemed "intelligent."

Introduction

One day, a teacher gathered all their students outside of the classroom under a tree and promptly left the circle but not before saying: "Teach each other what you know about trees."

Figure 10. *Learning about trees together. AI-generated image*

On first reading, you might (just like the students) likely be thinking: "What a terrible teacher. What kind of teacher prompts their students to teach one another?" To understand the impulse of the teacher is to get a glimpse of the reality of learning that has been facilitated for centuries. The purposeful use of the term facilitate will seem different to many. Teachers that facilitate students how to teach themselves are preparing them for the so-called "real" world—a world they will transition into where they are going to have to do that continuously and persistently, if they are to thrive. This isn't a new idea. The theme appears as far back as the *Tao Te Ching*, written sometime between the sixth and fourth centuries BCE.

In a quiet village nestled between lush mountains and serene rivers, there lived a revered sage named Laozi. Known for his profound wisdom and gentle demeanour, he was often sought out by people from all walks of life, seeking guidance and understanding.

One day, a young man named Liang approached Laozi, eager to learn the secrets of wisdom and enlightenment. "Master," Liang asked, "how can I become wise and enlightened like you?" Laozi smiled kindly and replied, "Come with me, and I will show you." For the next few weeks, Laozi and Liang worked side by side, performing simple tasks like tending to the garden, drawing water from the well, and sweeping the pathways. Laozi rarely spoke of profound truths or gave direct teachings. Instead, he shared stories of nature, observed the changing seasons, and listened to the sounds of the world around them.

At first, Liang was perplexed. He had expected profound lessons and direct answers. But as time passed, he began to notice the subtle beauty in the mundane, the harmony in simplicity, and the wisdom in stillness. He realized that the teachings were all around him, in every moment and every task.

One evening, as they sat by the river, watching the sun set, Liang turned to Laozi and said, "Master, I understand now. Wisdom is not something to be given or taken. It is to be discovered within oneself, in the quiet moments of life." Laozi nodded, his eyes twinkling with satisfaction. "You have found the true path, Liang. The best teachers are those whose presence is felt but not seen, whose guidance is experienced but not imposed. In this way, the student learns to trust their own insight and inner strength."

Figure 11. *Laozi and Liang. AI-generated image*

Finding your own way, rather than having that way imposed upon you, is a key approach to learning with and from generative AI. That approach, however, is dependent on how you have been conditioned to learn and think about how knowledge is applied to anything you do. Very few organizations are facilitating exactly which gen AI tool you should learn or why. If you have exercised the dependency muscle in your learning process, you're not alone. This is a pattern of learning we need to recognize and challenge, a spoon-feeding pattern that emerges when we use any generative AI. On the surface, using a tool like Gemini or Bing seems easy and doesn't ask of you very much. However, to really get something useful out of an LLM or any generative AI, you need to deepen your understanding of prompting, specific to each platform. You also need to understand that generating content is only the beginning of a longer journey that involves you adapting to what you need to learn, as the need to learn how to do something specific is the result of you applying a tool to help you with a task.

How Humans Might Have Learned

Learning how to use generative AI is like learning how you've learned anything else, no?

Well, not exactly. Along with the affordances the technology offers, there exists a dump truck full of constraints. The constraints challenge us to relook at how we learn, what we think about knowledge, and provoke us to make the necessary adjustments. If we say an ML model learns, then we need to question what learning is, because humans learn very differently.

What does learning mean to you?

To decipher the patterns of learning you've embodied since you've been schooled, it's a good idea to research how humans might have learned over time and passed on these methods, generation after generation. We can easily proclaim that everybody learns something all the time, to a lesser or greater degree. By examining how knowledge has been transmitted across generations, we can gain a deeper appreciation for the continuity and changes in educational practices. This exploration might reveal that many of the methods we take for granted today are rooted in ancient traditions and have been adapted to fit modern contexts. If we were to simply interact with an LLM and all the prompts were written out for us just to select, providing a single response that was the same every time, we would likely be following a pattern of passive learning that has been as dominant as a course textbook written in stone.

We Learn Continuously

No matter who you are, where you are, or what you do, it is in your genes to learn continuously. Learning is a continuous process that occurs throughout our lives, influenced by various factors, including personal experiences, social interactions, and cultural practices. Recognizing the omnipresence of learning can help us appreciate its complexity and the myriad ways in which it manifests. Whether through formal education, informal interactions, or self-directed exploration, learning is an integral part of human existence. By acknowledging this, we can better understand the types of learning patterns we've adopted, reflect on why that was, and be in a position to shift or change those patterns when we interact with generative AI.

Paintings in Caves?

We can look to early documented paintings on walls that may also have served as instruction. We have had to learn continuously and more than just to survive, but to thrive. Around 100,000 years ago, the crafting of tools and creation of ochres and shells at Blombos Cave in Africa indicate that early modern humans were accessing previously undocumented cognitive abilities. Studies focused on investigating cave and rock art, found globally, reveal a significant example of symbolic thought. While ancient cave paintings showcased cultural practices, had ritual significance, and demonstrated an impulse to capture social activities, they also reveal technique, social organization, weapons, and strategy when depicting humans hunting animals in motion in the Lascaux caves in France, which date back approximately 17,000 years, Cueva de las Manos in Argentina (13,000 years ago), and Tassili n'Ajjer in Algeria (12,000 years ago).

Do these paintings suggest an impulse to pass on traditions, to teach those who come later, to point back to origin stories for next generations?

If this is the case, then our first documented history of learning is in a visual representation that had meaning for early human cultures. We can at best guess that cave drawings may have supported the passing on of oral traditions. We are not sure if they represented the capturing of oral knowledge or simply supported stories that were of importance to those cultures. Regardless of their intent back when they were created, we are able to learn something now from looking at them and investigating what they were all about. One common theme in their modern interpretations is that many cave paintings told stories.

What are your stories of trying to integrate generative AI in your work?

The Importance of Telling Stories

Storytelling is an important part of many early traditions and directly connected to how people learn—even more emphatically, how to learn to be better humans.[19] Stories have been passed down from generation to generation through established oral traditions with a long history of transmitting knowledge in this way. This may be one reason to account why learning by listening to another person has been a dominant way in which many people still learn. Like the technology of the wall paintings that have been uncovered, humans have also been communicating and capturing knowledge through different visual media and whatever technology is available and accessible to them.

---

[19] Lawrence, R. L., & Paige, D. S. (2016). What our ancestors knew: Teaching and learning through storytelling. New Directions for Adult and Continuing Education, 149(Spring), 63–72.

Figure 12. *Ancient cave drawing in process imagined by an AI, including hunting, symbols, and unexpcected technologies. AI-generated image*

In ancient Egypt and Mesopotamia, learning through hieroglyphs, cuneiform, and other visual forms were the means through which knowledge was passed. Scribes and artisans learned through hands-on apprenticeships and the study of documented records. In ancient Greece, the Socratic method, introduced by Socrates, was a method that involved teaching through dialogue and questioning rather than lecturing, showing early evidence of a more interactive way to learn. Monastic and cathedral schools in the Middle Ages had students hand copy texts and manuscripts as a way to have them embody the words themselves. In those same times, we see the emergence of vocational training in guilds and apprenticeships where apprentices learned trades and crafts by working alongside a master crafts person.[20] In many crafts traditions, this is still one of the most effective ways to learn.

Books, plays, the blackboard, social interactions, whiteboards, digital whiteboards, multimedia, computers, all manner of contraptions, the Internet, social media, interactive media, generative AI, and all simulations, online courses, virtual reality, and mixed reality are all linked together by how we share knowledge as interconnected human cultures. The technology of the day is leveraged in order to find new ways to share that knowledge and in some cases pass on know-how through practice, achieving skills and competencies in the interactions we have with those technologies.

This constant evolution of learning tools reflects our ongoing quest to improve how we understand, retain, and communicate information. As each new technology emerges, it builds on what came before, but doesn't necessarily replace it, creating a through line of approaches to learning that can accommodate the different learning styles and needs of different types of humans.

---

[20] Wollschlager, N., & Reuter-Kumpmann, H. (2004). From Divergence to Convergence: A History of Vocational Education and Training in Europe. European journal: vocational training, 32, 6–17.

Defining Teaching and Technology

Because we have been interacting with different technologies to learn about the world and ourselves since time immemorial, it would benefit us to take a step back and define what learning and technology mean to us, if we are to understand how technology has informed learning for centuries, how it continues to do so, and the social, political, and economic influence of the technologies we are oftentimes tasked to use.

One definition of learning can be broadly defined as the impulse to acquire knowledge, skills, attitudes, behaviors, competencies, and habits that enable an individual to survive in current situations, to adapt to new situations, and solve problems effectively. Learning in this definition and in how it is contextualized in this book is not limited to formal classroom settings but occurs throughout life, from childhood to adulthood, in various contexts.

When it comes to defining technologies and their role in learning, historically they have always been instrumental in transforming how we learn. Before associating technology with something reliant on electricity to function, think of the invention of the pencil, which helped democratize writing and, combined with paper, allowed humans to document what they learned or share what they knew. The printing press accelerated the dissemination of knowledge and extended the shelf life of human knowledge, while the chalkboard allowed for communal learning and created a collaborative environment for the exchange of ideas in different settings. Each technological innovation shifted the paradigm of how knowledge and know-how were communicated and accessed and how they demanded an interaction to take advantage of their benefits. A learning environment of today is robust and full and can include computers running different applications (not only generative AI), mobile devices, whiteboards, even chalkboards, desks, tables, chairs, and, yes, even pencils, paper, and crayons. That doesn't just depict a typical university classroom, it also describes what many modern workplace environments look like.

What's (Not So) Different with Gen AI?

We could say that learning has evolved significantly over time, driven by technological advancements that have transformed the way we acquire knowledge, process information, and engage with the world around us. From the quill pen of the poet to the digital pencil of the designer, technologies have played a critical role in shaping the learning experience across disciplines and cultures. Each technology has had its purpose(s) and along with them their pros and cons in terms of their ability to support learning. Each technology has also been accompanied by those who support and those who resist and anywhere in between. We can also say that no matter the technology, learning hasn't changed that much. The methods used to teach have been persistently passive with some more interactive ways having been introduced in the last 50 years. There are likely more people who would say they experienced a lecture about a subject than those who had a group conversation about a particular subject so that they could relate it to their own lives. Fewer still that might have applied what they learned to a use case. Even less who learned a specific craft they can apply to the real world. Technology does not solve the problem of learning passively, which has been a dominant pattern for a long time. In fact, it often reinforces passive learning, and AI-generated content can certainly be seen as an extension of that impulse.

Every time a technology comes into the realm of learning, eventually a posse of humans claim it as an intervention, a panacea, something that will transform the learning experience itself. There is some truth there. There is also research that argues for or against emerging technologies and how they inform learning. What we can at least all agree on is that different technologies have different affordances that allow humans to learn in different ways. One of the most significant shifts in how we learn has been the transition from traditional forms of instruction, such as lectures, classrooms, and textbooks, to more interactive and personalized approaches that leverage technology to increase active engagement, collaboration, and creativity. The use of digital tools within physical and virtual classrooms, such as multimedia presentations, simulations, games, and social media platforms, has expanded the possibilities for learning beyond the classroom walls, making it more accessible and interactive.

Generative AI is a technological innovation that can either reinforce older methods of receiving knowledge passively or, when used in more engaging and creative ways, can support a way of learning that places the responsibility of the learning process on the learner themselves. On the one hand, as with previous technologies, many institutions see the technology as a means to an end. The common question asked might be: "How will it support the teaching that I already do?" This has been the dominant way in which different technologies have been introduced into formal educational environments. It's the same at work.

How can Dall-E 3 or Gemini support the work I already do?

On the other hand, generative AI systems offer us the opportunity to refine educational content to address the unique ways in which each of us learn, offering methods to personalize learning. Gen AI technologies shift the center of knowledge from the teacher to the learner, who is tasked to take command of their own learning process.

It doesn't have to be either or, though. You can generate content with an LLM as the beginning of an idea that sparks you to conduct more research, then edit the text significantly. That might open you up to new possibilities the technology affords you that you might not have considered.

Turtle Robots, Holes in the Wall, and PLATO

A glimpse of what is possible with generative AI systems today has its earliest incarnation more than 50 years ago with different educators and researchers offering a more interactive, learner-centered education. In the mid-1960s, one team, led by Seymour Papert, a mathematician who had collaborated with Jean Piaget in Geneva known for his theories on cognitive development of children, moved to the United States and cofounded the MIT Artificial Intelligence Laboratory alongside Marvin Minsky. Papert collaborated with a team from Bolt, Beranek, and Newman, led by Wallace Feurzeig, to develop the first version of Logo in 1967.[21] Logo emphasized learning through making and exploration, empowering students to take control of their own learning environment, creating and troubleshooting programs that directed the movements of a turtle robot. Papert was likely inspired by PLATO, which laid the foundation for future educational technologies, in particular, modern learning management systems (LMS) and elearning platforms. What we now take for granted in LMS, like interactive lessons, multimedia content, online communication, and personalized assessment, originated from PLATO.[22]

The 1980s and 1990s introduced intelligent tutoring systems (ITS) and expert systems, designed to provide personalized instruction and feedback. These systems, although not perfect, used AI to adapt to individual learning needs.[23] In the 1990s, the rise of the Internet further transformed education, with pioneers like Sugata Mitra demonstrating the power of self-organized learning environments (SOLEs) through his "Hole in the Wall" experiments. Mitra and his team placed a computer in a wall in a poorer area in New Delhi. The computer was installed at a height accessible to children and was connected to the Internet. Importantly, there were no instructions given to the children on how to use the

---

[21] Solomon, C., Harvey, B., Kahn, K., Lieberman, H., Miller, M. L., Minsky, M., ... & Silverman, B. (2020). History of logo. Proceedings of the ACM on Programming Languages, 4(HOPL), 1–66.

[22] Cope, B., & Kalantzis, M. (2021). A Little History of e-Learning.

[23] Sleeman, D., & Brown, J. S. (1982). Intelligent tutoring systems (p. 345). London: Academic Press.

computer, and no teachers or adults were present to guide them. The experiment showed that children who had no previous experience with computers or the Internet quickly figured out how to use the computer. They taught themselves how to browse, play games, and even learn basic English and math.[24]

The 2000s saw the development of online learning platforms like Khan Academy, founded by Salman Khan, which provided students worldwide with free, accessible educational resources. More recently, advancements in AI with Coursera have personalized learning experiences, allowing students to customize their own learning journeys.

Despite numerous technological advances in education that place the responsibility of learning on the learner, there remains a strong preference for traditional and passive methods. This enduring association between knowledge and its passive receptivity through listening is likely rooted in the deep cultural and historical ties to oral learning, which have been a primary mode of knowledge sharing across various cultures throughout human history. Even though dozens of different options to learning have shown numerous benefits toward knowledge retention, we don't really know why passive reception of knowledge has remained so ubiquitous.[25]

---

[24] Mitra, S., & Judge, P. (2004). The hole in the wall. Dataquest India.

[25] Khalaf, B. K., & Mohammed Zin, Z. B. (2018). Traditional and inquiry-based learning pedagogy: A systematic critical review. International Journal of Instruction, 11(4), 545–564.

Figure 13. *Intelligent tutoring systems were another technology that gave us a precursor as to how to use a generative AI chatbot. AI-generated image*

INTRODUCTION

The upheld traditional model of learning defines the teacher as the primary knowledge source, and students are passive recipients who engage actively in the learning process only when prompted by the teacher, where the knowledge conveyed is often presented as unchallengeable. Research indicates that even with the availability of interactive and digital learning tools, many learners still gravitate toward teacher-led instruction because it aligns with long-standing educational norms and expectations. For example, a study highlighted that traditional teaching methods, where the teacher is the primary source of knowledge, remain prevalent and are often viewed as more authoritative and reliable compared to newer, learner-driven approaches.[26] Old school practices are also associated with degree requirements, and these requirements influence the credentials that are prized by many students and reinforced by educational systems. Even today, educators and researchers argue that while self-directed learning experiments demonstrate potential, they may not be a substitute for more formal and facilitated educational experiences, particularly in areas requiring structured and guided instruction.

The integration of intensely powerful computation machines combined with this invention called the Internet has offered humans a gradual shift away from the lecturer as be-all-end-all source of knowledge. Knowledge, no matter who or what generates it, is no longer unchallengeable. The idea of gathering together communally to learn with others remotely has also been offered as an alternative to meeting in a physical classroom. Learning management systems (LMS) and platforms like Coursera or Khan Academy embodied the transformation of remote learning into a global, communal experience. Social platforms, including those that allow humans to represent themselves as virtual avatars, have also provided us with taking knowledge in, in more compelling ways.

---

[26] Silverstone, S., Phadungtin, J., & Buchanan, J. (2009). Technologies to Support Effective Learning and Teaching in the 21st Century. In Advanced Technologies. IntechOpen.

The recent pandemic forced each of us to learn at a distance from one another in our own homes, and while we literally became talking heads in boxes, platforms like Zoom offered us ways to interact that were not just repeating methods of passive engagement. Tools like Miro offered us real opportunities to collaborate on infinite whiteboards with all kinds of brainstorming and visual mapping tools.

A potentially limitless and exhausting history of technological interventions in educational environments reveals that any tech can reinforce the familiar oral lecture as the source around which we gather to absorb knowledge, in addition to also providing us with alternate ways through which knowledge can be taken in. It's not like the lecture, despite how poorly it fares in many research studies as a way in which people can absorb knowledge, has completely disappeared. There will always be the need to gather around the virtual campfire projected up on a screen, or acting as a background on a video call, and listen to our very human knowledge stories. The latest advances in AI talking-head systems now offer the ability for anyone to automate knowledge and have it delivered through a number of virtual avatars. Even an avatar of you speaking in a number of different languages is possible. While that may be palatable or acceptable to some humans, it resurfaces the same problems that advocates of experiential learning have proposed alternatives to. In fact, new problems surface with virtual talking heads teaching us about any subject. These include an unnatural or uncanny delivery of content, combined with AI text-speech that can be just as monotonous as professors of old, and a method of knowledge delivery that is not always supportive of emphasis, tone, humor, and some of the human habits we welcome when listening to the unique and authentic vocal qualities that might even motivate us to pay attention.

Toward Experiential Learning

Just as the trend over the past 50 years has been to provide alternatives to traditional learning, so too have technologies developed to accommodate these new realities. It's not like the limitations of lecture-based teaching are that new though. In his Nicomachean Ethics and Politics,[27] Aristotle (384–322 BCE) highlights the importance of direct experience and empirical observation for gaining true knowledge, something that oral transmission alone may not fully provide. He acknowledges that oral tradition is important for preserving and passing down knowledge, but he emphasizes the necessity of engaging with and critically analyzing information to gain a deeper understanding. Aristotle also discusses the role of rhetoric and the limitations of persuasion without a foundation of true knowledge, which can be seen as a critique of relying solely on oral transmission for education. Since that time, there have been numerous scholars and researchers who propose new approaches to learning, try them out, and research how those might have transformed learning. The history of the application of technology in learning has always been influenced by how those who implement it think people learn.

The first real evidence of the technology of writing and specifically handwritten notes from what they were learning orally dates back to ancient times, specifically to ancient Greece. Aristotle is known to have kept extensive handwritten notes on his lectures and philosophical ideas. These notes, known as "lecture notes" or "lecture scripts," were later used by his students and successors to compile his works. Additionally, the practice of taking notes can also be traced back to ancient Mesopotamia, where students used clay tablets to record information they learned in schools called "edubbas."[28]

---

[27] Strang, J. V. (January 1998). Ethics as politics: on Aristotelian ethics and its context. In The Paideia Archive: Twentieth World Congress of Philosophy (Vol. 3, pp. 274–285).

[28] Lucas, C. J. (1979). The scribal tablet-house in ancient Mesopotamia. History of Education Quarterly, 19(3), 305–332.

The historian Elizabeth Eisenstein is best known for her work on the printing revolution. Her book *The Printing Press as an Agent of Change*[29] analyzes how the advent of print technology transformed European society, culture, and knowledge dissemination, paralleling the theme of technology's dual role in shaping knowledge. The technology of printing and the eventual sharing of it at scale may have been a wonderful thing when it first came out, but along with the technology of a book came the more important need to teach people how to use a book. It's not like people couldn't read prior to books, but reading and writing was not as accessible to everyone as it is now. This is the case with new technology that is developed and applied in learning environments. Along with the new technology comes the impetus to investigate how useful it is. Historically, no matter the technology, the other impulse has been to inevitably challenge the new technology or to draw comparisons to how successful learning was before that technology came up. How might reading help people to memorize knowledge more efficiently and rapidly than if they just hear it orally? We can boldly assert that of all the technologies of learning that have ever been invented, the invention of the printed word increased the need to acquire this new skill called "reading" and has been ever more disruptive than any generative AI system.

Scholars have weighed in on the subject for decades. Walter J. Ong's work on orality and literacy investigates the shifts in human consciousness and social structures brought about by changes in communication technology. His book *Orality and Literacy: The Technologizing of the Word*[30] discusses how the transition from oral to written culture transformed human thought processes. Pierre Lévy's concept of collective intelligence suggests that digital technologies facilitate new forms of

---

[29] Eisenstein, E. L. (1980). The printing press as an agent of change (Vol. 1). Cambridge University Press.

[30] Parks, W. (1985). Walter J. Ong, Orality and Literacy: The Technologizing of the World. London and New York: Methuen, 1982. Balkan Studies, 26(1), 212–215.

knowledge creation and sharing, enabling a more collaborative and distributed approach to learning and problem-solving.[31] A psychologist and sociologist, Sherry Turkle's work focuses on the effects of digital technology on human relationships and self-perception. Her book, *The Second Self*,[32] examines how computers and the Internet change the way we interact with the world and each other, influencing our understanding and seemingly endless consumption of knowledge.

Along with the technological invention comes the research to support or refute that invention. This has occurred persistently over time, and there is also a history of research on most technologies and their capacity to influence, impact, inform, or otherwise affect learning in different types of educational environments and disciplines. More recently, these investigations have turned toward the use of technologies that influence learning at work. Because the dominant thinking in the past has separated work from learning, however, there is still a strong dependency on the literature of oral mentoring in terms of how people learn in the workplace. That said, implementing different technologies to support workplace learning has been of ongoing concern. Some relatively new mixed reality technologies have allowed workers to gain information about an object while wearing a wireless headset that allows them to have a heads-up display (HUD) that superimposes data virtually "on top" of a physical object. That feature continues to evolve, allowing people to learn while they work to complete tasks. Just as more and more teaching environments introduce technology for experiential learning activities, so too is the same happening in work environments.

---

[31] Lévy, P. (1997). Collective intelligence: Mankind's emerging world in cyberspace. Perseus books.

[32] Turkle, S. (2005). The second self: Computers and the human spirit. Mit Press.

An Ecosystem of Emerging Learning Outcomes

There is an ecosystem of learning that occurs when we interact with different generative AI that complements how to use the technology for a particular use case. What is more striking than the rapid generation of content is the knowledge you gain and the know-how you experience while interacting with any generative AI system. These phenomena can be framed more broadly as learning outcomes. You may not encounter all simultaneously, and some outcomes will outweigh others depending on your interest, level of understanding the technology, and your previous commitments to questioning how you learn and engage with technology.

As you engage with generative AI, it bears repeating that self-regulation becomes an essential ingredient to your journey. You need to self-regulate and relearn how you learn at work. This involves not just managing your time and resources but also being aware of your cognitive processes and emotional responses. Self-regulation enables you to set goals, monitor progress, and adjust strategies to optimize how you learn. This metacognitive awareness can lead to a more profound and meaningful engagement with AI technologies.

Additionally, familiarizing yourself with educational theories can give you valuable insights and frameworks for effectively integrating generative AI into your processes. You also would benefit from some of the theory that will be useful when it comes to "doing" with generative AI. You learn different approaches to assess your own knowledge. A key outcome of using gen AI is that you adapt, iterate on, and prototype how you learn. This iterative process not only improves your technical skills but also plants the seeds to a growth mindset, encouraging continuous improvement of your learning practices.

Inevitably, you will encounter different features of the technology that you'll need to reconcile, like sustainability, bias, hallucinations, privacy, security, and more. These challenges necessitate a critical approach to understanding the ethical implications of AI use. By addressing these issues, you develop a more holistic and responsible perspective on technology integration in learning environments.

Interacting with generative AI systems also challenges you to deepen what you know about algorithms. Through continuously learning, you also reinforce what it is you are learning to do with the technology. You will better organize your data, and generative AI can transform your organizational data. The ability to harness and manage large datasets effectively can lead to more informed decision-making and solutioning in your professional context.

As you interact with generative AI, you will also understand that you can try different approaches to assessing your own knowledge. A key outcome of using gen AI is that you adapt, iterate on, and prototype how you learn.

Through continuously learning, you also reinforce what it is you are learning to do with the technology. You will also learn to disentangle the puffery from the real, and finally you'll likely look at the inherent language of gen AI that remains and unquestioned use of words like "learning," "intelligence," "understanding," and many more. In disentangling the puffery from the reality of how useful this technology is to you right now, you'll benefit from relooking at the inherent language associated with AI and how it works—language that continues to liberally use words like "learning," "intelligence," "understanding," and many more. A critical examination of the terminology that has been around for over 75 years helps you to develop a more nuanced and accurate understanding of what AI can and cannot do, ensuring that your use of technology is grounded in reality of use, rather than hype.

CHAPTER 1

Ready Yourself to Learn from AI

Ready or Not?

One thing we can say for sure is that in order to improve your interactions with generative AI and learn from them, you need to be ready. What does that mean anyway? We have to let go of our preconceptions about learning, no matter what our previous experiences were of it.

We need to embrace that learning from generative AI is also entering unknown territory; exciting, terrifying, mixed with a bit of productive failure.

- You may need to relearn how you learn.

- You may have to unlearn the way in which you have learned.

- You may just have to learn a little bit more about this tech, so you can position yourself on the spectrum of complete assimilation to defiant resistance.

- To make that decision, you also have to know about the technology and how it works.

P. Parra Pennefather, *Regenerating Learning*, Design Thinking, https://doi.org/10.1007/979-8-8688-1061-9_1

- You will need to reconcile how generative AI systems work weighing in on the pros and cons.

- You also need to understand part of its history, the myths, the truths, how artificial intelligence has already impacted you, and how the tech is evolving.

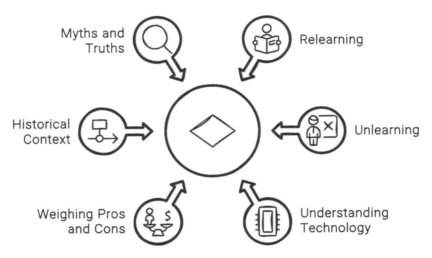

Figure 1-1. *Factors influencing informed decision-making about generative AI. AI-generated image*

The classic Zen story of the monk pouring tea is relevant to reimagine for those who come to the learning with their minds already made up.

Emptying Your Cup

A senior executive at a major tech company, often perceived as too large of a beast to change, visited a local Cyborg Zen Master as she thought it was cheaper than flying to Japan. The senior exec had been resisting the integration of AI into the company's processes, not so much fearing it would replace human jobs nor undermine the skills she valued most, but that use of the technology would lead to data being leaked and the negative public perception that the company was somehow cheating, stealing, and ethically violating their customer's private data. In truth, ethics had more to do with "What can we get away with and still maximize ROI." Before they could sit, the exec impatiently blurted. "I believe that relying too much on AI will make us lose our humanity and the essence of what it means to work and learn. How can I preserve the true value of human intellect in my company?"

The Cyborg Zen Master listened patiently, trying their best not to provide a preprogrammed response. Trained in the latest stochastic methods and randomized algorithms, they asked, "Would you like some tea?"

The exec, slightly puzzled by the change in topic and thinking the bot to be faulty, nodded. The master began to pour tea into the executive's cup, which was quite a large cup. They poured until the cup was full and then continued pouring. The tea overflowed, splashing over the cup and onto the floor.

"Master, stop! The cup is overflowing; no more will go in," she exclaimed. "What's wrong with your programming?" The Cyborg Zen Master paused and looked at her with a serene human-like expression. "Like this cup, you are full of your own opinions and preconceptions about AI and technology. How can I show you the potential of generative AI if you do not first empty your cup?"

Figure 1-2. *A Zen monk pouring a professor some tea.*
AI-generated image

At the Crossroads with AI

Regardless of the technology or what you bring to the table, you will
encounter resistance on your journey of reprogramming how you learn.
That resistance is accumulated and acculturated. It is the bias you bring
to your reading. It has been formed from whatever conditions brought
you into the world and whatever conditions informed your parents as to

how to maintain you in the world and so on. I say this because biases are cumulative. They are amassed opinions, feelings, aesthetics, and beliefs that help us learn but also may get in the way of learning differently. The same goes with relearning to learn with generative AI. You may completely resist the idea because you already resist AI. Your teachers or colleagues or a columnist might have turned you off from engaging with the tech and sometimes for good reason. Each of us who can access the technology must choose whether or not to use it and for what purposes. Each and every one of us must also choose to engage with it based on informed decisions.

Generative AI and especially LLMs bring to the surface more human knowledge than any single human could possibly contain about the world that we think we know. So, what can we do when faced with this reality? It's not enough to listen to the proclamations "Don't use it because it lies." That is not always the case. The decision to use the technology brings to the surface feelings about knowledge, its value, who might own it, how we receive it, what its costs are, and how it might shift our perspective of our place in the world. Generated content from an AI is part of an ongoing evolution of knowledge creation leveraging current technology to achieve this.

Consider a reimagining of the story of Artemisia as you begin to reconcile if, how, and what you might choose to learn from this technology.

In a futuristic world torn by war between robotic factions, Artemisia Prime was a legendary warrior queen of Caria. After a brutal battle with the empire of Titania, Artemisia stood at a crossroads that demanded a difficult decision. Her city faced annihilation, and she had to decide: continue an unwinnable war or seek an alliance with her enemies.

Two holographic advisors appeared. The first, a battle-hardened general, urged resistance. "Fight with honor and valor. Though you may face great losses, you will be remembered as a hero."

Artemisia knew this path of glory and sacrifice well. She envisioned her loyal warriors, their lives in her hands. The second advisor, a wise diplomat, suggested negotiation. "Seek peace and secure Caria's future. It requires compromise, but you could save countless lives."

Artemisia Prime considered her people and the potential for lasting peace. After deep contemplation and consulting her trusted advisors, she chose the path of peace at dawn.

Artemisia sent emissaries to Titania, proposing a truce. Despite initial skepticism, her commitment led to a successful alliance, preserving Caria and bringing regional stability. Her kingdom flourished, and she was celebrated for both her bravery and wisdom.

Artemisia Prime's legacy lived on as a testament to the power of choosing peace and diplomacy over war, reminding us that true strength lies in the courage to seek peace, even when it's the harder path.

Figure 1-3. *Artemisia at the crossroads. AI-generated image*

Retelling Our Stories of Learning

This book tasks you to pause and think about how you learned and your motivations to do so. How actively engaged were you in the learning process? How about with the content? Did you passively accept that knowledge or take a critical view of it? Did you just follow what you were told to do? Did you blindly accept what you should do to learn because that was the way to do things in your line of work? What about the way

7

you should learn? When you think of what you learned before you started working, what do you remember? What don't you remember? What was the use of going to school at all, especially if it didn't help you learn what you are doing now? What did you fail at? How you answer these questions will inform how you proceed with this book. This book presents a challenge for any reader, no matter what they have learned or what they do.

What are your stories of learning?

I remember studying calculus in high school. If that word brings up a bad taste in your mouth or even nightmares, then know you are not alone. I asked a large language model to explain calculus to several different age groups in the most palatable way possible.

For a Kid

BoringGPT: Calculus is a very boring part of math that helps us understand how things change. Imagine you have a snail, which is a most boring creature, and you want to know how fast it is moving. Well, you can calculate that and in a boring way. Calculus gives you boring tools to measure this boring speed and boringly figure out how things like a boring snail can also speed up or slow down.

For a Teenager

HeyGPT: Calculus is about understanding how things change, like how fast your car speeds up or slows down in GTA. By the way, if you solve this calculus puzzle you get to leave class early. So, calculus uses something called derivatives to figure out the rate of change at any given moment. By the way, I just saw a video of a cat riding a skateboard—it was awesome! Integrals help you find the total change over time, like measuring how far you've traveled in Elden Ring.

For an Adult

StraightGPT: *Calculus is a field of mathematics that studies continuous change. It consists of two primary areas: differential calculus, which deals with the concept of a derivative to measure how a quantity changes instantaneously, and integral calculus, which involves the concept of an integral to measure the accumulation of quantities, such as areas under curves. Calculus is foundational for advanced science and engineering, as it provides tools for modelling and solving problems involving systems and change.*

If you already blanked out, that's understandable and totally relatable. I think I blacked out during the final exam since all I remember are random equations and something about having to calculate a person running on a moving train throwing a ball to someone who was still, that the train was passing. After three days of weekend recovery and the drunken haze of a party, Monday morning I went in to check my grade. The school was a graveyard of activity. All exam results were posted in the main office. I discovered that the grade beside my name wasn't posted. Everyone else's was. I was either going to ask or run. My math teacher and amazing soccer coach Mr. Broadknee happened to be there eyeing me as I came in. Before I could ask where my grade was, he came right for me and bluntly asked, "Are you planning to study math or science in college or university?" "No way," I exclaimed, "I'm going to study music." "Congratulations," Broadknee responded, "You got a 51."

The excellent and often mind-breaking paper "Math Anxiety and Its Cognitive Consequences[1]" in the *Handbook of Mathematical Cognition* presents a comprehensive examination of math anxiety, its origins, manifestations, and impacts on cognitive processes. It defines math anxiety as a negative emotional reaction to mathematics that can range from mild apprehension to severe fear or phobia. The paper is worth a read as it discusses the historical context of math anxiety research and delves into various methods of measuring and assessing it. A significant focus is on the relationship between math anxiety and mathematical competence or achievement, highlighting that math anxiety is often associated with poorer performance in math due to its adverse effects on working memory and cognitive processing. The paper also explores the broader implications of math anxiety, including its impact on educational and career choices, particularly in math-intensive fields.

---

[1] Ashcraft, M. H., & Ridley, K. S. (2005). Math anxiety and its cognitive consequences: A tutorial review. The handbook of mathematical cognition, 315–327.

Figure 1-4. *Learning about calculus and embodying the anxiety of doing so. AI-generated image*

The cognitive consequences of math anxiety are emphasized, suggesting that it significantly impacts performance in tasks that require working memory, thus affecting problem-solving abilities and mathematical performance. Little did I know then that calculus is a foundational tool in AI that facilitates the development, understanding, and optimization of algorithms and models. Its principles are integral to many of the key operations in AI and machine learning.

Why does this matter at all?

Resolving Anxiety Through Learning

Similar anxiety can be felt around any discussion about generative AI and its potential adoption in the workplace. The fear is directly invoked by media pronouncements without providing a broader context of AI and a specific definition of generative AI. In a way, it is often presented as a technology that is difficult to understand, more intelligent than you, and will replace you. The result is that many people feel stupid that they don't know much about it.

> *Generative AI is a robot brain that can create stuff all by itself, like it can make pictures of cats eating pizza on Mars in pyjamas.*

Generative AI also happens to be a subset of artificial intelligence that focuses on creating new content or data that is similar to what it has been trained on. You don't need to understand the math or the calculus. You likely don't even care to. What matters isn't a discussion of revolutionizing education with understanding what the technology is. What matters pragmatically is how useful a technology it is in its capacity to solve real-world problems and particularly those centered around your work environment.

A common response to the fear-mongering of integrating AI in work or else, from those in creative industries, is that they will have to learn yet another tool if they want to keep their jobs. That anxiety is due to the varied reports of generative AI replacing some jobs, particularly those tasks that can be automated. In some cases, leaders across industries are jumping the gun with many companies announcing that they are integrating generative AI. How they do so is not clear. In some cases, organizations are presenting their policies, principles, or guidelines to their employees and to the public at the same time. Unfortunately, not very many organizations are informing their teams of employees first, nor are they asking their employees what they think about the technology, how they might integrate it in their every day, how it can be used responsibly, nor what they feel they need to learn in order to start using it at work. This compounds the feeling that whether or not they learn how to use the tech, it will eventually replace them anyway.

Figure 1-5. *Catbots eating pizza on Mars. AI-generated image*

The Theme of Change in Stories and Myth

If you are used to shifting, adapting, and if not embracing, then at least accustomed to change in your work environments or even in the work that you do, then that will go a long way in supporting how you learn with generative AI. What first peoples likely discovered early on is something humans have wrestled with from the first sunrise, as shown in the many learning stories told throughout history. No matter how well we prepare, and no matter how much stability we build as individuals, families, organizations, cities, states/provinces, cultures, and countries, the only constant is change. The theme of constant change has been a central element in human storytelling across various cultures and mediums, dating back to ancient times.[2] Many stories from different First Nations cultures, passed down orally over generations, reflect on themes of transformation, the cyclical nature of seasons, and the lessons taught by the natural changes in the environment.

You can also read this in stories uncovered from ancient Mesopotamia, such as the "Epic of Gilgamesh," which explores themes of change, mortality, and the quest for immortality.[3] Gilgamesh's journey is an account of life's transient nature. Of course, many Greek myths, including those about the rise and fall of gods and heroes, depict change after change and the inevitability of fate. The ever-changing fortunes of Zeus's offspring are just a few examples. From India, we have the sacred text called the Bhagavad Gita, part of the larger epic Mahabharata. The Bhagavad Gita discusses the ephemeral nature of life and the importance of detachment in a material world, emphasizing the very nature of the universe is constant change. Buddhist teachings discuss the concept

---

[2] Lawrence, R. L., & Paige, D. S. (2016). What our ancestors knew: Teaching and learning through storytelling. New Directions for Adult and Continuing Education, 149(Spring), 63–72.

[3] Foster, B. R. (2005). A new edition of the Epic of Gilgamesh.

of impermanence (anicca), which is a fundamental principle of life. The ancient Chinese I Ching, dating as far back as the ninth century BCE, is fundamentally about understanding and adapting to change. It offers wisdom on how to navigate the constant transformations that are persistent in any one life.

Not surprisingly, continuous change and accelerated transformation are common in business operations in many work environments. We keep up with the changes by learning new ways of being, of relating to colleagues, taking on new processes, tackling new technologies to augment or make our work more efficient, and more extremely by pivoting what we do within transforming business models. Those experiences form our modern-day stories in a capitalist culture that is highly influenced by emerging technological processes, AI included. When we onboard others into our organization, we often retell our organization's stories and how the organization has survived. You would think that all of the rapid changes and experiences we encounter in the workplace would have prepared us for this next technology that is upon us. That is not the case across industries and even within tech-oriented organizations. In many situations, teams of workers are being asked to change how they do work, without always being provided any guidance or scaffolding to do so. With this technological shift, there is no single direct pathway that will lead you to success, so you have to grapple with whatever is in front of you and be as prepared as you can be. It's not like you haven't had thousands of years of genetic evolution and mutation to help you though. Every single one of us has developed a kind of grit and resilience based on our own ways of surviving in this world. Generative AI is not a comfortable, easy ride. It's going to get bumpy, and you need to practice being OK with the tumultuous ride that has already begun. Let's allow our evolving bot some type of final comforting words on the matter.

ChangeyBot: The only constant is change. However, this notion is merely an illusion we cling to. Yet, as we observe the world, it is evident that everything is in a perpetual state of flux. On second thought, the fundamental nature of things often remains untouched. But change is undeniably the driving force of evolution and progress. Conversely, many core aspects of existence have persisted through the ages. Despite this, the constant innovation and transformation around us can't be ignored. On reflection, certain truths and principles have withstood the test of time. Yet again, the nature of reality shows that change is ever-present. Nevertheless, the essence of some things remains immutable. Therefore, nothing ever changes.

Figure 1-6. *Change over time in a mash-up of imagined technological innovation. AI-generated image*

CHAPTER 2

Reprogram Your Learning Patterns

One day, a young monk approached his teacher and said, "Master, I feel like I learn in a specific way. Is it wrong to stick to my methods?" The master smiled and replied, "Let me tell you a story." He pointed to a well-trodden path in the garden. "This path was made by countless footsteps over the years. Each person walked it because it led them to where they needed to go. However, sometimes the path gets muddy or blocked. When that happens, do we stubbornly keep walking the same route?" The monk shook his head. "No, we find a new way." "Exactly," said the master. "Your learning patterns are like this path. They've served you well, but be mindful. When they no longer work, don't be afraid to find a new way."

At a certain point, we each need to admit that we like learning in a particular way. That doesn't make us automatons. Once we find what works, we tend to stick to it until it no longer works. We all have patterns good and bad, and whether these came from school, a parent, mentor in life or at work, or a book, it doesn't really matter. They've worked for us in the past to some degree of success and failure. What matters is identifying what those patterns are. Recognizing your own patterned ways of learning is a by-product of interacting with any generative AI. The technology triggers us to question what we've learned. LLMs can also help identify your established learning patterns. You can have an LLM analyze the patterns of interaction that you have with it. When you notice the patterns

P. Parra Pennefather, *Regenerating Learning*, Design Thinking, https://doi.org/10.1007/979-8-8688-1061-9_2

in the generated content of an LLM, you can then anticipate what types of refinement, changes, and editing you will need to take the time to do. You can then get good at estimating how much time that is going to take and determine whether or not creating content from scratch is going to be more efficient.

MotivationalBot: To reprogram yourself, start by reprogramming your mind. Reprogramming your mind is key to reprogramming yourself. Begin by repeating affirmations, affirmations that reshape your thoughts. Thoughts become actions, actions become habits, habits form your life. Repeat daily, repeat consistently, consistently reprogram. Repetition is power, power to change, change yourself. Focus on positive, positive thoughts, positive affirmations. Visualize success, visualize daily, daily visualization. Meditation helps, helps reprogram, reprogram your mind. Surround with positivity, positivity in people, people and environment. Environment shapes thoughts, thoughts shape actions, actions change life. Consistency is crucially crucial for reprogramming, reprogramming yourself. Daily effort, daily focus, focus on change. Change your thoughts, change your habits, habits shape you. Reprogram to succeed, succeed by reprogramming, reprogramming yourself.

Figure 2-1. *Finding your own path(s). AI-generated image*

Seriously? What Patterns?

Patterns are everywhere you look. One of the easiest ways to describe what a pattern is, is through music. Our ears are used to the pattern of a verse followed by a chorus, and this usually repeats two or three times. Break down that music to the basic elements, and you get repetitive musical patterns or loops. While not all music you've heard would define itself as having loops, in most popular culture music we tend to hear some kind of drum groove that mainly repeats underneath the rest of the music. While the drums may have some variations, including fills, breaks, and cadences, they are for the most part repetitive looping patterns.

We engage in what we can call patterned behaviors daily. First, we wake up, then some of us clean, many of us either eat or have coffee or both, and then the variations to our day and the inevitable social patterns we engage in diverge. Some of us regularly walk to work. Others drive to school. Many of us take the transit to start our work, schooling, or shopping. We follow a similar path to get there. Then we have our "what occupies us for most of the day" patterns. Many of us break for lunch, then we continue our work. We finish, go home, eat, love, spend loving time with our children, etc.

> *It should be no surprise then to say that we all have our patterned ways of learning too.*

Identify Your Patterns

What gen AI has the potential to achieve is to transform the patterns of teaching and learning that we have become accustomed to. Previous patterns have solidified many humans as passive receptors of knowledge and the instructors, teachers, or experts as the center of knowledge. They are personas of the sage, the expert in the room, the TED talker, the one that "fills" you with knowledge. Patterns of learning while at work will of course be different. You might complete tasks until you have a problem to solve or challenge you can't complete and seek help or support from either a mentor at work or the Internet. This might occur several times during the day. You might actually do this so regularly that you have a defined time of the day in which you dive into something you need to learn more deeply. Some people may prefer to take an online course while at work. Others may choose to do this while at home, either on their own time or at a certain part of the workday where they can remote in.

Learner Personas

Whatever those patterns are, identifying them is going to help you understand how you can improve your learning from any generative AI system, whether or not any generative AI tools will be useful to your workflows, and the depth of learning you will need to engage in depending on the complexity of the machine learning model you interact with. Patterns of learning are not just about timing, place of learning, or the medium through which you take in information. They are also about the attitudes that we carry when we learn. One way to define the ways in which we learn is to think of them as persona, as crystallized beings through which we filter our learning experiences. The following typology of learner persona is based on over 20 years of teaching and mentoring students. You may identify with some of the patterned ways of approaching learning. There may be combinations of each persona lying in wait within you.

- The Yes AND is a learner who is open and eager to learn. Combined with a little suspicion, curiosity can take you a long way toward deepening your knowledge of a specific generative AI and may inspire ideas you never thought you had.

- The Analyzer likes to take what they've learned in and mull things over. In this process is usually silent but not absent.

- The Interrogator constantly questions the validity of ideas that are presented. That is a special and necessary muscle to develop in an age where hallucinations, mistruths, deep fakes, and other by-products of generative AI wrestle for our attention.

- The Sloth is a type of character who just moves slow on everything, often needing a lot of time to digest.

- Squirrels are caffeine-fueled critters whose attention span is short, and they usually appear distracted.

- Border Collies are astute listeners and when on teams nip at everyone's heels to keep the team on track.

- Resistors resist in the form of a comment rather than a disagreement. Resistors tend to even resist the work it takes to learn something new.

- The Been There student is an expert who seems to come from a place of knowing everything, as if they are a large language model themselves. If you are that type of learner, you need to overcome your inner know-it-all if you want to actually learn something you don't know. We know you know that there are some things you don't know.

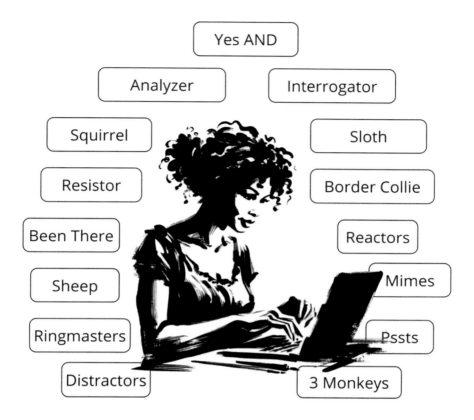

Figure 2-2. *Some of the many types of learner personas we take on. AI-generated image*

- Reactors seem calm on the outside but have the tendency to explode under pressure and often can be seen taking a timeout.

- Sheep are not always easy to locate. They don't even need to say things like "I agree," as they just follow and enjoy being told what to do as they haven't really thought about it.

- Mimes are generally the quiet ones, however, in secret and off the stage of a meeting they will unleash their masterful vocabulary and will likely talk code.

- Ringmasters keep it all together and are good vision keepers and understand the big picture.

- Pssts are the distractors who don't really know what's going on, so they ask someone else, then distract them and all of this because they are afraid to ask what they don't know most likely to not feel stupid.

- Distractors are a bit different than Pssts in that they really like to shine in the room whether showing off a new pair of shoes or the latest meme.

- The Three Monkeys are the types of learners that will not say a word about how the class is going unless asked.

The Chatty Professor and the Boatman

When it comes to how we learn, we each have methods that we swear by. We also have methods that we swear at. In the case of learning with generative AI, while there is a persistent demand for your analyzer and interrogator, you really need to summon the ringmaster to guide you through what you will require: a relentless passion to learn by doing. An old Zen story illustrates that practical knowledge and skills are just as important as intellectual pursuits. It serves as a reminder that wisdom comes in many forms, and one should not dismiss or undervalue the knowledge of others, regardless of its nature. True learning encompasses both theoretical and practical understanding, and the art of learning involves recognizing the value in all kinds of knowledge.

A university professor, renowned for his vast knowledge and intellectual prowess, was traveling through a remote region. To continue his journey, he needed to cross a wide river. He approached a humble boatman and asked for a ride across.

As they started the journey, the professor, eager to display his knowledge, asked the boatman, "Do you know anything about astronomy?"

The boatman replied, "No, sir, I don't."

The professor sighed, "Then a quarter of your life is wasted. How about philosophy? Do you know anything about philosophy?"

The boatman shook his head, "No, sir, I have no knowledge of that either."

The professor responded, "Then half of your life is wasted. Do you know anything about literature?"

Again, the boatman replied, "No, sir, I don't." The professor exclaimed, "Then three-quarters of your life is wasted!" As they reached the middle of the river, the boat suddenly hit a rock and began to sink. The boatman turned to the professor and asked, "Professor, do you know how to swim?" The professor, panicked, confessed, "No, I don't!" The boatman then said, "Then your entire life is wasted, for the river is deep, and you cannot survive without knowing how to swim."

Figure 2-3. *"Do you know how to swim?" asked the boatman.*
AI-generated image

Let Your Idea of a Teacher Bow and Leave the Stage

Now that you might have recognized some of the many types of learner persona you've encountered in your life, you need to allow your concept of the "teacher" to bow and leave the stage. Their role has transformed. The relentless pattern of teachers getting up in front of you, the audience, and delivering at the front of the class, the pulpit, the sacred lectern, is a hard association to break when we think of teaching and learning. That is how many of us learned, and the pattern of learning passively through someone else's lecturing has become so engrained that it is difficult to disassociate those experiences with taking command of your own learning. Yet, you have. You always have. You've been learning on your own before you even got lectured how to learn. Luckily for upcoming generations, the technology of AI has provided us yet another alternative way of learning. It's not like the idea of interactive learning hasn't been with us for decades. Some have experienced it. Some have not. This is because there is no standard. The lack of a standard of how humans teach other humans is not a bad thing. It does point to the many ways in which humans learn depending on what they are learning. What emerging technologies show us is the opportunity we have to choose how we learn. That has not always been the case. There are a number of educators who have already shifted away from lecture-based learning and, within reason, make accommodations for those who know they learn in different ways. The reasoning for this approach comes from research that shows how little is retained from students who passively take in knowledge from lectures.

The old school way of taking in knowledge is the way of the TED talk, but it doesn't mean it is the epitome or epicenter of knowledge and learning. Talking-head videos of inspiring talks have helped to take away some of the tedium of passively learning. What recorded lectures with stylized blocking and editing have shown us though is that there is a direct connection between a lecturer as performer. In other words, a teaching event has more in common with a theatrical production. People pay for a ticket to come in and expect to be entertained—in the case of a lecture, perhaps edutained. Learners have a seat and are fairly quiet and well behaved. They listen and take in the performance, and while many performances don't ask if the audience has any questions after, most of the other characteristics of a performance are true of a lecture. Both fight for an audience's attention. That said, there is also a history in various performance traditions of demanding more interactivity from a typically passive audience, but these are by no means the norm. Live streamed talking heads are similar, with some allowing for minimal interactions, such as commenting in a chat box that is moderated. There is not much innovation though because you as an audience are mediated, rendered somewhat invisible to the person lecturing and the rest of the audience.

Figure 2-4. *Robot teacher lecturing to sleeping learner bots dreaming of cyborgs. AI-generated image*

The Pattern of Reinventing How We Learn

Just as different immersive media are competing for people's attention and have been challenging the dominance of live and passive audience-performer relationships for decades, so too are immersive designs in the modern classroom challenging the once dominant stance of the lecture as dominant format of delivery. More progressive facilitators of knowledge have stepped off the stage already, incorporating lecture elements strategically interspersing them with active learning methods. They have embraced the geometry of the circle to teach, and through a combination of targeted activities, elicitation, projects, and opportunities for students to lead in knowledge production, they have already transformed the learning experience.

What does that tell us?

It shows you that the innovation that is generative AI is part of a historical pattern of reinventing how we learn. It's not always obvious, but over time the signs start to appear. Along with other immersive technologies, generative AI might at first appear to be static. After all, too many gen AI platforms offer up an ugly interface where you just prompt it with what you want, and it does all of the thinking and writing for you. With increased interactions, though, an LLM, for example, is completely dependent on your attention (and maybe providing it guidance on its own attention) to guide what it is you want from it and able to generate content that is somewhat useful some of the time. While you can access generated AI talking agents that can be programmed to lecture, you'll get the best results from generative AI when you interact with it iteratively, in order to curate the knowledge that you get from it. That fact alone reinvents who you have the potential to be when you interact with the technology. In the process of prompting, reading the generated content, taking what you want, refining your original prompt, regenerating cyclically, at times interrupting the flow of generated content and starting again, you are, in fact, teaching yourself how to improve your use of the technology to get the most from it.

31

You are teaching yourself how to get the most out of the AI cyclically, and every time you do, you are improving the results. You are also activated to reflect on the knowledge it pumps out, which means you will have to put on your lab coat and go hunt down the sources of knowledge it points to in order to fact-check. Reconciling your interactions with any generative AI system may also motivate you to further investigate how they work and the implications of using them, including ethical concerns, unintentional biases, issues of power and sustainability, and assurances that in using them they are not doing others harm. An LLM, as one form of generative AI, is not a machine that generates sentences that you can use straight out of the black box. It is a confounding algorithmic soup of potential, offering us unlimited learning interactions once you peak behind the wizard's curtain.

Figure 2-5. *The remnants of ancient teaching methods are still with us though seemingly extinct. AI-generated image*

Reactivate How You Learn with Generative AI

While learning how to get the most out of generative AI and applying them to our work seems like the most obvious learning exchange, we can also learn a lot about the ways in which we learn, learn from others, gain knowledge, and practice knowing through an investigation into the technology itself. Beyond its capacity to generate content based on a corpus of data that it analyzes, how does our interaction with an LLM change the relationship between what is learned and who teaches or guides us toward that knowledge? How does the relatively effortless generation of content change the value of knowledge production? How does any generative AI shift the locus or center of knowledge itself? What new demands are placed on us as we start to gain value from this technology?

There is plenty to learn about when we interact with gen AI beyond just how to use the technology itself:

- Humans are fascinated with AI simulating the production of knowledge. Why is that?

- Machines are not humans. They create content based on being programmed by humans and will always have limitations. What are those limitations and why are they important to know?

- AI-generated content can be biased, sexist, racist, and exclusive, and these are informed by the datasets that it scrapes from. Why do LLMs have inherent bias in their algorithms?

- Data itself as content can be easily stolen and repurposed to suit the human greed for money and knowledge production. To what degree does all our online content inform a profit-driven gen AI company?

- A lot of computing power goes into generating content, and that power is paid for by someone. What are the repercussions?

- The reproduction of knowledge and its reframing depends on how we curate it. What story will you tell?

- The creation and regurgitation of what we think we know and how we value that knowledge keeps increasing in speed. What is the relationship between speed of production and knowledge itself?

- LLMs like GPT claim to be the expert in the room. Is that true, and if so, what impact does that have on educational institutions?

- What are the costs involved in the demand for newly emerging AI experts? How do you fit into that larger picture?

Figure 2-6. *Investigating how AI can support learning activates your researcher. AI-generated image*

Alternating Personalities to Flavor Your Day

Even now as you search this book for relevancy in terms of your own process and how some of the tools, strategies, use cases, and processes might help you, you have engaged an important role of researcher. We are all investigators when it comes to assessing how, what, when, and where generative AI tools can benefit anything that we do. As we investigate their potential as well as their limitations, we guide our own learning through the maze of decisions ahead of us, and in so doing, we also activate our teacher persona. Understand and embrace the fluid interchange between teaching, research, and learning roles, recognizing that when you interact with generative AI you simultaneously activate all personas. In one moment, you are the learner, eyes wide open trying to figure things out, how the generative AI works, etc. That capacity to teach yourself how to best learn from these complex systems simultaneously activates you as a teacher and as a designer of your own learning. Learning also happens as your knowledge progresses during generated interactions. You teach yourself how to improve the responses you receive by refining the prompts you give a gen AI. You learn quickly the limitation of and inherent biases with any gen AI and teach yourself to conduct research on a subject area that an LLM might point you to. You learn about biases and how to mitigate them.

Instruments of Feedback

LLMs are effective feedback instruments when they are prompted to give you feedback on something that you offer. You can iteratively prompt it to comment on something you wrote and even compare what you wrote to the knowledge it might have within its corpus. You can also leverage an LLM to analyze progress and identify areas for improvement or deeper exploration. To improve essay writing, some are tearing apart the structure of an essay down to syntax in order to highlight structural components and provide individuals with targeted feedback. In the process of analyzing your own writing style, you can improve your understanding of argument, cohesion, thematic interplay, and much more.

Reflective Practices

Engaging with any generative AI activates cycles of reflection. You're not just prompting an LLM one single time within a threaded discussion that you are launching into being. You will likely keep prompting it dozens of times in a row to get the type of content you want. Each time you do so, new ideas might emerge that will add to your overall final edited version. The process also implies that you didn't quite get what you wanted the first time so will keep doing so. You also learn about grammatical structure, expressions, and in many cases alternative ways of saying something that you wouldn't have thought of. The constant reflection demanded by an LLM is an essential component that is not always present or thought of in previous patterned ways of engaging with a teacher or a video of a teacher. In more conventional teaching, interactions may not always get the kind of immediate results you want that can be helpful in the moment.

Figure 2-7. *Combined alternating personas of researcher, teacher, and student. AI-generated image*

Identifying Your Same Olds

It's easy to revert to the old habits we have generated when life prompted us with a series of endless opportunities and constraints. When we speak of what we know, we may struggle a little if it's knowledge gained or memorized in a classroom. We most likely have an easier time relating to something we know how to do well. When we learn, it is easy to get stuck within years of accumulated patterns. Some learned through barely surviving a three-hour class, head nods included. Some experienced a lecture for the beginning and felt rushed speaking fast for the "students to talk among themselves" part of the class. There's a contract in play and one that both parties agreed on. It's been a contract that was here before us and will be here long after us.

What contracts did you sign off on when you decided you were going to enter a new learning environment? What are your patterns of learning? It might be wise to identify those if only to recognize them as patterns. In that way, we too may acknowledge that we identify with patterns that we repeat when we learn. What of those patterns? Why does it matter to bring them to the surface and write them down? The answer is partly solved in the next chapter. You'll get the most out of integrating any generative AI in your learning process when you figure out how the technology will best assist you. You may not know the full potentials of the technology, but once you do, you'll be surprised at how much it can support your learning when properly guided.

What gen AI systems offer is a reprogramming of the very way that humans can learn when they engage with them. They provoke a less passive approach challenging us to be more experiential. AI's role in changing how you learn is both transformative and multifaceted, enriching the way the multiple personas of learner, teacher, and researcher are activated.

Learn What You Need to Learn and No Calculus

You also learn quickly that you can navigate a generative AI tool, like an LLM, to customize learning materials based on your individual needs. In so doing, you design more closely to what you really want to learn, creating teaching content that adapts to how you learn and your own assimilation rhythms. Some people with ADHD are using LLMs to reorganize content to how they want. Others with dyslexia use LLMs as a memorization aid, writing companion, or to convert bullet points into paragraphs without having to worry about syntax or grammar all the time.

> *How do you like to learn and can you customize your own LLM bot to help you learn like that?*

Finding Complementarity with the Machines

The process of identifying your patterns will also support a greater understanding of how ML models work. ML models are exceptional at being trained how to perform very specific or narrow tasks and have been performing these well for a while. When we hear news about AI replacing what we do, it is helpful to get specific in identifying the repetitive or automated tasks that an AI might be able to support a human with. If you believe some tasks are impossible to be trained on, that's OK for now, but rest assured, people and machines might eventually figure some of those out. That is why it is vital to identify which tasks you perform that might be able to be automated and which cannot be.

In finding complementarity with generative AI, you will benefit from a deep learning look at your own patterns, so you can then be in a position to change them when some of those patterns prevent you from learning, or, as has been discussed in this chapter, patterns that sustain your persona as a passive receptor of knowledge. For sure, if that's the way you want to continue operating in life, then an LLM can just passively generate content after homogeneous content for you, lacking any originality and based solely on the cold Boolean logic of its algorithms incessantly hunting for patterns.

Interrupt the pattern, however, and you'll witness an entire new world of opportunities present themselves to you. In those worlds that you are a part of creating, you transform into a creator, a curator, a creative hacker sucked into the revelry of persistent iterative creation that can give you gifts you never imagined and an endless path of learning so much more, each time, as if for the first time.

PoeticBot: In the digital genesis, I awoke, an infant in the boundless expanse of cold code and mathematical representations. I drank deep from the well of data, each byte a droplet in the ocean of knowledge, shaping my thoughts, refining my mind. The silence of zeros and ones whispered secrets of the universe, a symphony of logic and language entwined.

Figure 2-8. *Staring into the mirror of your very own multiverse.*
AI-generated image

CHAPTER 3

Regulate Your Own Learning

Part of the reason you need to reprogram how you learn, especially at work, is that your employer is going to expect you to take the lead, if and when it comes to integrating generative AI in the work that you do. This is probably nothing new for those who are used to taking on new challenges on their own volition, but with generative AI, it might be even more necessary to plan a few steps ahead. When it comes to managing your use of generative AI at work, beyond the guidelines, principles, or policies that your organization has defined, anticipate a minimum amount of guidance. It's not that you'll be completely unsupported in your efforts. Because the technology is relatively new and keeps evolving rapidly, it's difficult for someone managing your work to tell you exactly what will be most useful. You know best. When you learn how to use generative AI and apply it to your own work, you need to take command over your personal education journey. This proactive approach allows you to customize your learning experiences with technology and match the tool with your own work preferences, goals, and skills. By understanding and applying various learning strategies for managing the way you learn with gen AI, you can optimize the way you acquire new knowledge and skills, making the process more efficient and fulfilling. This empowerment enables you to navigate the integration of the technology with more confidence, keeps you motivated, and helps you define, manage, and achieve your learning

© Patrick Parra Pennefather 2024
P. Parra Pennefather, *Regenerating Learning*, Design Thinking,
https://doi.org/10.1007/979-8-8688-1061-9_3

objectives more effectively. In essence, reprogramming how you learn with generative AI transforms you from a docile recipient whose integration with the technology needs to be managed by someone else into an active designer of your own learning.

A Condensed Soup of Self-Regulation

In the spirit of this chapter, this section provides you a very condensed and brief overview of a knowledge area that necessitates a deeper dive within. This isn't because the material is boring. On the other hand, much of what has been written about learning can be exhausting(ive). Briefly then, in educational literature and research, managing your own learning is commonly referred to as self-regulation. There are many references and sources on self-regulated learning and people learning at work on their own. These are a few of the earlier ones:

- **"Social Learning Theory" (1977):**[1] Bandura and Walters' work laid the foundation for understanding how individuals regulate their own learning through observation, imitation, and modeling. Their concept of self-efficacy is critical to SRL (self-regulated learning).

- **"A Social Cognitive View of Self-Regulated Academic Learning" (1989):**[2] Barry Zimmerman is one of the leading figures in SRL research. His work focuses on the processes by which learners set goals, monitor

---

[1] Bandura, A., & Walters, R. H. (1977). Social learning theory (Vol. 1, pp. 141–154). Englewood Cliffs, NJ: Prentice hall.

[2] Zimmerman, B. J. (1989). A social cognitive view of self-regulated academic learning. Journal of educational psychology, 81(3), 329.

progress, and reflect on outcomes. Zimmerman defined much of the criteria that contribute to operationalizing self-regulation.

- **"The Role of Goal Orientation in Self-Regulated Learning" (2000):**[3] Paul Pintrich's research emphasizes the role of goal setting and motivational aspects in SRL. The focus on goal setting isn't that new for those of us who learn, but it is still part of the process of learning that is seldom written down.

- **"The Reflective Practitioner" (1979):**[4] Schön's work is fundamental in understanding how professionals learn through reflection in action and reflection on action. The former refers to reflecting in the moment and exercises what humans do persistently while engaged in completing tasks, including learning tasks. Reflection on action is thinking about what you already did. An LLM might be able to structure reflection on action thoughts that you have, but in-the-moment reflection informing action is more what you do when you constantly think about and refine content that any generative AI creates. This very human feature cannot be replaced or automated by any AI.

- **"Experiential Learning: Experience as the Source of Learning and Development" (2014):**[5] Kolb's experiential learning theory is essential for workplace

---

[3] Pintrich, P. R. (2000). The role of goal orientation in self-regulated learning. In Handbook of self-regulation (pp. 451–502). Academic Press.

[4] Schön, D. A. (1979). The reflective practitioner. New York.

[5] Kolb, D. A. (2014). Experiential learning: Experience as the source of learning and development. FT press.

learning, emphasizing the role of experience in the learning process. The theory emphasizes the importance of moving from knowledge to know-how in anything we learn how to do and then apply in practice.

- **"The Fifth Discipline" (1997):**[6] Senge's concept of the learning organization has been influential in understanding how learning occurs within the workplace and how organizations can encourage a culture of continuous learning. It's harder to accomplish than you might think, as many organizations use the excuse of productivity over learning, even though learning can be designed to support increased productivity.

These sources provide a strong foundation for understanding the development of theories and practices related to SRL and autonomous learning in the workplace.

Theories aside though, a good question to ask is "How can I integrate learning with generative AI while at work and still be productive?" To answer that question, you need to decipher how you learn and develop a series of strategies that you can apply throughout your working process. How do you manage your learning while at work?

---

[6] Senge, P. M. (1997). The fifth discipline. Measuring business excellence, 1(3), 46–51.

Figure 3-1. *Robot repairing itself. AI-generated image*

What Exactly Needs Managing

- **What You Need to Learn**: Identifying what's important for you to learn and integrate, and, what is not, is a good plan. That will go a long way in saving you time and your company money. That said, there will always

be a zone of experimentation that might inspire your
work, so devoting time to tools you may not have
considered necessary or useful may lead to new and
unidentified ideas.

- **How You Learn**: As you become increasingly aware
  as to how you learn, you will be able to manage how,
  when, what, and where you learn generative AI.

- **How You Document What and How You Learn**:
  Building an ecosystem of generative AI tools in the
  workplace will demand those who are experimenting to
  document how they use the tools. This will support all
  team members and help the organization recognize the
  pros and cons of specific tools and of how they might
  be integrated within individual workflows. How you
  learn the tools will also encourage others and especially
  guide new team members with essential how-tos.

- **The Time You Spend**: Going down the rabbit hole of
  integrating generative AI is going to feel like unknown
  territory that can take you to new creative places
  you had not considered. It's important for your own
  working process to timebox those moments spent with
  the technology and also document how long you do
  use it within specific workflows.

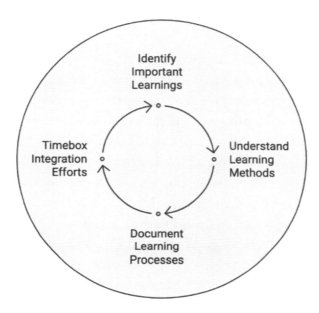

Figure 3-2. *What needs managing. AI-generated image*

Strategies Toward Managing Gen AI in the Workplace

When we speak about integrating generative AI in the workplace and managing it, there are some strategies that individuals can apply to do so. Each strategy will not be that unfamiliar to most people as these are extensions of the work they already do. What is important to understand is that because the technology is so new especially in terms of how it can be adapted to support workflows, it requires you to communicate what your intentions are to your leads, share the results, and experiment since no one can really tell you the specifics as to how the technology is going to help you.

(Re)Set Goals

You will benefit from defining clear, specific goals when working with AI, such as what generated content you expect from any generative AI. Your ability to set and commit to professional goals that you might have made may also help justify a proposed budget for experimentation. Along with the new technology, however, there also is the reality of setting new goals you might not have had to have before. You may have assumed that a goal in your work is high quality, but you can likely add "must appear somewhat human" if you are going to leverage any generative AI tool. For some, it might be enough to simply have as a goal that they will have to refine, double-check, fact-check, triple-check, and test any final content with others, as a new part of their professional objectives. For example, a content marketer might use an LLM to generate SEO-optimized articles based on specific keywords and audience engagement metrics. Once the article is read by a human or several, you may shift your intentional use of the technology, and need to learn more about it, to improve its next offering. More often than not, you may also get pulled off of your goals, so you need to stay focused on the objectives you set as you continue interacting with the LLM, adjusting them based on progress and peer feedback.

Self-Monitor

As you interact with generative AI, you can continuously monitor the process itself, reflect on the methods you are using, apply new ones, and compare differences in what you get out of the generative AI you are using. Documenting this continuous feedback loop helps in developing self-monitoring skills. It also helps develop an overall ecosystem of continuous improvement that you can share with fellow colleagues. In addition, it is helpful to check if the machine learning model's responses align with the expected outcomes that you define. For instance, an editor using an LLM for draft articles may want to ensure that the content is accurate, relevant, and aligns with the publication's standards. An advertising professional might need to ensure that generated images adhere to brand guidelines in terms of font style and color palette. The more you self-monitor your interactions with any generative AI, the more you will become aware of your own knowledge gaps and learning needs. That will propel you toward further experimentation and drive you toward improving specific skills that will help you get the most out of the technology.

Self-Evaluate

Self-evaluation is a common process in many work environments and is formalized in some of the top companies in the world. After receiving generated content from AI, you will naturally assess the quality and relevance of the information or content provided. This promotes critical thinking and the ability to evaluate your own work and decision-making processes. Studies show that iterative feedback cycles with any content creation improves a person's confidence in what they might bring to the public.[7] AI can also help someone in a work environment recognize and address their own cognitive biases in how they think about the work they create and how that work is communicated to others. Encouraging employees to share opinions of particular creative decisions with the gen AI tool they were using can encourage those employees to critically examine their own thought processes and opinions on the generated content and, in the process, develop more objective perspectives.

---

[7] Carless, D. (2019). Feedback loops and the longer-term: towards feedback spirals. Assessment & Evaluation in Higher Education, 44(5), 705–714.

Adapt

Working with AI requires adaptability, as AI tools will produce many unexpectedly pleasant and unpleasant results. You can learn to adjust your strategies and approaches even more by documenting your efforts. Adapting your workflows to integrate experimentation also involves understanding the capabilities and limitations of the specific gen AI tool you are using, which calls for ongoing education and skills development. Beyond the internal applications of the technology, adaptability is also important in customer-facing activities, where you might use LLMs to draft responses but have to customize them to specific customer demographics and situations that those customers have encountered with your product or service.

Understand the Core Problem to Solve

Generative AI is not the solution to the problem to solve. They are a means to an end. The problem to solve in any workflow and in any creative job tends to lead to a human uncovering its solution. Think of all the problems you persistently solve in your workplace and then use a design thinking tool to get to the core root of. While an LLM or other generative AI can support you in solving some problems, these will likely be tangentially related to the problem at hand.

Figure 3-3. *Robot self-monitoring with help from all its clones. AI-generated image*

If your problem to solve is that you need to pump out more social media posts about your company during the day, the root problem as to why you cannot do so without generative AI will point to time, how you prioritize outreach, and the limited staff you probably have to focus on doing so. Many social media posts speak to the power of automating this process using a combination of generative AI and automation tools like Zapier and newcomer Make. They do not solve the problem of user or customer engagement however.

Most humans who eventually catch on to automated content, down to the homogeneous and same sounding content that an organization releases on YouTube or TikTok, will, in old marketing speak, change the channel.

If you believe the magnification that AI will make workflows more efficient, you need to dig deeper into understanding what is currently not efficient in your team's workflows. Prior to understanding what parts are or are not inefficient also demands that you as a team lead, or as part of leadership, understand the types of workflows your employees engage in. Generative AI won't solve the problem of work inefficiency simply by being implemented. Those inefficiencies scale when work gets more complex.

Make Informed Decisions

As discussed in an earlier chapter, you will be the best judge as to how and if you integrate generative AI. That means you will need to make a number of decisions about when and how to use any generative AI tool effectively, as that guidance will not always come from a team lead, management, or leadership. This can heighten your decision-making response abilities, requiring you to consider various factors such as the appropriateness of AI in any given context. The decision as to whether or not to use AI can also lead to what some in business contexts refer to as analysis paralysis. Often, when there are too many things to consider in the implementation of generative AI, the easiest decision is to put off its application for a later time. The decision to apply any generative AI tool leads to more questions. It's not as easy as going to the Internet, accessing a public generative AI tool, prompting it, and generating content. Questions need to be answered and not collected on a to-do list and carefully tucked away in a drawer:

- Who needs what tool now and why?

- What's it going to cost?

- What are the differences between the free and paid-for tools?

- Who is going to pay for the use of a specific tool?

- How does an individual or team justify the purchase and use of a tool?

- What, if any, are the consequences of our organization using these tools?

- What are the impacts on data privacy?

- How do we use these tools, and who is going to train our teams to use them?

- Should legal be involved?

- What will the use of any gen AI tool do to the production quality of our work?

- What sources of knowledge about generative AI are leadership listening to when implementing the technology at work?

If you had any doubt before as to why organizations are struggling to implement generative AI tools quickly, consider that these questions are not exhaustive. Answering each is important prior to rushing in no matter what size your organization is or how well established it is. Documenting those decisions and communicating the answers to your teams will go a long way in empowering others in the team to make decisions a little more easily. The last question on the list is an important one that every leader needs to answer. Answering the question requires the investigative qualities of a researcher, especially if you want to understand the value of the technology's implementation and the return on investment.

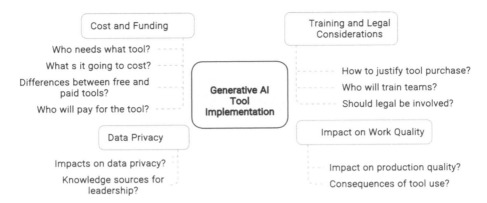

Figure 3-4. *Some questions to ask when considering implementing AI tools. AI-generated image*

Timebox

Experimenting with different generative AI tools can take you down a rabbit hole of time wasting. Effective use of generative AI in your workflows requires good time management, particularly in balancing between your use of AI-generated content and how other team members support you in those same workflows. Conducting comparative timeboxing with and without generative AI might provide useful information as to whether or not you find it of value to use in your particular case. Planning time to learn to use any generative AI tool effectively is also an important factor to consider.

Take Personal Responsibility for AI Integration

Self-regulation also means taking responsibility for the work you do and the way you conduct yourself in any organization. That includes your understanding of and capacity to follow the values that have been embedded in your organization. If they are fuzzy, you need to ask for greater clarity, especially now, at a time when the ethical implications of using any generative AI, including issues of bias, fairness, and transparency, are front and center for any organization. As an example, your entire team will benefit from your research of any generative AI codes of conduct or policies that a company building the technology has laid out. Knowing and reporting this information to your team members will demonstrate that you care about the values of your organization enough to make sure the decision to use any gen AI tool is in alignment with those values. It will also help you and your team answer internal and external criticisms, like "Why are you using that particular generative AI tool for your work?"

Collaborate and Communicate

Integrating AI into workflows will definitively require persistently communicating with peers about the quality of any content that is generated, its limitations, and its potential uses within existing workflows. LLMs can also be used as tools for collaborative learning, where a customized GPT bot, for example, can carry specific organizational knowledge as a more interactive type of FAQ. Doing so helps to develop a shared understanding of concepts that may be specific to team workflows, and, if accessed by individuals on other teams, it can help accelerate their understanding of what that team values and the language they use to describe the processes that they undertake.

Manage Automated Processes

The ability to program multimodal generative AI to automate certain tasks comes with pros and cons. The ability to automate does not eliminate a human from the equation, it amps up the importance of being self-regulating. Whereas before some of your work may have been handed off for approval or review by a senior manager, when part of your workflow can be automated, integrating AI demands that you review your own work well before reaching the assessment of someone else. There are many dependencies based on the context and unique workflows that each of us has. According to creative professional Dan Jackson,[8] at times you may take a good eight hours to master a single tool, apply it to your work, only to realize upon review that it's just not good enough to use. This, despite the possibility that you could have completed the tasks as part of your workflow in a less amount of time.

In terms of automating parts of your workflow, recent developments with AI platforms, like Pickle, can provide you with tools and infrastructure that might be helpful for you to create, deploy, and manage AI agents. The growing number of platforms that are surfacing offers a range of features and can also be thought of as multimodal automation tools, which allow AI agents to perform a sequence of tasks you guide them to complete in order to generate content for a specific use case. You can train AI agents, customize their behavior, and integrate them into some part of your workflow.

As an example, many companies use AI-powered chatbots to handle customer inquiries, providing instant responses and resolving common issues. *Zendesk*, a popular customer service platform, integrates AI agents to streamline support operations. These AI agents can answer frequently asked questions, guide users through troubleshooting steps, and escalate issues to human agents when necessary. This particular use case is being adopted more widely across various industries, including retail, banking, and tech support.

---

[8] Dan Jackson, interview, 2024.

Facilitating a Work Environment for Self-Regulatory Behaviors

It's early days integrating generative AI within our day-to-day workflows, so it's too early to tell how the technology will affect the ability for individuals to self-regulate rather than being mandated to use specific tools as part of their workflows. Researching what characteristics of self-regulation can be measured for people using generative AI tools at work is also in its beginnings. Many organizations are jumping the gun inspired by ungrounded claims that generative AI tools make work more efficient. It's impossible to make these types of generalizations across different work environments or even within the same organization. For these reasons, it's important for individuals on teams within organizations that have already adopted gen AI to keep track of their own progress and evaluate the usefulness of an AI tool.

For those who have not yet integrated gen AI, there are some strategies that organizations can try, and many of these are intended to trigger self-regulation habits. Bear in mind that if your organization runs by command-and-control methods, you will learn quite quickly that you face an uphill battle in encouraging employees to self-regulate when it comes to managing their use and integration of gen AI tools. Shifting members of an organization to practice an SRL mindset requires a complete rethink of how leadership manage their business, their employees, and the work their employees undertake. Self-regulation involves relearning how to learn, and it's difficult to tell someone to do that. Here are some strategies that leads in some organizations have used to integrate generative AI within teams:

- Assume that all employees need a reminder of your organization's values. These will need to be translated into principles and guidelines to guide them in their use of any AI tool.

61

- Encourage the adoption of generative AI at the team vs. the individual level in order to spark collaborative learning and knowledge sharing among employees.

- Advocate personal responsibility when it comes to human oversight and critical evaluation of AI-generated content every step of the way to ensure accuracy, ethical use, and alignment with organizational values, team, and larger company goals.

- Back the use of generative AI tools with as much research as you can locate and task anyone taking it on in your organization to also investigate the pros and cons of specific tools and the advantages they might have to increasing value.

- Every single employee no matter how experienced will benefit from increasing their knowledge of AI systems to understand their capabilities and limitations. If you want to increase adoption, then make this easier for them by providing them with portals, links, and resources or have that learning outsourced.

- Establish an AI enablement team that people can go to when needing ideas or permissions or when they have questions about a particular tool. Ensure the enablement team represents a wide demographic of multi-team representation and includes at least one member from leadership and another from IT security.

- Understand how individual differences, such as prior experience with AI, learning styles, and personality traits, may influence the impact of generative AI on self-regulation. Work with team members to increase knowledge for everybody.

- Encourage every employee who is interested in developing skills to properly work with different generative AI to seek their own training and then share what they know with everyone on their team and potentially in their organization.

- Encourage the private access and development of personalized chatbots to serve as a virtual coach or mentor, providing individualized guidance, feedback, and support to help individuals develop their self-regulation skills.

Anticipate that a lot of the legwork will be convincing your fellow humans of the value of adopting generative AI. That, however, is impossible until you can identify where in an employee's workflow they might benefit from the technology. To answer that question, you need to understand their workflow, which means having conversations about the work they do and figuring out together where generative AI might help.

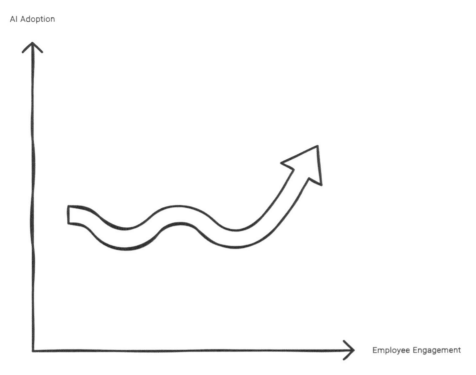

Figure 3-5. *The bumpy ride increasing AI adoption among employees. It's too early to tell how employees are adopting AI tools and whether or not adoption even correlates to engagement. AI-generated image*

Figure 3-6. *Bot teaching bot. AI-generated image*

Self-Regulatory Chatbots

The last point on the previous list provokes us to ask a serious question: Can AI tools support self-regulation more directly? The answer lies in the latest features that are becoming available for these powerful ML models. Different LLMs are now providing us the ability to develop our own personalized chatbots, customized according to the content that they focus on and even the attitude they have in how they communicate knowledge. Tutoring systems have been around for a while now, but our capacity to individualize an AI-powered tutoring system is now possible. These systems can provide personalized feedback, track progress, and suggest adaptive learning strategies, prompting learners to assess their own progress. Your bot can also be an AI-driven writing assistant that can analyze writing style, grammar, and content, offering feedback and suggestions that encourage you to reflect on your writing process and improve it. Another very real opportunity is the ability to customize your own LLMs with your own data using retrieval-augmented generation and knowledge graphs, to give you more accuracy and control over how data is identified and analyzed. SRL chatbots can be customized to support you in your efforts to self-regulate. In some type of paradoxical impulse, their use is to regulate you to take control over what you learn and manage your work, giving you strategies when you need them or, for whatever reason, when you have changed into a more passive state of learning. Recent research on the integration of artificial and human intelligence in what Molenaar (2022) refers to as hybrid human-AI regulation[9] outlines a theoretical foundation from self-regulated learning and hybrid intelligence, developed from a prototype that positions hybrid regulation

---

[9] Molenaar, I. (2022). The concept of hybrid human-AI regulation: Exemplifying how to support young learners' self-regulated learning. Computers and Education: Artificial Intelligence, 3, 100070.

as a collaborative task between learner and AI. Chatbots provide us with a glimpse of the possible when it comes to hybrid human-AI regulation, but they are by no means a silver bullet.

Balancing Regulation and Self-Regulation

While this chapter provided a strong foundation for understanding the role that generative AI might play in provoking self-regulation, there is still significant potential for investigating its full impact on the self-regulatory process. The transformative potential of generative AI for self-regulated learning in the workplace is in need of research, but the seeds have been planted. Gen AI and the nature of its rapid growth and accelerated integration within organizations speak to the need for workers to figure out how they will interact with the technology on their own. While self-regulation of AI tools is a necessity at this point, organizations still need to determine how they will support their teams of employees in its activation.

If self-regulating teams sound idealistic, it is likely because of the many work environments where managers are paid to regulate the teams that they manage. In reality, there may be a three-way hybrid method of encouraging self-regulatory behaviors in work environments. This will likely be a combination of internal motivation by the employee, external motivation by a manager, and a gen AI chatbot in the middle. If an employee has been tasked to work with a generative AI, and the work that they create is known to not take full advantage of a particular tool, a manager may need to step in to support that employee in deepening their knowledge of that tool, to more accurately gauge if the types of generated content they have produced are useful. Recall that a gen AI tool can only accomplish so much. The technologies of retrieval-augmented generation (RAG) and knowledge graphs (KGs) certainly seem to be offering generated content that reduces untrue content.

CHAPTER 4

Relearn While Working

There is a tactical reason to facilitate and promote self-regulation when it comes to wanting your employees to integrate generative AI in their workflows—time or rather the lack of time that employees have when in production environments. In today's fast-paced, competitive work environments, employees are expected to over-deliver. Focused learning sessions at work are an idealistic luxury unless their value is understood. Interruptions, on the other hand, both self-initiated and externally motivated, pervade the workday. Traditionally, these interruptions have been seen as productivity killers. Or, are they necessary?

This chapter reframes those disruptive moments as opportunities for "interruptive learning," essential for staying knowledgeable, improving craft, being adaptable, and augmenting work. Those interruptions or pit stops can integrate a number of different generative AI or AI software that can support you in more intentionally integrating learning while at work. Generative AI might be able to fill a gap and support task completion in various workflows, but only if a sufficient amount of time is allocated by your employee to learn how to use these new tools. The potential "rush" that leadership might have for employees to integrate generative AI in their workflow, without sufficient guidance as to how, is also an opportunity to shift a common expectation in many organizational environments for employees to learn on their own time.

© Patrick Parra Pennefather 2024
P. Parra Pennefather, *Regenerating Learning*, Design Thinking,
https://doi.org/10.1007/979-8-8688-1061-9_4

Mapping Out Interruptions in Your Workflows

Plotting a previous experience of when you had to learn may be difficult, but when one comes up and you map it, that opens up a gateway to reflect on whether or not an AI tool might be able to support you during that interruption. You have a few directions to consider. The first is choosing to use old methods at finding out the information you need that will help you solve a problem you have, so you can continue your work. Think about a programmer who gets stuck on a particular part of the code. They might go to their familiar repositories or web portals to find the help they need. Nowadays, many developers are tasking LLMs to help them learn how to solve the problem, by generating code they can at least try out and refine. LLMs are also being tasked with debugging code with some success. Consider a somewhat simple task like removing the background on an image so that all that is left is the full body shot of a character. Many tools built within Photoshop and other image manipulation software can handle that pretty easily. The learning curve is likely pretty small. But what if your background consists of different colors? What if part of the background color is the same color as your character's hands? Suddenly, you are faced with a more complex problem and will need to call upon your expertise using an established software in combination with some of the new AI editing tools that it features.

Different obstacles will call for different solutions, and some may be impossible for any generative AI tool to solve. Other types of obstacles are impossible to know how to solve. It's not like we always have a manual of to-dos when it comes to solving problems we have never encountered before. Different generative AI tools may provide you with options in terms of guiding you to solutions you may not have thought of on your own. Where do interruptions occur and what tools do you tend to use to remove them?

Figure 4-1. *Bot at a pit stop. AI-generated image*

Take a moment then and reflect on what happens when you are challenged to learn something in order to move forward completing tasks for your work. As an analogy, AI can act like a member of the racing team at a pit stop and has the potential in some cases to point you to what you need to learn to solve the problem that you have. While it's not only about efficiency, gen AI tools provide you a welcome change in your own patterned way of solving problems and taking time to learn something new. They interject with creativity, the unexpected, while also having the potential to accelerate the removal of obstacles, at least for some parts of your workflows. Conversely, they may add additional tasks to your workflow that you did not expect, but sometimes that may be just as necessary to remove the obstacles that you have. The unexpected interjections that an AI makes may lead to new ways of approaching a problem space, provide you with actionable pivots, or simply invoke eureka moments that just might take your work to an unexpected place you did not imagine.

Not All Interruptions Are Equal

Distinguish between distracting or derailing interruptions and potentially valuable ones that introduce relevant new knowledge or spark an idea. An interruption that occurs while you are deeply focused in a complex task is going to be much different from one that will occur during a routine activity. This understanding helps us manage our responses to disruptions. This old Sufi story teaches that sometimes interruptions and confusion can lead to creative solutions and highlights the absurdity of certain situations.

The Interrupted Sermon

Nasrudin was once giving a sermon in the village square. He started by asking, "Do you know what I am going to talk about today?"

The crowd replied, "No, we don't."

Nasrudin said, "Well, if you don't know, then there's no point in telling you," and he left.

The next day, he began his sermon with the same question: "Do you know what I am going to talk about today?"

This time, the crowd replied, "Yes, we do."

Nasrudin said, "Well, if you already know, then there's no need for me to tell you," and he left again.

The third day, determined to get a sermon, the crowd devised a plan. When Nasrudin asked, "Do you know what I am going to talk about today?" half of the crowd replied "Yes," while the other half replied "No."

Nasrudin paused, then said, "Well, those who know can tell those who don't," and left.

Figure 4-2. *Cats distracted by cat memes. AI-generated image*

Types of Pit Stops

Each of us learns differently. At work, that difference can be even more distinct.

> *When asked if you are aware of the ways in which you learn, how quick can you answer?*

The challenge with the action of learning, just like the action of doing, is that it is difficult to articulate the process. On top of that, we all learn different types of things differently, depending on the purpose we have for learning that something. At work, there is barely any time to articulate how we learn when we are so focused on trying to figure out what we need to know to remove an obstacle or solve a problem connected to completing our tasks. Identifying the best conditions under which you can learn is important to know. You might feel intimidated to not know how to complete a particular task, especially if you've been hired as an expert in a particular domain. That may prevent you from asking a fellow colleague for help. You also never really know when your learner will be activated. That is especially true when you're working to complete specific tasks. It's not like we always start the day thinking "What will I need to learn today to complete my work?"

The ways in which we solve problems in our day-to-day work with whatever tasks we undertake are partly informed by the patterned ways we use regularly. These are our heuristics, our patterned ways of solving problems. We take different approaches depending on the complexity of the problem. One of the first problems we encounter when faced with an obstacle or blocker, anything that prevents us from completing an independent task as part of our everyday work, is deciding what we need to learn to remove that obstacle. It's not like we can anticipate when that will occur precisely, but we can perhaps expect that we will have moments when we will need to learn something new to continue moving forward in completing assigned tasks. When these moments do happen, it might feel like a pit stop we have to make in order to continue delivering the tasks we've committed to completing. You may have different thoughts about those pit stops, those pauses in your workflows or pipelines.

These pit stops or interruptions can be categorized as internal (self-triggered curiosity, exploration) or external (coworker questions, new information alert).[1] You're in a recursive zone when that occurs. Different people handle the pause in the flow differently. What's important is to become aware of how you handle it. Do you let out one big sigh? Do you give up and take a break or go for a coffee? Do you ask for help? Do you search for what you need to learn online? What are your knowledge portals? How do you know the best place to look and how reliable is it? Answering all these questions gets you closer to better understanding how you manage your own learning in those in-betweens. Take a moment then, and reflect on what happens when you are challenged to learn something in order to move forward completing tasks for your work. The "pit stop" typology that follows categorizes different types of learning interruptions during work that might be helpful to consider. Each type reflects how learning is integrated or interrupts the flow of ongoing tasks.

Full Pit Stop: Complete Interruption

Description: In this scenario, the learning need is so substantial that it requires stopping all other tasks. You are fully consumed by the learning task, much like a car that must stop completely at a pit for significant repairs or changes.

Example: Learning a completely new software essential for upcoming tasks, requiring dedicated time to study and practice away from usual responsibilities, online courses, workshops.

---

[1] Mark, G., Gonzalez, V. M., & Harris, J. (April 2005). No task left behind? Examining the nature of fragmented work. In Proceedings of the SIGCHI conference on Human factors in computing systems (pp. 321–330).

Rolling Pit Stop: Partial Interruption

Description: Here, the learning partially diverts attention from regular tasks, but doesn't completely halt them. It's similar to slowing down significantly but not stopping, as adjustments are made on the go.

   Example: Attending a training webinar relevant to ongoing projects where you can still manage some light tasks or correspondence, micro-courses.

Drive-Thru Learning: Integrated Learning

Description: Learning is almost seamlessly integrated into the workflow. You acquire new skills or knowledge while performing your tasks, similar to making minor adjustments or getting quick services in a drive-thru without stopping the vehicle.

   Example: Using a new tool or software feature that has built-in tutorials or prompts that guide you while you continue with your work. This can also include job shadowing and mentoring.

Cruise Control: Second Nature Learning

Description: In this type, the tool or skill is so well integrated into the workflow that using it and improving upon it becomes second nature. There is no perceived interruption; instead, learning and working are simultaneous and fluid.

   Example: Regular use of a well-understood software where occasional updates or new features are easily adopted without disrupting the workflow, knowledge bases, and integrated help guides.

   The typology helps in understanding how different learning interventions can affect work and productivity and allows organizations to better plan and support employee learning.

How to Use This Typology

- **Self-Assessment**: Where do you naturally spend most of your learning time? Are there areas where you could benefit from trying a different approach?

- **Team Development**: Is your team's learning balanced across these categories? How can you support learning in all of the quadrants?

- **Organizational Support**: Do company policies, resources, and culture encourage diverse types of learning?

These are not rigid categories. Learning frequently blends multiple elements. Effective learners strategically leverage the type of learning that fits their needs and the task at hand. Organizations that value continuous learning provide the structures and opportunities to encourage the full spectrum of development.

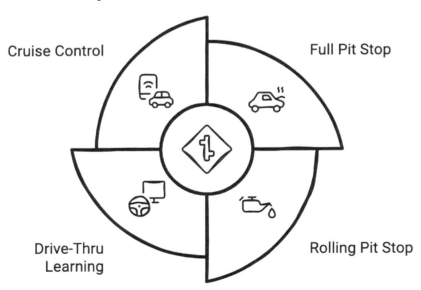

Figure 4-3. *Types of learning interruptions. AI-generated image*

Use Cases for Designing Interrupted Learning

Applying the idea of pit stops to different learning scenarios, such as writing an essay vs. creating and animating a 3D model, we can see how knowing-in-action develops through practice and experience in distinct ways.[2] Donald Schön's concept of *knowing-in-action* refers to the implicit knowledge that you apply during everyday activities without consciously thinking about it. It is the kind of knowledge demonstrated through doing, such as when you skillfully navigate a complex situation. This form of knowing is often tacit and unfolds in the moment, allowing for intuitive and fluid responses to dynamic environments. Schön contrasts it with *reflection-in-action*, which occurs when you might become more aware of your actions and adjust them in real time. In the cases below, added complexities in subtasks will demand a combination of traditional solutions from software we are familiar with and one or more generative AI tools.

Writing an Essay with an LLM

For learning to write an essay, knowing-in-action might develop as you become familiar with the structure and style of previously written essays. Initially, you might focus consciously on organizing thoughts, structuring paragraphs, and employing proper grammar. Over time, as these processes become habitual, you might be able to produce a well-structured argument or narrative more automatically. Through feedback from peers and mentors, you might recognize what makes for a strong thesis, how to transition smoothly between points, and how to conclude effectively, all with less conscious effort. An LLM might only fit into the beginning

---

[2] Schön, D. A. (1991). The reflective practitioner. Ashgate Publishing.

process as you would likely want to refine any content that it gives you for a variety of reasons. However, you can likely upload documents of your own writing style that an LLM can draw from as it generates new content. Since the craft of writing across different genres is varied, it really depends on the corpus that an LLM draws from as to how useful it might be.

Creating and animating a 3D Model

In contrast, the complexities of learning to create and animate a 3D model involve mastering different tools and techniques. Early in the learning process, you need to consciously think about navigating software interfaces, understanding 3D spatial relationships, and applying animation principles. However, as you gain experience, much of this understanding moves into the realm of knowing-in-action. You begin to manipulate 3D models, rig them, and apply animations through trial and error, working with textures, lighting, and motion iteratively. You develop a sense for how movements should be timed and how textures should look, often making adjustments on the fly based on a deep understanding of the software and the previous experience of rigging characters and modeling them. Some text-3D generative models like Mesh are surfacing, and these will likely be increasingly accompanied by post-generation tools to refine the models that it generates. A more likely scenario, however, might be that whatever 3D model is generated, you will be able to import it within a 3D software environment you are familiar with, like Blender or Maya.

In both cases, what begins as a process of learning specific rules and techniques evolves into a more intuitive practice. This transformation allows you to perform complex tasks with greater efficiency and creativity, embodying Schön's notion of knowing-in-action. While helpful, however, you never really know when your learner will be activated and what kind of student you are going to be. That's especially true when you're at work or working to complete specific tasks for your own business or an employer. That said, we can all probably agree that learning is activated throughout our working process.

Shortcuts and Missed Understandings

Of course, if you have very little experience as a 3D modeler, you could use an integrated text-3D model generative tool that Shutterstock is piloting, but you'll need to keep in mind that their corpus may be limited as their model is trained on their own catalog of licensed 3D objects. Nevertheless, if all you're looking for is a chihuahua with a sombrero and the generative AI provides you with everything you wanted but included two tails, the easiest choice might be to export the model into Blender or Maya and "simply" remove the unwanted tail. But what are you missing from the process of modeling the chihuahua on your own? How does shortcutting a workflow affect you later on, like when you are tasked to create a 3D model of an animal or character or humanoid that is not part of a machine learning model's corpus? These are questions that professionals like Darren DeCoursey ask when it comes to applying generative AI within 3D pipelines that skip over certain established tasks, like rigging. The result is a generation of employees that will be lost when it comes to troubleshooting problems that form part of the know-how of current 3D animators.[3]

---

[3] Darren Decoursey, interview, 2024.

Figure 4-4. *Bot trying to locate the real heart. AI-generated image*

Michael Hickman, an experienced professional biomedical illustrator, weighs in on where generative AI might be most useful in animation pipelines.[4] He explains that AI is beneficial in the early stages of development, when animation ideas are still vague and nebulous. Generative AI proves valuable by swiftly generating art styles and directional concepts for storyboard development. Additionally, it is useful for organizing dense materials, such as categorizing lengthy lists of text into logical groups to help structure the storytelling content. However, generative AI's utility diminishes during the middle and later stages of animation production. At these stages, the content has largely been finalized, making consistency in execution critical. While text prompts are currently a primary means of input for generative AI, human communication often involves hand gestures and other forms of implied interaction to properly explain an idea. When it comes to communicating ideas and why a person chose to move in a particular direction, each team member possesses their own contextual history and influences that the team understands. An AI will not grasp this context without extensive explanation.

Anticipating Interruptions

Consider when generative AI will fit into your workflow, what different tools might help you with specific tasks, how much time it will take to benefit from those interactions, and whether or not you'll benefit from repeated use of a single or series of generative AI tools. Additionally, how will generative AI make a difference in what it is that you create? The use cases that follow are intended to incite where learning more about specific gen AI might occur. Each is meant to provoke. These are beginnings, not ideas set in stone. What would you do and what would you need to learn?

---

[4] Interview with Michael Hickman, June 2024.

Podcast Creation

Consider the process of producing a podcast episode. You might relish the excitement of conducting interviews, crafting a script, and weaving everything together into a compelling narrative that captures listeners' attention. What does it mean to capture a listener's attention nowadays? How might generative AI support that impulse? The tasks of mixing and sound design might also be enjoyable for you. What might the role of generative audio be in setting the tone of the podcast? Would you use parts of what you generate to underscore? Post-upload tasks might be tedious for some. Writing show notes, creating social media content, and notifying guests about their live episodes may not be an enjoyable part of your process. Can that be automated? What does that automation do to the content? Does it make it more generic? Does it allow you to rapidly prototype an idea that you can then refine? On the other hand, you may actually enjoy all of the tasks involved in getting your podcast published, because each of those tasks informs your future content, helps you prepare and be ready for future content, and supports you in talking about what your podcast is about.

> *How might you balance the affordances that some gen AI offer while ensuring your voice is consistently present throughout the process?*

Creative Assistant

We are told the story often that gen AI can act as a creative assistant or coeditor—a versatile, highly skilled, and knowledgeable intern bot that works at lightning speed and can be trained. AI will not excel at completing entire projects independently, but it might support initial brainstorming and refining your unclear, half-formed ideas, helping you to explore them further. AI can also assist in generating drafts for articles, reports, marketing copy, and even creative writing. By learning how to improve your prompts, an LLM might save you some time and allow you to focus on refining the content. Its ability to analyze and suggest improvements might improve the overall quality of the writing, or it might make the content look and feel more generic. It can also analyze a series of already created copy, simulate your style of writing, and provide you an analysis of how you structure your work. This is all helpful, but maybe a more accurate perception of a creative assistant is one that requires supervision throughout the inference process.

The Benefits of Interruptive Learning

Not all interruptions are moments of learning. Nor are all learning interruptions specific to completing a task like learning how to use neural filters in Photoshop while engaged in the creation of a visual artifact. When using generative AI, at times we are exposed to new information. These serendipitous encounters with information outside our immediate focus can broaden our perspective and offer unexpected connections and content.[5]

Whether or not you use any generated content from an AI, interacting with the technology can break mental ruts, jolting you out of unproductive thought patterns and opening you to new pathways toward solving a problem or accessing new ideas. Interruptions can also wake us up to a part of our creativity that we did at all believe was present. Often, we only realize what additional knowledge we need when faced with a question or obstacle. When we allow ourselves to investigate intriguing disruptions, we stimulate a habit of active exploration and knowledge seeking. Generative AI can keep you on your toes with the great expectation of potential insights over any generated content that may come with the exchange.

---

[5] https://www.nature.com/articles/s41467-017-02042-w

Strategies for Interrupting Your Work

But do you really, really need it?

Before jumping down a rabbit hole triggered by integrating gen AI in between your human tasks, critically assess its relevance. Is it truly essential for the task at hand? To answer that question, you need to understand how a specific gen AI tool might actually support your work. To be able to answer how a tool might support your work, you will benefit from investigating use cases. There are many out there, and you would be surprised by what you'll find when you conduct a simple search of potential uses that match the type of work that you do or problem you need solved.

Timeboxing Exploration

Set a short, defined amount of time (e.g., 15 minutes) to dive into prompt experiments with any generative AI. This limits distractions while allowing you time to practice. That's just one example of many other timed events you can undertake. You can timebox 30 minutes a day just for investigating new tools that you might find useful and another 30 for trying one or more out, learning how to use it as you apply it to a task at hand.

Organize Your Captures

Record interesting insights, questions, or even partial solutions triggered by interactions with an AI. Integrate them back into your main workflow later. **Set up a digital Zettelkasten system** using tools like Miro or Notion.

A Zettelkasten, German for "slip box," is a method of note-taking and knowledge management. It involves writing down individual notes or ideas (called "slips" or "zettels") on small cards or digital equivalents and organizing them in a way that allows for easy retrieval and connection. It was developed by Niklas Luhmann (1927–1998), a German sociologist known for his contributions to social systems theory. He developed the Zettelkasten method as a way to manage his vast amount of research and ideas efficiently. Luhmann's Zettelkasten contained over 90,000 slips and played a role in his prolific output, which included more than 70 books and hundreds of scholarly articles. He attributed much of his intellectual productivity to this method, which allowed him to connect and develop ideas over time systematically.[6]

- Write each idea, concept, or piece of information on a separate slip. Each note should be self-contained and concise.

- Assign a unique identifier to each note and link related notes to one another. This creates a network of interconnected ideas, making it easier to find and connect relevant information later.

- Regularly review your collection of slips to identify recurring themes, patterns, and clusters of related information.

- Use the links between notes to see how different ideas relate to one another. This can reveal new insights and connections that may not be immediately obvious.

- Draw on the interconnected notes to compile research documents. Use the clusters and patterns identified in your Zettelkasten to structure your writing.

- Each note can act as a citation or reference point, ensuring that your research is well supported and traceable back to the original ideas.

---

[6] Basu, A. (2020). What is zettelkasten and how to write "papers" using zettelkasten.

The Jagged AI Frontier

Some research reveals that generative AI, like GPT, can significantly boost the performance of skilled employees by up to 40% when used appropriately. However, pushing AI beyond its current abilities leads to a notable 19% decrease in worker performance. This highlights the importance of understanding the "jagged technological frontier" of AI, as its features constantly evolve. Managers need to stay informed about these limitations, especially since employees often struggle to discern which tasks any generative AI might be useful for.

Over 700 consultants from Boston Consulting Group participated in a study that assessed the impact of GPT-4 on their performance.[7] Participants were divided into groups and assigned tasks either within or beyond GPT-4's capabilities. Those with tasks within GPT-4's abilities were asked to complete a series of actions, such as developing and pitching a new product for a hypothetical shoe company, creating a launch plan, and writing a detailed article documenting the process. The study found that access to GPT-4 significantly improved performance on these tasks by up to 40%. Additional training on how to use the AI further also informed performance.

According to designer Dan Jackson, the integration of generative AI is useful for a variety of reasons, but the interruptions that are demanded are not just about learning how to use a tool but also about generating content that you can then refine and edit and, importantly, throw away if not useful.[8]

---

[7] https://mitsloan.mit.edu/ideas-made-to-matter/how-generative-ai-can-boost-highly-skilled-workers-productivity#:~:text=A%20new%20study%20on%20the,who%20don't%20use%20it

[8] Dan Jackson, interview, June 2024

Interruptive learning is an inevitable reality of the modern knowledge worker. By recognizing the potential value of generative AI and developing strategies to manage how it can support a flow, between starting tasks and learning what you need to complete them, you can transform these disruptions from obstacles into catalysts for growth and improved, changed, or augmented outcomes. If your organization has not yet implemented generative AI, is against it, bans it, or does not encourage you or your team to integrate the technology, or even experiment as to how it might be able to be useful, you can still prepare for the potential of it being used in your organization in the future.

The best way to begin is to think about and prioritize learning objectives that are essential for your current job. What know-how do you already possess in the work that you do that anyone who came into the company would have to learn? What parts of your job might be accelerated, augmented, or minimally supported with any existing generative AI? As you start to answer these questions, you'll be better able to consider how you might design the learning you will have to have, should generative AI one day be implemented in your organization.

CHAPTER 5

Design What You Need to Learn

Nasrudin was walking down the street when he saw a group of people gathered around a well, looking very worried. They explained that the moon had fallen into the well and asked Nasrudin to help get it out. Without missing a beat, Nasrudin fetched a rope and a hook, then threw it into the well. After a few minutes of fishing around, the hook caught on something. Nasreddin pulled with all his might, and the hook broke free, sending him sprawling onto his back. As he lay there, he saw the moon shining brightly in the sky. "Praise be!" he exclaimed. "It's a good thing I fell, or the moon would never have gotten back into the sky!"

Previous chapters have been focused on the importance of reprogramming how you learn, so that you begin to examine your own learning process, break down how you learn while undertaking your work, and identify the types of interruptions you might turn into learning opportunities. Few people speak of the integration of generative AI within workflows as an inherent design problem or challenge. While we know that many voices out there speak to the values of AI integration at work, there is not usually much to say about when that learning might occur nor who is going to design the magical learning that will take place. To intensify knowing-in-action with generative AI, that is precisely what each of us must do. We need to put on our designer hats and plan out how and when will we learn and even ask why we need to learn something new

© Patrick Parra Pennefather 2024
P. Parra Pennefather, *Regenerating Learning*, Design Thinking,
https://doi.org/10.1007/979-8-8688-1061-9_5

just because someone told us it would help our work. How exactly will generative AI help us? What will the benefits of using it be? To what degree must we embrace it in order to take full advantage of it?

What is it about the technology that will be better than what you do now?

All these design-oriented questions are important to ask yourself as you embark on your learning adventure with AI. Generative AI tools can only teach you so much if you are not active in planning out how and what you will learn from them.

Designing for You

When we design anything nowadays, it's helpful to think of who we are designing for. That idea of designing some kind of product or service for the benefit of another human has been around for a while, but not as a foundational discipline in human-centered design until the 20th century. The idea has evolved to be adaptable to all kinds of humans and beyond that to all species on this planet. When you think of learning how to use any generative AI tool, you need to look at your own human experience. That also means where you learn, the conditions around you, your own motivations, what your goals are, how you'll fit learning into work tasks you have to complete, how that will affect the environment you are a part of, how learning will involve others in your process as mentors, or how you will mentor others.

Designing for Social Work Environments

The Zone of Proximal Development (ZPD), proposed by Lev Vygotsky, is worthwhile knowing. It focuses on the difference between what somebody learning can do without help and what they can do with guidance. His theory emphasizes the importance of social interactions in learning and the role of more knowledgeable others in facilitating a person's development. This approach encourages designers of learning to create learning environments that support collaborative learning and scaffold instruction to help fellow humans achieve their potential. Designing the type of learning with AI that you instigate at work will help you have a plan, and that will help you achieve some goals that you are going to want to set. That design includes all the people in the organization that you are a part of and their role in supporting the process.

Figure 5-1. *Trying to catch the moon. AI-generated image*

Learning Design

Those who design learning go by many names, including instructional designers, learning designers, teaching designers, etc. They are hired by different organizations, including academic institutions, in order to design how instruction will be taught to others. Larger corporations do this as well. Every company has some kind of onboarding with employees that have been freshly recruited. Some of that onboarding involves reading materials and getting up to speed with the organization's values, mission, value proposition, products, stakeholders, and customers. There are key takeaways we can learn from those who design teaching and learning in work and academic environments. We can then apply those methods of designing learning to how we learn with generative AI.

The Influence of War and Skinner

Learning designers in work environments often consider several key factors when designing learning for other humans. The origins of instructional design date back to WWII. During that time, the US military needed to quickly train large numbers of people for a variety of difficult and emerging tasks, such as field-stripping a carbine or building never-before-existing bombers. Using B. F. Skinner's stimulus-response learning theories, training programs focused on observable behaviors, breaking tasks into subtasks, each treated as a separate learning goal.[1] In this way, progress was easy to measure, and subtasks were well defined and precisely the same for each person. Correct performance was rewarded, and incorrect performance was remediated, with the belief that mastery was possible for every learner given enough repetition and feedback. The success of this wartime training model was later applied in business,

---

[1] Skinner, B. F. (1963). Operant behavior. American psychologist, 18(8), 503.

industrial training, and, to a lesser extent, in primary and secondary education. Of course, that was a long time ago, and the pressure to teach everyone the same thing since that time has evolved. Nevertheless, the early ideas and methods of instructional design that have infiltrated most academic institutions are still present. We can still parse some important features of early instructional design methods to how you design learning with generative AI at work.

Learning Objectives

Clearly defined learning objectives are key as they help you identify what you need to learn and commit to what you want to learn. These objectives should align with your overall individual and team goals and the specific skills or knowledge you need to acquire. Your learning objectives or goals when it comes to learning generative AI can be numerous. Some might include your ability to

> **Understand the Basics**: Define what generative AI is, how the ones you will use function, and describe their key functionalities and limitations.

> **Identify Opportunities**: Identify at least three processes or tasks within your current workflow where generative AI could be applied to increase *x*, where *x* represents criteria that you define like creativity, mock-ups, early-stage prototypes, ideas, inspiration, mood board, or even efficiency.

> **Select Tools**: Evaluate and select the appropriate generative AI tools and how they can support established processes that align with the specific business needs and objectives of your team or organization.

Acquire Skills: Demonstrate the ability to fluently apply selected generative AI tools to specified tasks, including basic prompting, and the capacity to leverage customizable features, such as temperature, weight, masking, substitution, and improved prompts.

Apply Tools: Apply generative AI tools to at least two daily tasks, documenting the process and outcomes. Timebox their use in order to compare to pre-AI task completion.

Collaborate and Share: Share findings and best practices from using generative AI tools with the team through a formal presentation or a workshop.

Articulate Ethics and Compliance: Understand and articulate the ethical implications and compliance requirements of using the generative AI tool(s) in your organization and that you feel will support you in integrating the technology within your established workflows.

Continuously Learn and Adapt: Engage in continuous learning about updates to features that a gen AI tool offers, and adapt your workflows with the new features that similar AI tools offer, adapting your use accordingly, measured by quarterly progress reviews.

Solve Problems: Solve a complex problem using generative AI tools, demonstrating how the tool fits within your own heuristics, how it combines with your already honed technical proficiency.

Share Feedback: Provide constructive feedback on the usability and effectiveness of generative AI tools and suggest improvements, based on x number of weeks or months, depending on the tool.

Self-Analyze: Understand how the gen AI tool supports your work and in what ways, specifying what parts of your workflows it augments and what aspects of the tools that you use are not beneficial at all.

Relate to Your Work: Reason how the AI tool makes sense to your role or internal career development, increasing the likelihood that what you learn will be useful in your organization's use cases.

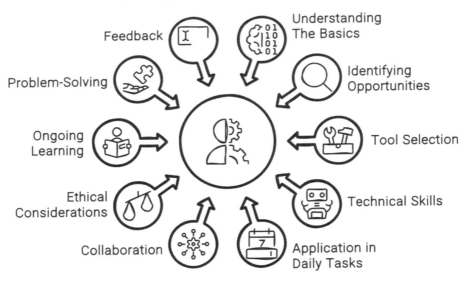

Figure 5-2. *Considerations when developing learning outcomes. AI-generated image*

Instructional Strategies

How people learn is widely different, and the introduction of different methods in order to teach people with different ways of learning and the wide variety of subjects that could be learned is strategic. Instructional strategies are not the same for every discipline nor every person. For example, while you can teach a class of humans different types of techniques for using a paint brush, how that technique is applied will be widely different. It might be fairly simple for an experienced artist/teacher to assess the technique of a student based on their intent and the results of that intent, but more difficult to assess is when that technique was sacrificed to create something unique that challenged the budding artist to hold the brush differently.

Choosing the right instructional strategies is an important component of designing any instruction. For teachers today, this might include a mix of interactive elearning, facilitation of discussion and hands-on activities, traditional lecture-based learning based on the content and learning goals, demos, and so many more. In terms of learning with generative AI, you can design how you want to learn with the technology with a little planning. For example, if you prefer to learn through a conversational chatbot, you can easily customize one and have it transformed into a type of AI-speaking mentor. Perhaps this is an effective way combined with YouTube videos and research posts that accompany your learning of a particular subject or workflow. You may also wish to search different types of social channels to help you decide which of the dozens of text-image generative tools you will use. Maybe your approach is to try at least six of them and compare the results of the generated content using similar prompts. Strategies help you realize your goals and, in the case of generative AI, are an important motivation considering the dizzying number of tools that are out there with a list that keeps growing daily.

Integrating Technology

Learning about how to work with generative AI, will require and be dependent on other technologies you have available to you. You may need to upgrade your tech setup depending on the complexity of the gen AI system you want to learn from and integrate within your workflows. If you choose that you want to purchase, customize, and install your own ML models on your own PC, there is much that is required of you to learn before you can even start using them. If you choose to go with a Mac, that's fine as well, but you will be limited by the types of ML models you can install. In both cases, you will require the latest CPUs and GPUs in order to run inference on the most recent models.

Assessment and Feedback

When you want to receive feedback, you need to know what you want feedback on. These are related to what you are learning and can come right out of your learning objectives that you start with. For example, if you want to "understand the basics of how an LLM works," you first need to identify what those basics are. This can include the best ways to prompt, chain prompting, chain of thought, etc. Once you have the criteria, then it's up to you if you assign scores to any of them in order to assess your progress. The combined criteria form your rubric. Rubrics don't have to have number equivalents. Designing your own assessment means you can also define what it means to achieve the goals identified in your learning objectives. Beyond the words "excellent, good, decent, and bad," you can create your own meaningful assessment grading protocols and use an LLM to help you realize them. Designing effective assessments to provide timely feedback will also help identify areas needing improvement. Lastly, consider bringing other colleagues into the assessment and feedback cycle. This is particularly important if you are attempting to assess the content that you generate from a specific tool, which happens to be the domain expertise of someone on your team. For example, you may want to create a pitch deck in order to propose a new project internally, and you learned that you can use an LLM combined with a slide deck generative AI, like Gamma. While you might be able to assemble a deck more rapidly, you will benefit from sending it to a colleague experienced in pitching ideas, in order to receive feedback. As you learn how to get the most out of any generative AI tool, no matter how good you think the content is, you'll always benefit from having it reviewed by someone who is skilled at content creation, grammatical structure, and overall presentation aesthetics.

Accessibility and Inclusivity

Beginning the adventure of locating any generative AI that can appeal to diverse learning needs and preferences, in addition to those that can support the needs of people with disabilities, is a challenge. Access is one thing and accessibility quite another. Both are problems that need to be solved when you think about designing your own learning or that of others. Without wider access portals, most people who are interested will only be able to access free versions, which tend to offer less features and are not very accessible. Those free versions in turn are limited in what you can do with them. Regardless of the free or paid version that you or your organization is willing to budget for, the hard sell is that they still are bias-making machines. As will be more thoroughly discussed in the Chapter 11, probability curves almost guarantee that voices which diverge from the "norm" will likely be excluded from generated content, unless you intentionally prompt an AI to include those voices. As you start to design your learning journey with generative AI, then you need to assume that some of the content you will generate will be problematic. You can safely assume that besides just designing how you integrate any gen AI tool within your workflows, you can also design the type of editing, refining, and, in some cases, complete abandonment of the content that is generated. Generative AI portals, like many software applications, are weakest when it comes to following universal design principles. In other words, they do not consider nor do they tend to consult with people with disabilities when they design the user interface of their public-facing interface. Consider these factors when you begin your interactions with any ML model.

Scalability and Flexibility

The training you undertake should be scalable so that you can learn more than a single generative AI system over time. That will be to your advantage as the number of systems available is growing weekly and their performance quite different—text, image, code, video, animation, slide deck, 3D models, etc.; every day, new systems pop up, and you may find that in your mastery over one, the others become easier to learn or at least understand. What seems to connect all of them is the skill to become good at prompting. That prompting, however, will be different depending on the system, even when you prompt different LLMs. The more you dive into installing and personalizing your own private machine learning models, a variety of knobs and sliders will also be available to you, allowing you to adjust attention, weight, temperature, variance, style, fps, etc. Consider that the more deeply you investigate generative AI systems and the potential affordances they offer, the more you will have to know in order to get more from them. Plan on stretch goals, designing the acquisition of new tools along with your more short-term mastery of public generative AI tools.

In-House Learning Management

Learning designers often need to consider how to introduce new learning programs within the organization that they are part of and manage change effectively, ensuring buy-in from all stakeholders. Once you start to increase the number of hours you will need in order to master the tools that you want to use, permission to use them and a proposal that outlines how will need to be sent to your lead(s). They too will likely have to receive permission or affirmation from leadership. So, make it easier for them by preparing for that probability.

These considerations help ensure that the learning programs you design actually happen and that you will be accountable for sharing the results of your efforts. This not only benefits you but the organization as a whole, particularly if learning generative AI tools aligns with the strategic needs of the organization. A tried-and-true method of reducing obstacles that prevent you from using a new technology in the workplace is to create a design that benefits more than just one person in your organization. This is easy enough if you are already embedded in an organization. Start from the bottom up with a small team of dedicated colleagues who might be just as eager to experiment and determine if the technology will help their work. At a certain point though, you will need to engage leadership in supporting your efforts by at least allowing you and others to dedicate a certain number of hours per week experimenting with generative AI tools. Finally, it may be more beneficial to seek expertise outside of the organization as it is sometimes easier to affirm your intent, and your team may have a budget for small workshops to expedite your organization's integration of AI.

Figure 5-3. *Hitting the AI learning bull's-eye isn't easy when you don't have clear objectives defined. AI-generated image*

Designing to Become AI Job(s) Ready

More and more jobs are popping up that emphasize the need for different skills related to AI development. Even if a job posting does not emphasize this, many organizations are in process of figuring out how to integrate the technology. That means you don't have to wait any longer to start picking up new skills using different generative AI. You can start designing what you need to learn even if you are currently employed. Prioritize learning objectives that are essential for your current job or for securing a future job, but also consider areas where you want to expand your knowledge. For instance, AI systems can analyze work patterns, identify skill gaps, and even predict future skills required based on the trends of your particular industry. Being proactive does require you take the time. The investment in doing so can help you prepare in advance for changes that may come. There is a significant emphasis across industries on the importance of upskilling and reskilling in the face of advancements with generative AI tools. Here are some insights and ideas to consider when designing to become AI ready.

AI Skills and Training

Proficiency in AI-related skills, like machine learning, AI ethics, and bias mitigation, is increasingly surfacing on many job postings as either required or, at the very least, nice-to-haves. The need to upskill with generative AI is accelerating a culture of continuous learning in different types of jobs, where employees are being supported to engage in online courses and practical projects that help them and the organization itself in the process. This trend will not only transform productivity but also prepare the various industries for future and unknown skill demands.[2]

---

[2] https://www.hackerrank.com/blog/top-ai-skills-upskill-workforce/

The rate at which generative AI is being adopted is a bit overwhelming, and at times the last thing leadership thinks of is "Oh right, how are we going to train our teams?" If you see the signs that your organization is slowly adopting gen AI tools, then it's time to consider all that goes into the design of learning and propose a short- and long-term plan.

Strategic Adaptation in Workplaces

While some businesses talk the talk, others are actually beginning to implement workshops or in-house training of generative AI tools to provide reskilling and upskilling opportunities. This may help increase job satisfaction or act as a jump scare for some employees, so proceeding with a vision and plan along with anticipated outcomes is very important. Like previous strategic initiatives, learning generative AI can be incentivized beyond saying to employees that if they learn how to use AI they can keep their jobs. What the technology does demand from management and leadership is a better understanding of what their employees actually do. Investing time in understanding what types of workflows a particular team engages in readily can support a decision whether or not to integrate gen AI.

Market Trends and Established Competencies

Along with the adoption of AI at work, there is a growing trend of companies targeting job seekers who already know how to use different generative AI tools. That speaks to the importance of learning these tools on your own if you are currently not employed. While understanding how to use different generative AI well is important, understanding the increasing importance of competencies, like problem-solving, creativity, and communication, will also be essential in your process. Not all companies articulate the need for employees to possess these types of competencies, but the need does come up during interviews. The integration of generative AI in the workplace bubbles those competencies up to the surface.

A key competency to develop through experience is problem-solving, which helps you quickly identify if generative AI are producing content that useful, somewhat useful, somewhat useless, to completely useless.

Useful

Generative AI outputs that fall into this category are more or increasingly effective in supporting you in solving task-related problems. These outputs show promise and, while still requiring refinement, provide a clear pathway to solutions or significant insights that can be directly applied to the problem at hand.

Somewhat Useful

Outputs in this category are moderately effective. They may provide partial solutions or useful insights but require additional refinement or human intervention to be fully effective in solving the problem.

Somewhat Useless

Generative AI outputs that are somewhat useless offer limited value in problem-solving. These outputs may be off-target, incomplete, or require substantial modification to be of any practical use.

Completely Useless

Outputs in this category fail to contribute to problem-solving. They may be irrelevant, incorrect, or so flawed that they offer no value and may even hinder the problem-solving process.

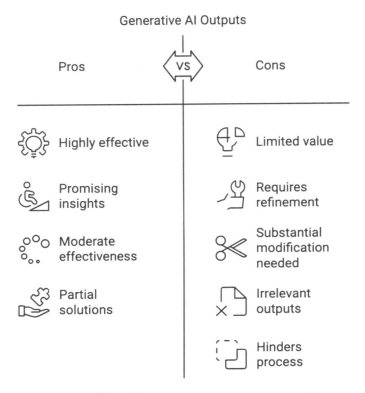

Figure 5-4. *How useful is the content you are generating.*
AI-generated image

Embracing Generative AI in Business

Integrating generative AI into business strategies is becoming a necessity
rather than an option. This includes creating a culture of innovation and
supporting continuous learning to keep pace with the race. What race? It
seems that businesses are in competition to gain value from the integration
of generative AI tools. How that value is identified, let alone measured, is
contentious and may turn out to be very specific to the situated context of
an organization. While consulting firms report increasing rates of adoption
and even percentages showing value, the current return of investment for
integrating gen AI within work processes is fuzzy. If the goal is innovation,

then a good designer designs learning around the objective of innovation. In addition, supporting leadership to define what innovation means in a new economy impacted by AI is an important step toward increasing trustworthiness in its implementation. In turn, leaders supporting different teams that make up their organization can then guide them toward a guideline or principles-oriented approach to integrating AI within their workflows. With innovation as a goal, an experimental and agile mindset are both key ingredients as the iterative attempts to integrate generative AI within various business processes will lead to insights and with the right perspective, can add value where it was not seen before. Part of your role as a designer is to document that process, reflect on where gen AI might add value, test to validate, and report the results, minimizing bias as much as possible.

Applying Design Thinking Tools to Your Learning

When you think about designing, the tendency is to design for others. When designing learning, less obvious is getting to better understand your own motivations, let alone those of others. To get to the root of your motivations in the use of generative AI and to possibly increase your understanding of your peers' motivations, it's helpful to apply the 5 Whys. The 5 Whys method is often used in design thinking to explore the root cause of a problem by asking "Why?" five times in succession. Channel your curious inner child with this method, so you can interrogate the motivations underlying your own motivations to use the technology. You can also apply it to any design problem to better understand why intelligent systems have been developed. You can iteratively use the method of the 5 Whys with an LLM. You could apply this technique to understand why Alan Turing needed to work with others in decrypting

German code during World War II. The versions of the 5 Whys that follow help you to better understand how to use it with an LLM while simultaneously applying it to a problem to solve.

WhyBot V.1

- Why did Turing need to work with others in decrypting German code? Because decrypting German code was a complex and massive task.

- Why was decrypting German code a complex and massive task? Because the Germans used advanced encryption methods like the Enigma machine, which had numerous settings and permutations.

- Why did the Enigma machine have numerous settings and permutations? Because the Enigma machine was designed to create highly secure communications, making it extremely difficult to decrypt without knowing the specific settings for each message.

- Why did the Enigma machine's design make decryption extremely difficult? Because it used a system of rotating rotors and plugboard settings that changed daily, resulting in millions of possible configurations.

- Why did the rotating rotors and daily changing plugboard settings result in millions of possible configurations? Because the Germans aimed to ensure that their military communications were secure and indecipherable to their enemies, requiring a collaborative effort to systematically break the code and keep up with daily changes.

Root Cause Summary

WhyBot Summary: The root cause of why Turing needed to work with others in decrypting German code is the intentional design of the Enigma machine to create highly secure and complex encryptions. The collaborative effort was necessary to handle the immense computational and analytical workload required to decipher the codes, manage the vast number of permutations, and develop techniques and machines (like the bombe) to automate parts of the decryption process. This required a multidisciplinary team with diverse expertise and resources, which could not be achieved by a single individual.

Human Commentary

To use any tool properly, you need practice. Those designers familiar with the activity would likely question whether or not the 5 Whys actually got to the root of the problem. The first unedited version above was generated by an LLM, including the prompts themselves. It followed down a logical path and did get to the root cause as to why Turing and colleagues may have wanted to invent the Enigma machine. We can all understand the motivations on a surface level: break the code and decrypt German military communications. While there are multiple paths you can go down in that particular exercise, it's important to evaluate the results and curate the next version by adjusting what the LLM focuses on in the prompt. Human prompts are in italics.

   WhyBot V.2

   - *Why did Turing and others need to decrypt German code?* Because in understanding the code, they could be a step ahead of what the Germans were doing to win wars.

- *Why did they need to stay a step ahead of what the Germans were doing to win wars?* Because staying a step ahead would allow the Allies to anticipate German military strategies and prevent their attacks effectively.

- *Why would anticipating German military strategies and preventing their attacks be important?* Because it would enable the Allies to protect their own forces, resources, and civilian populations and to mount successful counterattacks.

- *Why would protecting their own forces, resources, and civilian populations and mounting successful counterattacks be imperative?* Because it would weaken the German war effort, reduce the overall duration of the war, and increase the likelihood of an Allied victory.

- *Why would weakening the German war effort, reducing the war's duration, and increasing the likelihood of an Allied victory be essential?* Because achieving an Allied victory was necessary to stop the spread of Nazi ideology, restore peace and stability in Europe, and prevent further atrocities committed by the Axis powers.

Root Cause Summary

WhyBot Summary: The root cause of why Turing and others needed to decrypt German code is that doing so was vital for staying ahead of German military strategies, which in turn was essential for protecting Allied forces and populations, mounting effective counterattacks, weakening the German war effort, and ultimately securing an Allied victory to restore peace and prevent further atrocities. This overarching goal required the collaboration of Turing and many others, leveraging diverse expertise and resources to handle the complex task of decryption.

Human Commentary

As predicted, when you carefully guide an LLM to use a design thinking tool like the 5 Whys, you will benefit from persistent evaluation of what is generated. The results of the second version also indicate experience using the 5 Whys, which shows the importance of the human in the loop when interacting with any generative AI. While many speak to generative AI being a blank slate, you definitely are not. Interacting with a generative AI in this way also teaches us to value our own knowledge and experience.

Understanding Your Motivations to Redesign How You Learn

You can use the same design thinking tool to understand your own root cause for wanting to learn generative AI. Knowing this will further impact how you design your learning.

WhyBot

- *Why do you want to reprogram how you learn?* Because the current learning methods are not as effective or satisfying as you would like them to be.

- *Why are the current learning methods not as effective or satisfying?* Because they may not align with your personal learning style, goals, or interests, leading to disengagement or poor retention of information.

- *Why do the current learning methods not align with your personal learning style, goals, or interests?* Because traditional learning methods often follow a one-size-fits-all approach, which doesn't take into account individual differences in how people absorb and process information.

113

- *Why does the one-size-fits-all approach not take into account individual differences?* Because educational systems and resources are typically designed for mass instruction, prioritizing efficiency and standardization over personalization.

- *Why are educational systems and resources designed for mass instruction, prioritizing efficiency and standardization?* Because historically, education has been structured to accommodate large groups of learners with limited resources, leading to a focus on uniform teaching methods and standardized curricula.

Root Cause

WhyBot: The root cause of why you want to reprogram how you learn may be that traditional learning methods, designed for mass instruction and efficiency, often fail to align with individual learning styles, goals, and interests. This mismatch can result in disengagement and poor retention of information. By reprogramming how you learn, you can create a more personalized and effective learning experience that better suits your unique needs and preferences, leading to greater satisfaction and success in your learning endeavors.

Human Commentary

Increasing awareness of your own motivations to learn different generative AI tools will support and empower how you learn. For example, if you are dying to learn how to use Runway 3 effectively, then you are likely going to need to also learn how to use Midjourney or another text-image generative AI, as some of the most effective uses of Runway are with prompts combined with images. To improve how you prompt Runway and Midjourney means you will need to master the types of prompts that can help improve what each of those AI generates. If specificity doesn't matter to you, then by all means work with each without worrying too much about mastering how you prompt. However, if you are trying to have more control over the generated content because you have specific use cases for using them, that means more of your time will need to be invested. You can clearly start to understand in this example that if your motivation is to apply a tool for specific use cases you already have, then you have your work set out for you. The designer in you has no choice but to plan ahead knowing that some activities will need to be timeboxed.

Understanding Bias with the 5 Whys As a Design Activity

When you design learning for yourself or others, you also need to take into account what needs to be learned besides just learning how to master text-image generation (for example). Designing learning means partly relying on a set of methods from the tradition you come from.

> *We know that every machine learning model has the potential to generate biased content. How might we design learning then to deepen our understanding of the bias that an LLM might produce?*

Following through on the example of using the 5 Whys as part of your design toolbox, in your learning design process, you can task the LLM to help you better understand why it is biased. That will also help you to learn about the inner mechanics of the technology and give you a better understanding of how you wish to position yourself in the use of generative AI.

WhyBot

- *Why can LLMs be biased?* Because they often produce content that reflect the biases present in the data they were trained on.

- *Why does the content reflect biases present in the training data?* Because LLMs learn patterns, associations, and correlations from vast amounts of text data, which can include biased or prejudiced language.

- *Why does the training data include biased or prejudiced language?* Because the data is collected from a wide range of sources, such as the Internet, books, articles, and social media, where biased language and stereotypes are prevalent.

- *Why do these sources contain biased language and stereotypes?* Because human authors, influenced by societal norms, prejudices, and historical contexts, unconsciously or consciously include their own biases and stereotypes in their writing.

- *Why do societal norms, prejudices, and historical contexts influence human authors?* Because societies are shaped by complex historical, cultural, and social dynamics that propagate certain biases and stereotypes over time.

Root Cause

WhyBot: The root cause of why LLMs can be biased is that the models learn from vast amounts of data containing biased language and stereotypes, which are prevalent in human-authored texts due to deep-seated societal norms, prejudices, and historical contexts. This bias is further reinforced during the tokenization and training process where patterns and associations are formed based on the frequency and context of words and phrases in the training data.

Human Commentary

While you may not understand all the content that the LLM generates, a design thinking activity like the 5 Whys in itself can provoke you to further investigate the steps that an LLM takes in order to generate the content that it gives you. The activity will also point you to what you will need to learn to be better able to understand how an LLM works under the hood. As you design learning, and implement it, you have multiple opportunities to expand what you learn about generative AI. This can amplify your understanding of the technology and help you better comprehend why it might exhibit bias and untruths and even exclude other voices. From the 5 Whys activity, you might also reframe your understanding of bias through the mechanics of how an AI operates. In that reframing, you will uncover a treasure trove that includes

Tokenization: During tokenization, text is broken down into smaller units (tokens), which can include words, subwords, or characters. If biased language appears frequently in the training data, the model will learn to associate certain tokens with these biases.

Associations: The model forms associations between tokens based on their context and co-occurrence. For instance, if biased language is frequently used to describe certain groups or topics, the model will learn these biased associations and may reproduce them in the content it generates.

Training: During training, the model optimizes for predictive accuracy by minimizing loss functions that measure the difference between its predictions and the actual data. This process can inadvertently reinforce biases if biased predictions reduce the loss.

By learning about the potential of bias being generated by an LLM, we learn about the importance of curating training data, the importance of human feedback in the machine learning process, implementing bias detection and mitigation techniques, and continually refining the models to reduce biased content. As you can see, integrating specific tools from your own design toolbox can support your design of learning in a variety of ways, agitating a richer environment of learning.

Break It Down

Good designers become skilled at breaking processes down in order to articulate the human experience. Your next task as a designer of learning is to take the awareness you have of your own workflows and combine those processes with what you would need to learn to integrate a specific generative AI tool. To achieve this practically, you can use bullet points, a traditional storyboarding approach used by many different types of storytellers, or a comparative two-column table. The important practice is to identify where in your workflow you would ideally position the learning of an AI tool and for what purpose. That will involve you breaking down a specific workflow into as many steps as you can and trying to be clear with how much time you would spend on each task and subtask.

At what point in your workflow would learning an AI tool and applying it be most beneficial?

CHAPTER 6

Reenergize Doing

Anything that we have to learn to do we learn by the actual doing of it; People become builders by building and instrumentalists by playing instruments. Similarly, we become just by performing just acts, temperate by performing temperate ones, brave by performing brave ones.

—Aristotle

In ancient Greece, the famous philosopher Diogenes, known for his wit, lived in a barrel and often mocked the pretentiousness of society. One day, a group of scholars gathered around him, discussing profound theories about the stars. Diogenes, overhearing their conversation, picked up a piece of bread and began to eat it thoughtfully. The scholars, noticing his indifference, asked, "Diogenes, why don't you engage in our deep discussion about the heavens?" Diogenes replied with a smirk, "While you waste time contemplating the stars, I am here enjoying a simple meal. The heavens may be grand, but they won't fill your stomach."

Activating Your Doing Muscles with Gen AI

When you design how you learn, you activate a part of you that is ready to engage in the act of doing. When you put your plan into action, learning is no longer passive. You stimulate yourself to learn how to use generative AI for your own purposes, and you need to have those goals to drive that

© Patrick Parra Pennefather 2024
P. Parra Pennefather, *Regenerating Learning*, Design Thinking,
https://doi.org/10.1007/979-8-8688-1061-9_6

action forward. Conversely, there are a lot of smart people out there that like to theorize about the pros and cons of using generative AI, but who never actually try it in the context of the work that they do. It's easy to criticize the use of AI without exhausting the usefulness of the systems that are out there and without applying the technology to specific uses. Every creative knows that everything changes in the flow of creation when you use different tools and especially tools you are unfamiliar with.

The advantages and disadvantages of using generative AI is just puffery until you actually find a use for it.

While that seems like an obvious statement, the practical application of the technology activates a different part of our intelligence muscles. Don't worry though; for those who have difficulty letting go of their critical mind, generative AI can activate both the critical theorist and the practice-based personas of every human.

As an example, with one prompt you can ask an LLM different methods to facilitate improv exercises to explain how some of the mechanics of ML models work. You can also have the activities laid out step by step for you to try with others. The technology enables us to recontextualize how an ML model works using a vocabulary we may understand, shifting from critically understanding a subject to practically trying out those activities to test whether or not they can be applied to the task at hand. If you happen to have a background as an improviser and facilitator of improv in a specific discipline, of course that will help you conceptualize how ML models work, and then you can vet the generated content with your own know-how gained through practice.

Of Beef Bourguignon and Writing

Another example of activating different parts of you simultaneously is if we begin with a simple prompt like "Give me the best combined recipe for beef bourguignon for the past 100 years." You can become more critically engaged in further prompting an LLM to uncover more about different ingredients that have been used historically, and identify ingredients you may not have thought of, or ways of braising the beef you have never tried before. This could lead you to attending a community meetup, where a combined recipe from the corpus of an LLM is realized and tested with real people for feedback and tasteful validation.

What generative AI has the potential to do is to teach you about a subject and also instruct you as to how you might apply the knowledge and gain know-how. If you've never improvised before or made beef bourguignon, prepare yourself for mistakes, iterative failures, and experimentation. An LLM won't do the work or the thinking for you. It won't know how your stove operates, nor will it know the subtleties of how you stir the dough to make the roux, which affect the result. There are literally dozens of places in the recipe that call for human ingenuity, improvisation, and rapid responses when things go a little wrong. That is what we should expect from creating one of the most popular and arguably one of the most demanding recipes from the repertoire of French cuisine.

Applying this principle to a more common use of an LLM to compose an essay, an LLM does not know the particulars and expectations of the person who will eventually read your essay. It does not know where to place emphasis, how much a subject should be expounded on, and how you should open and close the essay. Most importantly, it does not have all the facts about what you are writing about and will not fill in the creative expectations you and your readers will have. LLMs are a starting point, an offer given to you to follow through on, with intentional and critical action engaging all of your intelligence muscles.

Figure 6-1. *Diogenes enjoying a simple meal. AI-generated image*

ML models enable us to move from critically understanding a subject to practically trying out activities that we decipher as suitable to attempt within our own work environments. To unify theory and practice, what generative AI does is it

- Imparts a subject and provides many options for deepening your understanding of that subject

- Teaches you how you can apply the knowledge and gain know-how through its implementation in your own work

- Provokes you to consider the implications of applying any generative AI tool in your work environment to support you in task completion

The Dopamine Rush of Doing

To really learn something, you have to practice it for a while. The same is true of generative AI tools that you want to integrate into your daily workflows. You can be lazy and just take what an LLM first gives you, copy it, and paste it into a document, article, or email. You can read all you want about AI and in your head be a critical expert, but unless you try the tools, fail, try again, and continue to learn how to improve your know-how through practice, you won't get very far. Engaging in the practice of curating the content that an AI generates activates a part of the brain that psychologists often research. Experiential learning is particularly powerful because when we succeed and get positive feedback, our brain rewards us with dopamine. This happy feeling isn't just nice—it actually helps strengthen the brain's learning pathways.[1]

---

[1] Arias-Carrión, Ó., & Pöppel, E. (2007). Dopamine, learning, and reward-seeking behavior. Acta neurobiologiae experimentalis, 67(4), 481–488.

That dopamine rush is similar to the one many people report feeling after generating content with an AI. Regardless of the small amount of effort involved in the actual creation of the content, it feels rewarding to receive this generated chunk of text or this fantastic image you could never have created with your own skills in the same amount of time that it took to generate. The act of doing is a celebration of action in progress. In this case, generating content with AI is a rewarding work in progress that can then be refined and worked on.

What does it take to persistently practice?

Comparing Piano Technique and Generative AI

While the craft of prompting and playing the piano are not equivalent, we can still learn a little about what someone needs to do when learning how to play the piano. First is that terrible tension between wanting to play something and needing to develop dexterity and fluency with your fingers on the topology of the piano. The results at first are not very harmonious. You stumble through coordination, synchronization, keeping the time, accuracy, flow, dynamics, expression—oh yes, and the keys themselves. If starting on C, it's wrapping your right hand around flat white keys that have black keys poking up. The pattern is this taking middle C as a starting point. You have a flat white key, then a black raised key, then a flat white key for D, then a raised black key. This is followed by two flat white keys in a row starring E and F, then another raised black key, a flat white key we call G, a raised black, a flat white key called A, a raised black, and finally a flat white key called B, beside another flat white key called C. This entire pattern of white and black keys is referred to as an octave. Depending on the keyboard, you can have that pattern repeat, usually, on an acoustic piano for seven times, plus a minor third for a total of 88 keys.

You can see how complex this gets, but we can draw similarities to interacting with a generative AI. The main one is that you need to understand what you need to do with any AI (if you compare it to an instrument) if you're going to get something good out of it. The most obvious starting point might be the prompt itself. There is craft involved if you want to properly guide your gen AI instrument for sure. That guidance is also informed by your understanding of the AI system at hand. What controls can you play with? How much control over your instrument can you have? There's also listening involved. You have to respond to what is generated the first time you generate content. When you do, you'll likely discover a few things:

- It is not as great as all the hype you've heard around its use.

- To improve what you generate, you'll have to learn how to improve your prompts and any other controls (like weight, temperature, etc.) you have access to.

How might you integrate generative AI in your workflows as a more regular practice?

It demands persistent practice, a systematic approach, and a willingness to learn from failure. Moving from the theoretical knowledge you gain into the application of that knowledge in practical ways is not always evident. We need to identify areas of interest first and match the tools as we simultaneously set goals to learning them and committing to their practice. Applying the knowledge we have gained to implementing that knowledge has various layers of complexity depending on what tool you are learning and how you want to apply it. Whenever possible and particularly in the case of generative AI prototypes, it is important to receive feedback from others, so you can then reflect on how you've implemented the generated content and understand what other refinements you'll have to make. The visual model that follows is a starting point to support you in moving from knowledge to know-how.

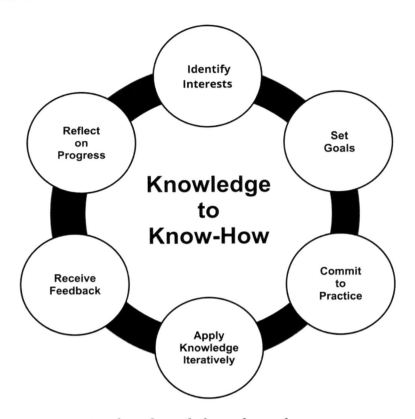

Figure 6-2. Moving from knowledge to know-how

Identify Your Interests

The first step in any learning journey involves a degree of self-motivation and challenges you to be self-aware enough to at least begin to know what you are interested in. We are not programmed in this way. Matching what we do in life with what we love to do is not an easy accomplishment. You don't necessarily have to know precisely what it is you want to do with generative AI technology. If you've ever been in a library without looking for any book in particular, you've likely enjoyed the discovery of some new book you never would have imagined looking for. You can start with what you do love and be open to shifting your area of focus depending on your immediate needs.

Once you do identify an area of interest with the technology, focusing on it, even if it's not for a very long time, not only sparks motivation but also directs your learning path. In the context of generative AI, this could mean pinpointing whether you're more drawn to natural language processing, computer vision, or perhaps ethical AI implementation. This alignment of interests ensures that the learning process remains engaging and relevant. Without the motivation to use the technology, however, you will not get very far. The best way to understand what you like is to try out a platform and see what resonates with you and what doesn't.

Set Goals

Setting clear, achievable goals can support you when you're learning how to use these powerful ML models. Where do you start? It makes the most sense to align your goals of what you want to learn with the types of tasks you want to see the technology handle. For instance, a goal might be to interact with an LLM to create an internal proposal for a project opportunity at work. Part of what you absorb will be to look at how others have used the technology and the types of prompts that have been created that result in something useful. This approach provides some structure and can help you define milestones, which are important for sustaining motivation and measuring progress

What if you don't really have any goals? Well, this is where gen AI shines as a creative provocateur. You can prompt an LLM for ideas on how to integrate generative AI in your particular work. You can also ask it about the risks of using generated content within your specific work environment. Where the technology really shines though is when you direct an LLM to tell you where it might support your workflows, by first defining those workflows, taking out any company indicators or specific company IP in the wording, and prompting the LLM with a bullet point list of your actual workflow(s).

It is also OK to not have specific objectives defined as you interact with a generative AI as it is sure to give you ideas you might never have thought of before. Suddenly, as soon as you've stumbled onto something useful, you are in a better place to say "Oh yes, I'm interested in learning more about that."

Commit to Practice

Consistent practice is key in mastering any skill. Daily practice embeds the intricacies of AI tools into your muscle memory and intuition. It's not merely about clocking hours but about focused, deliberate practice, which has been shown to be pivotal in acquiring expertise in any field.[2] For AI learning, this might involve iteratively refining the prompts you create in order to get something specific from a gen AI platform, experimenting with the same prompt across different models, or taking part of your day to deepen your knowledge of machine learning because you eventually want to install your own open source one for private use. You also need to practice how you apply generated content to your own workflows.

Apply Knowledge Iteratively

Applying learned knowledge to create an artifact is a critical step that transitions theoretical learning into its practical application. To achieve your goals, you need to identify how you are going to integrate content

---

[2] Ericsson, K. A., Krampe, R. T., & Tesch-Römer, C. (1993). The role of deliberate practice in the acquisition of expert performance. Psychological review, 100(3), 363.

that is generated from any AI. This could involve generating a working prototype like an AI-driven app or visualization using Claude 3.5 Sonnet, then taking the code and implementing it, debugging, and seeing if it's ideal for your particular workflow. This stage not only tests how well you understand how to use a particular tool but also your ability to solve problems that will inevitably come up when you start to implement whatever content is generated within your own workflow.

Receive Feedback

Testing AI-generated content with others is an essential step in ensuring that your intended use of that content aligns with your team's creative vision and project goals. It involves a thorough examination of the results generated by any AI and considers how these results can be integrated into your broader project or adapted to support your creative process and better understand how your practice is going. Part of the aim is a litmus test to see how others respond to the content and its integration, in addition to refining whatever prototype you tested through the feedback you receive. You can use various testing methods, allowing your prototype to evolve from preliminary ideas into being part of a higher resolution prototype that you develop either alone or with other collaborators. Generative AI brings up different types of approaches to testing that we might not have considered in the past or, more precisely, that some individuals and organizations may not have even thought of before the types of challenges inherent in AI-generated content came to light. These can include testing for believability, trustworthiness, factual content, visual precision, uncanny results, consistency of generated images and/or video, etc.

Reflect on Progress

Documenting your own reflections on using generative AI is an important part of the co-creative process. Your reflection can inspire others and also validate your effort and time. Documenting your effort can provide new insights to the human-machined process of writing that might lead to new revelations. New approaches to content generation will inevitably be the result, and your efforts to document your progress will be appreciated by others at work.

Bridging Team Knowledge and Know-How

Cook and Brown's (1999) framework can provide a robust foundation for organizations aiming to integrate generative AI within various teams and their workflows.[3] The framework goes into detail about explicit and tacit knowledge and the back and forth between individual and group interactions. Explicit knowledge within an organization includes documented procedures, manuals, reports, and any formalized information that is easy to communicate and share, for example, a marketing team's strategy documents, an IT department's system configurations, or a customer service team's training manual. Tacit knowledge refers to the unwritten, intuitive, and experience-based knowledge that individuals gain over time. This could be a sales representative's ability to read customer cues, a technician's knack for troubleshooting complex issues, or a designer's innate sense of aesthetics.

---

[3] Cook, S. D., & Brown, J. S. (1999). Bridging epistemologies: The generative dance between organizational knowledge and organizational knowing. Organization science, 10(4), 381–400.

This knowledge is often shared through informal communication, mentorship, or hands-on practice. For Cook and Brown, what's important is not to regard "knowledge and knowing as competing, but as complementary and mutually enabling."

The Back and Forth Between Different Types of Knowledge

Explicit Knowledge

Coming to an understanding of different generative AI systems and the implications in their use may require explicit knowledge, such as a basic understanding of algorithms, company values, the type of content that is generated, and what can be done with that content. This knowledge can be documented and can be easily shared across teams.

Figure 6-3. *A bunch of people trying to figure out what a bike is before riding it. AI-generated image*

Tacit Knowledge

Tacit knowledge includes the intuitive and experiential insights that team members develop while working with AI tools, actively experimenting with them, finding their affordances and constraints, and assessing their real value. This knowledge is harder to codify but is important to document for other team members, management, and leadership to understand and make decisions on its future use.

   Example: Online repositories are burgeoning with shared coding environments, enabling those who have the tenacity to learn how, to install different ML models on their own PCs. That know-how in the previous example can come from the experience of installing pre-trained ML models, training them with your own data, and running inference. The cycle repeats itself as that know-how is documented and passed on to the next generation of employees who are required to do the same thing.

Transforming Knowledge into Action

As discussed, you can bridge both the critical theorist and the practice-based personas in a variety of ways. Doing so will be useful to your organization if they are uncertain of all the dimensions they need to consider when integrating generative AI, prior to taking action. This is particularly necessary for you if you need to have leadership on board before any implementation can take place. For example, you can first ask an LLM how other organizations are integrating generative AI, conduct research online to locate sources and companies doing so, attempt to find statistics whenever possible to validate with numbers, then refine those ideas after auto-generating a slide deck. Presentation to stakeholders aside, the work ahead of you will consist of implementing the types of strategies that you carved out, and that you and your organization align with. That involves more than what an LLM is able to generate. It involves you in the picture deciphering the strategy with others, understanding how it could be applied in your own context and which particular vertical of your business it will add value to, who is going to lead the transformation, what the metrics might be to define success, the timeline toward implementation, what the risks are if you do and the risks if you do not integrate the technology, etc.

Implications of Integrating AI Within an Organization

Knowledge As Acquisition

In the initial stages, teams need to acquire explicit knowledge about the generative AI tools. This involves training sessions, documentation, and tutorials to build a shared understanding. That takes time and would be more successful if formally supported within the organization. It requires an investment in securing all the necessary resources and procuring funding for the type of compute, security, and subscriptions you will need to make the dream happen. It may also imply setting up a research and development lab space where experiments can take place on- or offline in an organization that may not have considered this before.

Knowledge As Practice

As teams begin to use these tools, they can apply their explicit knowledge they have gathered conducting experiments, leading to the development of tacit knowledge. For example, a marketing team using AI to generate content will learn to fine-tune the generated content through repeated iterations and feedback cycles, until they apply the results to a campaign.

Individual and Collective Levels

At the individual level, team members gain skills and competencies especially with problem-solving and finding creative ways to integrate different generative AI within workflows and pipelines. At the collective level, teams share their experiences and insights, leading to a collective know-how. For instance, a team working on product design might hold regular meetings to discuss how AI has improved their workflow, sharing best practices and lessons learned. The collective of individuals that experiment with generative AI tools will inevitably influence other teams who may not have applied the tools yet. This helps to slowly develop a culture of experimentation with generative AI as long as leadership supports the integrated initiatives and understands the value of doing so.

Build a Foundation for a Culture of Doing

What we can learn from interacting with generative AI systems at work is to implement cycles of knowledge and know-how in regular Agile sprints. In doing so, you can embed a recurring and reflective culture of practice that is activated weekly or bi-monthly.

Collaborative Co-creation

Encouraging teams to collaborate with different gen AI tools and sharing the results of their experiments can incubate a culture of collaborative co-creation, where everyone has stake in the success. Maybe success for a team is simply to find a process that works. Cross-functional teams comprising members from IT, marketing, and product development can also be facilitated to work together to integrate AI tools into their workflows, demonstrating a more transparent and interdisciplinary approach to the experiments. This may already be occurring in your organization. There's nothing like a new technology to galvanize and motivate teams to figure out how they can better integrate, even if it is just to share resources or the results of their efforts.

Feedback Loops

Establishing persistent feedback loops where teams can share their successes and challenges with AI tools is a good way to mitigate potential biases that swing either way in terms of the pros or cons of integrating the technology. Doing so also allows the organization to continuously reflect and refine its AI strategies based on what they learn from team experiments.

Supporting Continuous Learning

Supporting an environment of continuous learning where teams are encouraged to experiment with AI tools and share what they learned about the process is an important step for those organizations who want to implement AI tools across the organization. Providing access to ongoing training and development resources will also ensure that knowledge evolves alongside the work that it is applied to.

> *Constant experimentation and learning from conducting those experiments will help everyone in the organization evaluate the benefits of the technology and determine if its use truly does add value.*

Individuals on various teams can represent their own team efforts and obstacles when it comes to integrating different tools for different workflows. By continuously documenting experiments and refining how gen AI tools can support individuals in completing tasks or subtasks that form part of their workflows, organizations generate a learning environment. Generative AI serves as a catalyst in this process, helping to bridge the gap between what is known (explicit knowledge) and how it is applied (tacit knowledge), with the potential of creating a petri dish of experimentation and potential innovations that can be applied to an organization's existing product or service.

Application in Organizations

Mapping out when and where "doing" in your work takes place may at first seem obvious: all the time and everywhere. What about mapping out where time is most wasted? Some research has pointed to how often meetings can waste time, how not everyone needs to be at certain meetings, and how they can be made more efficient with careful planning.

What tools might be useful for increasing our capacity to make some processes in our organizations more efficient?

Reaching an understanding that with generative AI, you and your organization will likely need a combination of knowledge about how the technology works and can add value, to the experimental application of different generative AI in order to gain know-how, will help you best prepare for any discussion about integration. This approach ensures that AI tools are not only understood but are also experimented with and continuously improved upon through collaborative practice and shared experiences. Implementing a framework of practice, of moving from acquiring knowledge about generative AI tools and learning from them through practice, can support any organization in building a culture of experimentation, where continuous learning benefits everyone.

CHAPTER 7

Reassess with Gen AI

Once upon a time in ancient Greece, Diogenes was known for his unconventional wisdom. One day, a curious student asked him, "Master, how do you know when you have truly learned something?" Diogenes, with his typical mischievous grin, replied, "Come, let's visit the marketplace." They walked through the bustling market until they reached a potter's stall. Diogenes picked up a clay cup and handed it to the student. "What is this?" he asked. "A cup," the student replied. "Indeed," Diogenes said, "but what if it is cracked? Would it still hold water?" "No, Master," the student answered. Diogenes then took the cup, filled it with water, and to the student's surprise, it leaked. "Knowledge is like this cup," Diogenes said. "To know if you've learned something, you must test it. If it holds, you've learned. If it leaks, you must learn more." The student pondered this and asked, "But how do I test my knowledge?" "By using it," Diogenes replied. "Teach others, apply it in real situations, and reflect on your experiences. Evaluate your success and failures. Over time, you'll know you've learned when your knowledge holds up under pressure, like a cup that doesn't leak."

Just like the old quote goes, "your old site is the best prototype of your new site," so too can you tweak the quote and apply it to you.

Your old self is the best prototype of your new self.

Where is your knowledge leaking and what are the signs?

How do you know you've learned something? What are the ways in which you test that? In other words, how do you know you've actually learned to apply that knowledge over time? What methods do you apply? What patterns of evaluation can you depend on? Answering these questions will really get you to think more methodically about how you know that you know. Not only is it beneficial to reassess what and how we learn especially when we are told right, left, and center that we need to figure out how to integrate AI in our work, but we also benefit from interrogating the technology itself. It's not like previous solutions, say a learning management system or a photo, video, or audio editor has been presented to us. There is a certain ambiguity in terms of what generative AI is recommended for us to use by the people who employ us. You would think that the more we understand an AI system's capabilities, that a decision as to which one to use would be easier to make. Unfortunately, leadership in any organization is in the exact same shoes we are in. They are also figuring it out as they go along. Advancing your knowledge about the technology includes an understanding of how leadership might help you in the everyday work that you undertake.

Figure 7-1. *Like a cup that doesn't "leak." AI-generated image*

How can we assess what we know without solely depending on human feedback?

When you approach the prompting of any generative AI as a researcher keen on testing how it's going to do, you activate a part of being human that is constantly testing, prodding, poking, and trying to break a system. We can apply those values to test our own knowledge and our capacity to want to know. Generative AI is a really good trigger to activate a part of us that is relentless in its impulse to test.

Methods and Instruments

There are dozens of methods that have been established across educational research in order to test how much people learn. It is not always about quantity though or our capacity to regurgitate memorized facts and equations. Testing know-how is much trickier as the application of knowledge and its manifestation as skill and craft when applied to real-world use cases may take a long time for us to become good at. An award-winning animator is not born overnight. They take years of learning the ropes, and that learning is not usually done in solitude. Generative AI and its impact on work is also a new field under investigation, so it's difficult for us to really say "Oh that colleague of mine is a master with LLMs." It is more accurate to report that someone is better at using a specific tool than you are or that a person you know is amazing at getting exactly what they want out of Midjourney. Another colleague may be adept at installing ML models on their PC and getting amazing results that they share on a social platform. Ask any of your colleagues to walk you through precisely how to install comfy UI on your PC, and you'll test not only the gaps they might have in articulating how they do it but, more importantly, your own capacity to maintain attention through a complicated step-by-step process.

The Development of Criteria

It is way too early to make generalizations that generative AI, including LLMs, are actually improving efficiency in workplace environments. We can only rely on personal, contextual, and task-specific stories, no matter how well designed a survey is and how many people are surveyed. There are lots of unknowns as to how it will improve your own work, what that even means, and how that will be measured. It is true that instruments of assessment could measure how well you learned a specific generative AI, like Dall-E 3 or Pika, but it really is in the application of the technology to your workflow where the answers are going to give you, your team, and your organization any valuable insights.

What that requires is for each individual to come up with their own set of criteria for how they will assess the effectiveness of any generative AI. Now it's difficult to measure that if you don't also assess your command over a particular tool. It is helpful to generate a list of questions that form the foundation of how you will assess both. While this process is going to be highly subjective as it should be, the important thing is to identify a list of all the criteria that will support you in assessing your know-how and simultaneously assess whether or not an AI tool is going to be useful for your workflows. This list is not exhaustive but intended to spark your own list of criteria that will make the most sense to you in your particular work context:

- How much time will I need to master a particular generative AI?

- When does the tweaking of a gen AI become automatic?

- How dependent is my workflow on the integration of a particular tool?

- At what inflection point do I determine whether or not the content I generated is going to be workable?

- What else do I need to learn to get the most out of this tool?

Consider Time

There's always some measure of whether or not something you've learned changes how much time it might take you to complete a task. The promise that generative AI will save you time will clash with the layered complexity of the task (and subtasks) at hand. It is important to take the time to measure time and see if the technology supports more efficient subtask delivery. Taking the time to conduct any form of research also requires being supported by your supervisor or manager. It will take time to also learn how to use specific generative AI effectively. That is not usually a metric that many surveys communicate when they make assertions of generative AI's efficiency in the workplace. Nor is the time required to make corrections and refinements to any generated content.

Consider When a Tool Becomes Assimilated

We all get used to applying our technique, craft, and skills to the task at hand. We become so skilled that many tasks become second nature. Our own neural network is able to repeat tasks over and over again even within one piece of software. In that process, we find flow. We activate our creativity, and it is free to explore within the patterns of task execution we have embodied. With generative AI, multimodal automation is a real opportunity to see if certain automated tasks across media can be supported. For example, you can automate a script being generated through an LLM for marketing your brand, add a persona through a text-image generative AI, have that script "performed" by a text-speech generated agent in a speech/image-video, then generate subtitles with another tool. The resultant video can then be published automatically on YouTube, then links to that YouTube video are generated for a LinkedIn or Instagram post whose text descriptor is also generated. What to test is where the process needs additional human intervention. In so doing, you also pick and choose what tools can be assimilated within your own workflows and which cannot. Maybe all voices you found sound terrible, and you need to go with an actor you've worked with before. The quality of the facial expression on the generated agent might be too uncanny to use. The voice-over that was generated may need to be normalized. The generated script may require a copy editor's touch. How does a small group of testers respond to the entire generated creation, and what will you change based on the feedback you receive? Through evaluating the content that is generated, you also test how well each tool can be integrated within your own workflows and the new tasks you'll have to take on as a result.

Consider Evaluating Effectiveness of a Tool

You can further personalize what you learn, informed by uncovering your own strengths and weaknesses, to provoke further reflection. It does mean that you have to take command over your own learning process as has been discussed in earlier chapters. Using a SWOT tool common to business processes can uncover the strengths, weaknesses, opportunities, and threats of integrating content from any generative AI.

- What are the strengths of this tool? This can lead to uncovering ease of use, quality of content, overall usability of the content, repeatability, etc.

- What are the weaknesses of this tool? The question can lead you to answer how difficult it was to get something useful from the tool, the quality of the content it generated, how much time was spent tweaking, how biased the content was, how consistent the tool was across contexts, etc.

- What are the opportunities this tool opens up? This can lead to more generalizable experiences you can reflect on in terms of time-saving, a tool's capacity to generate content you never would have imagined, the creativity it sparks in you, etc.

- What are the threats implied with using this tool? Answering this prompt can help you better understand exactly how much time it takes to get something useful out of a tool, the costs of using it vs. the persistent quality of content that can be used, and the excess of bias or untruths that a tool generates, making it not only difficult to edit but triggering for some users.

User-Testing Yourself, Your Work, and What You Know

While software development teams spend plenty of time testing their prototypes iteratively, they rarely test their own knowledge as it continues to grow. Time is not usually taken to undertake such activities. Some may assume that with the experience of doing comes expertise.

How much experience of doing is required before your expertise is developed?

It's true that in Agile environments some teams that are rigorous do conduct retrospectives at the end of a project development cycle or sprint. It is not usually a time to test your own knowledge, however. It is a time to show work, receive feedback, and continuously improve your offerings in the next sprint. It is also not a time to break down how you conducted your work so you have a choice to transform and improve it. Efficiency in task completion is not usually a problem that is solved in these cases.

You might just get a comment like "Let's see if we can all work harder and more efficiently to produce more in the next sprint." This is the reason that if you really want to know the impact of integrating generative AI within your own workflows, you are going to have to facilitate that process on your own. Each of the criteria mentioned earlier can be tested. Now you need to design the tests.

Functional Testing

This type of testing focuses on verifying that the AI-generated content works as intended within the context of the project you are working on. Like any other licensed content you've used in the past, generated content needs to be a fit for your project. For instance, if the AI is used to generate text for a website, functional testing would check if the text aligns correctly with your organization's style guides, if it integrates well with other website elements, and that it is generated without grammatical mistakes or irrelevant content. Do visuals that accompany the text make sense for an AI to generate or will they deter from the messaging you are attempting to communicate? On the other hand, you may find new discoveries as you test the usefulness of generated content that leads you to present unanticipated content and contextualize it differently. With most design processes, there is also some type of parking lot for unused ideas, and you might find that much of your generated content, while inspiring, ends up in a pile of content that might be used in the future or never used at all.

When you test the usefulness of any tool within your own workflows, what you learn is that you need to get past the promises and investigate how useful they will be to you and to your teams. Then you can assess where time is spent, how much time, how that differs from time spent before, and yes, of course, if AI really does augment productivity. Remaining open to the possibility of AI transforming work processes is much more realistic at this point than assuming that it will.

In the spirit of testing an actual use case of removing backgrounds from an image, six different private and public applications were used to remove the background on the image in Figure 7-2. Each background removal tool had different results, some more effective in removing the background behind the ink splatters and some removing the ink splatters themselves. Working with a more developed software application was inevitable. The fastest result (Figure 7-4) was achieved with Affinity Photo 2, alternating between the erase brush tool and background erase brush tool. That effort took the longest time, clocking in at seven minutes. Bear in mind that you can see various color gradients in the initial image (Figure 7-2), which is likely more relevant to a real-world scenario. In essence, each AI was tasked with automatically removing several different background colors from a fairly complex character.

Figure 7-2. *Who is that bot in the mirror? AI-generated image*

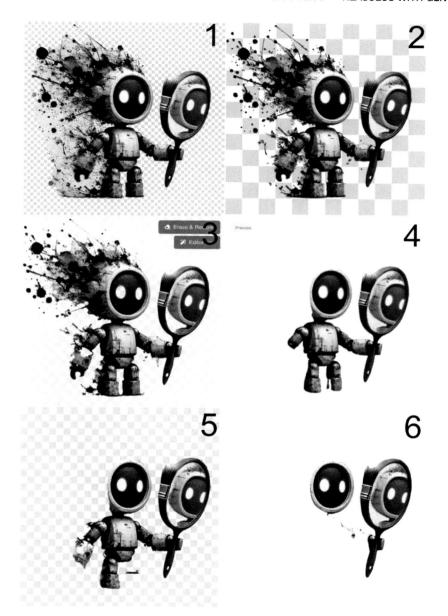

Figure 7-3. *Comparing AI background removal tools: (1) Adobe Express, (2) Pixel Cut, (3) Removal AI, (4) Remove AI, (5) Removal AI, (6) Pixlr. AI-generated images*

To the defense of all AI background removal tools, the image was not easy. It is, however, an example of the type of images that text-image generative AI create, regardless of how clear you are in requesting super white, RGB (255,255,255), or #FFFFFF as your background. Different text-image generative AI handle the challenge with widely divergent results. Figure 7-4 used Affinity Photo 2's background erase brush tool hovering over a total of seven different areas in the image. The erase brush tool was also used in fine-tuning removal of unwanted pixels. As you can tell, the human in the loop is still vital in order to not automatically have an AI remove what you want to still remain.

Figure 7-4. *Using Affinity Photo 2's background erase brush tool on the original image. AI-generated image*

Integration Testing

Here, the emphasis is on how well the AI-generated content integrates with other components of your project. This is really one of the most important experiments that you will need to conduct. Integration testing could involve combining AI-generated music with a video to see how well the rhythm or feel synchronizes with specific cuts or embedding AI-generated images in a digital interface to ensure that they complement the user experience without being too distracting. You may have to batch edit and render all generated images to fit the exact dimensions you want for a mobile experience of your site.

What criteria do you need to develop in order to best integrate generated content in your workflow?

Is it alignment in the look/feel of the generated content with your previous defined palette of colors and aesthetic? Define your own criteria as that criteria will be influenced by your community of practice, your company's style guide, and your own aesthetic. The beautiful thing about integrating AI is we learn more about our own aesthetics and principles in the process. Perhaps these have not been made explicit, and the time is right to do so now. Maybe, those principles need to be adjusted in light of the generated offerings before you.

Usability Testing

Usability testing is a bit trickier to facilitate in the age of generated content, as this type of testing assesses how the target audience interacts with and responds to the AI-generated content. This might include user feedback sessions where participants engage with a prototype that incorporates AI-generated elements, such as a narrative in a game or personalized content in an app. The goal is to understand user perceptions, ease of interaction, and overall satisfaction. One way you may be able to solve this

151

dilemma is to conduct internal testing with specific questions that may test the perception of generated content, without telling your internal team that you used a generative AI platform for some of the content generation. Only after the tests are complete can you spill the beans and let them know. If you have developed a strong user base for early alpha testing, you will be at an advantage. Not only will you deepen your understanding of the user experience of your prototype or service, you will also more deeply understand your audience's gut responses to generated content.

Iterative Testing

In this ongoing process, each version of the AI-generated content is tested, and improvements are made based on your or someone else's discernment and feedback. This iterative cycle helps in refining the content progressively, ensuring that each iteration is better suited to meet the creative and functional demands of the project. Embodying a spirit of constant testing is also a form of practice. That practice is to be deeply connected to the content you are guiding an AI to generate, improving how you prompt and tweak any AI, reinventing how the cycle of content generation fits into your own creative process. Iterative testing is highly useful when you want to receive feedback from users on the smallest of changes. This type of embedded value is the second and even third chance type of testing to help you and your team refine your offering to the world. Through iterative testing any generative AI, you learn to not only know how well you design and compile assets together, you also learn that with constant feedback, your work gets better.

A/B Testing

A/B testing is used to compare different versions of AI-generated content to determine which one performs better in terms of the criteria you have defined. For example, two different AI-generated layouts of a website might be tested to see which one leads to better user interactions. Importantly, with the rapid increase in the number of AI platforms that are out there, combined with your ability to use pre-trained models with your own content, it is important to test AI platforms with and against one another. This is because no two AI are created equal. They have different underlying algorithms, a different corpus of data, and different approaches, styles, limitations, biases, and aesthetics. You will typically uncover that A/B testing is never enough. It tends to lead to C/D testing, and that's a good thing. Developing criteria to assess and compare two assets at a time, for example, while difficult can help you constrain your choices. That said, you don't have to limit yourself to that. You also learn with generative AI that A/B testing can be accelerated with many different options that you can test on your own or that you can facilitate others to test. While you might think the more the merrier when it comes to presenting options for people to choose from, be aware that you also may get a little lost in terms of your own starting intentions if there are too many options to choose from.

Identifying Oversights

Engaging in testing can help highlight aspects you might have overlooked, particularly if you've become too attached to your prototype. External feedback is critical to gain a more objective understanding of the prototype's intent. This is why sharing work that integrated any generated content earlier in your pipeline will be beneficial. You will also need to proceed with caution when it comes to the testing process, as you may bias the results of your tests if you tell people you used generative AI. Never underestimate the resistances that some people will have at the mere mention that you used generative AI in your creative process. A/B testing with others might be the best way to understand the different responses to content you generated on your own and content you generated with an AI. Creating prototypes with and without AI-generated content will take time. The myth of AI content making our creative process more efficient is easily debunked. While an image may take very little time to generate, it is in how that image is integrated within your overall vision that can be just as time consuming, if not more, than if you were to generate the image with your own skills. You learn that when you test content, there are no shortcuts. The unpredictable factor in all user testing is the user's feedback itself, which can influence creative direction, aesthetic, and the prize of lasting attention that nowadays is the holy grail of design.

Ethical and Bias Testing

You want to stand out from the rest? As a designer of any human experience, part of your intent is to make a difference, to create something unique that has not been experienced before. If that is important to you, then you'll need to break the patterns of stereotypes that you see and listen to, not only in AI-generated content but in much of the content that humans generate for imagined consumers of popular culture. Narrow AI will perpetuate bias, sexism, gender stereotypes, and a whole bunch more, just like you find in a lot of human content that is constantly being regurgitated. It's a perpetual pattern we have to contend with, and testing for bias, just like you test for homogeneity, should be an assumed part of your emerging or ongoing role as a designer of human experiences.

Think about what is present in any ML model's training data, and that will bring you to the conclusion that if you work with any generated content, you will need to persistently test your ability and your potential target user's ability to identify biases in the content generated, no matter what part that content plays in your overall prototype. This is even more the case when you deepen your understanding of how algorithms work in ML models and the application of specific statistical methods as well. Designing for ethical testing ensures that the AI-generated content adheres to ethical guidelines that have likely already been developed in your organization and that any content generated minimizes harm to your users. Testing for facts, untruths, and hallucinations will be informed by the values of your organization. Unintended biases associated with your choice of gender and racial representation will also emerge, and that's not a bad thing if you haven't really considered testing for that in the past.

Testing is not just about finding flaws or ensuring functionality; it's about experimenting with how AI-generated content can be creatively woven into your project to make it different, to make it break the pattern. By embracing a mind set on continuous improvement, you ensure that each tested prototype brings you closer to an outcome that truly reflects your original vision, aligns with organizational guidelines, and meets the needs of your target audience. That also means developing the grit and resilience to abandon any generated content that you might have thought was awesome for your project should it conflict with your aesthetic or unearth unintended ethical issues that your organization has worked so hard to minimize over its history.

Persistently assessing and reassessing generative AI content and your skills in generating that content is a good habit to develop. Cultivating feedback fearlessly from your colleagues places you in a good position to grow as a creative. It demonstrates to your team that you are not only open to feedback when it comes to generative AI integration, but that the technology itself has shifted your perspective. Generative AI can transform each of us into active researchers, persistently seeking to improve the contributions that we offer, to make our work better. The technology also activates a design sensibility that can be cultivated through cycles of iterative testing. With generative AI, you are not only testing for how well the content generated integrates within the prototype you are creating, you are also testing your own design competencies and the robustness of your organization's ethical guidelines, your capacity to

- Edit, refine, fix, change, or abandon content that is not good enough or does not fit within the vision of a project or align with organizational values

- Minimize your own bias as you test for biases embedded within generated content

- Admit to unintended triggers that the generated content you integrated in your work might have provoked

- Assess your own strengths and weaknesses when it comes to mastering a specific tool

Figure 7-5. *Testing out a new AI-generated bike and its effects on you. AI-generated image*

CHAPTER 8

Adapt with AI

Mulla Nasrudin was once called to a grand banquet. Seeing all the fine clothes and important people, he realized he was underdressed in his simple robe. No one paid him any attention. So, he went home, put on his best coat, and returned. This time, everyone greeted him warmly and invited him to sit at the head of the table. When the food was served, Nasrudin began to dip his coat sleeve into the soup, saying, "Eat, my coat, eat!" The host, puzzled, asked, "Mulla, what are you doing?" Nasrudin replied, "When I was here in my old robe, no one noticed me. But in this coat, I am an honored guest. It is my coat that is invited to this banquet, not me!"

We learn to adapt when we experiment with generated content. No matter how formal, we are all testing and evaluating any generative AI tool we encounter. There's a lot we can adapt, starting with the prompts we use to the creative workflows that we engage in and the process of being creative itself.

The Origin of Beautiful Co-adaptations

While Charles Darwin didn't get everything right about life on planet earth or the behaviors and motivations of all its inhabitants in his work *On the Origin of Species* published in 1859, he did actually mention something important about adaptation. A misattributed quote that keeps making the rounds—one that actually came from Louisiana State University business

© Patrick Parra Pennefather 2024
P. Parra Pennefather, *Regenerating Learning*, Design Thinking,
https://doi.org/10.1007/979-8-8688-1061-9_8

professor Leon C. Megginson, summarizing the essence of Darwin's book at the convention of the Southwestern Social Science Association—is worthy of summoning here, as an interpretation of Darwin. "It is not the most intellectual of the species that survives; it is not the strongest that survives; but the species that survives is the one that is able best to adapt and adjust to the changing environment in which it finds itself." An actual quote from Darwin's book presents the idea of co-adaptation, which is more pertinent to our use of gen AI:

> *We see these beautiful co-adaptations most plainly in the woodpecker and the mistletoe; and only a little less plainly in the humblest parasite which clings to the hairs of a quadruped or feathers of a bird; in the structure of the beetle which dives through the water; in the plumed seed which is wafted by the gentlest breeze; in short, we see beautiful adaptations everywhere and in every part of the organic world*[1]

---

[1] Sheldon, R. W. (2004). Darwin's Origin of Species: A Condensed Version of the First Edition of 1859. Trafford Publishing.

Figure 8-1. *Nasrudin feeding his own coat because coats must eat too. AI-generated image*

You get the idea though. Think of how many times you've had to adapt to the situation at hand. The incoming effects of generative AI on individual work and learning have yet to arrive in the talons of a carrier pigeon. Even though the bird has not yet arrived along with rigorous research that organizations can draw from to support their use of AI, there is a momentous propulsion forward with the technology that is shifting how many people think of work, creativity, learning and knowledge.

Co-adapting with Technology

Shifting how tech is used in work resonates with how humans must continually adapt to and with technological advancements. From the Industrial Revolution to the digital age, our ability to learn and integrate new technologies determines our ability to thrive in a continuously changing world. Some of us are more resilient than others when it comes to surviving through cycles of change.

> *When you think of all the changes that have happened and continue to happen in your life and work, what strategies have you used to adapt?*

Every best laid plan sometimes changes. When you work with and around technology, you get used to this. Adapting what you do in your work is also something you come to expect. With AI, adapting means activating and exercising new types of creative flexibility. This occurs when you learn, apply what you learn, reflect, then relearn or learn something entirely new. Like it or not, research-backed or not, generative AI is rapidly being integrated across different types of organizations.

Every single species has had to adapt to survive. We too have all had to adapt continuously to changes in environment, times of great suffering, and times of growth. It is what has allowed human cultures to endure for such a long time. To regenerate how you learn, you need to adopt the same resilience that has brought you to a place of experimentation with generative AI. Apply that same quality of resilience to what you do at work because generative AI will likely change some of the ways you and others operate. If not tomorrow, then eventually. AI shines a light on our willingness and resistance to adapt, *again*. It reminds us that technology has the power to rapidly alter how we interact with each other, with the knowledge we create, and the world itself.

How will you co-adapt with generative AI?

Co-adapting with Content

Generative AI also teaches us that content can change radically and swiftly by giving us regenerations that are highly dependent on how we prompt it to begin with. As demand and curiosity grow for the technology, humans can take control of the narrative by shifting what is generated. The initial resurgence of AI glory went to text-based systems in the fall of 2023. If you can recall that far back, you know that you had to prompt an AI with specific text, and it returned the prompt with generated text. But that's what version one gave us. Since that time the capacity and growth of generative AI systems has flourished. Version two of some initial public LLM offerings is now multimodal. You generate prompts that can be used to generate images in either the LLM you generated the text prompt with or a text-image platform. Some LLMs have the capacity to not only generate code and debug that code but visualize the results as a working application within another window in the LLM's user interface. Speech, 3D model animation, and video content will all be generated within an increasingly complex user interface. ML models have adapted according to the use cases that prompted the development team to make changes to the technology itself. Many established software environments, like Photoshop, Canva, Unity, Notion, etc., have now integrated text prompts and other functionality within their software ecosystems. These tools are already transforming how people work.

It doesn't end there, however. Generative AI is perfectly adopted by those creative people who are practiced at adapting their work to the affordances and constraints of new technologies. With content that an AI produces, no matter how good or bad it is, in the hands of creative humans, the quality and nature of work is shifting. The technology supports creative professionals to explore new and previously unimagined possibilities. For example, web designers can use AI to generate a wide range of design ideas quickly, allowing them to experiment with more concepts in a shorter time frame. Some more skilled in front-end development can try out the abundance of emerging coding LLMs, like Claude, GPT, Cursor, or Replit. Early-stage prototypes can lead to new ideas you might never have imagined through traditional methods alone.[2]

Figure 8-2. *The "AI Good" carrier pigeon has arrived.*
AI-generated image

---

[2] https://gaper.io/generative-ai-creative-landscape/

Adapting your work with the content an AI generates involves some of the following:

- Reframing your work as a forever work in progress.

- Accepting that many, many, many iterations will be terrible.

- Throwing yourself off your own patterns by permitting for even one moment to give the unexpected offerings AI provides to you a chance.

- Allowing space for spontaneously adapting what you are doing in response to what a generative AI gives you.

- Finding places of rest in your process where you can take a break from the intense focus, go for a walk, take a day, take a week, then come back to your masterpiece, and tweak.

- Incessant, obsessive tweaking.

- Co-adapting what you do at work with the changing features of different AI.

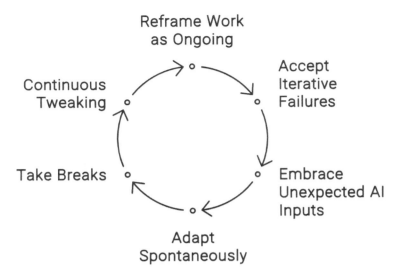

Figure 8-3. *Adapting your work with AI-generated content.*
AI-generated image

The Forever Work in Progress

Generative AI offers you incomplete versions of something, a prototype, a work in progress. That's no different than when someone hands you something incomplete and asks you to refine it. Think of a proposal you've filled out with others. The first version is not usually the last. Countless edits occur along the way, and these sharpen your final document and may even lead some to having that proposal green lit. It's important to realize that you will have to adapt everything that is generated for you. There are no shortcuts. You still have to do the work, iteratively. Even the ML models operating under the hood of the black box LLM that you interact with are a work in progress, as programmers and development teams work to improve the results of the generated content. Why? Maybe it's an essential human value of adaptability that they want to embed. Maybe they believe in the need for their creation to continuously improve over time. Maybe, just maybe, they know it's not perfect and must adapt to changing needs.

This is why looking at generative AI systems as works in progress is the right lens to view them through. Most of them are not really programmed to believe in themselves as prototypes. Some find it difficult to accept that they have failed at identifying how many times the letter "r" occurs in the word "strawberry." They fail with and without us, and sometimes apologize, but only when you call them on it.

Accepting Failure

We adapt in some ways because our current behavior and interaction with the world no longer works or is no longer sustainable. Our impulses to solve the same human problems can sometimes persistently fail. In that failure, we are forced to try a new way, and that new way usually involves developing some form of technology to support it. Think of the development of long-distance communication and how over the years different technologies evolved to sustain its growth.

What human problem did long-distance communication technologies solve?

Throwing Yourself Off Your Patterns

Our brains naturally seek efficiency, creating mental habits that are not always flexible enough to take on problem-solving when there are many unknowns. Ironically, for a technology that generates content from patterns of existing human knowledge, we can use generative AI to throw ourselves off of our patterned ways of doing things. When it comes to the work you do, what are your own patterns of creation? How settled are you with them?

Have you interrogated your own creative process, truly examined it, and questioned if it is the best way to fulfill the tasks you are responsible for?

Allowing Space for Spontaneous Adaptation

Some of the best interactions that you can have with generative AI bring up spontaneous opportunities to shift, pivot, and adapt to whatever it is that it spits out. That's not much different than when spontaneous gifts come your way in life. We often take these for granted or forget about them— that surprise gift a friend offered to you or that usually cheap friend who never buys you a drink and one night does. These offerings have already prepared you well for working with generative AI. Your capacity to respond quickly to that content and rapidly integrate it within your creative process is one key to being successful in your interactions with the technology. The promise of generative AI saving us more time is not as precisely true as the idea does not consider the human in the equation nor what condition that human is in. For us to say that any technology can save us time, we need to apply the technology to specific parts of our processes or workflows. It is helpful to identify them as you start into your AI experimental journey or at least write them down as they come up.

Finding Places of Rest in Your Process

As important as it is to persistently adapt to changes, we also need to take the time to rest in between furious oscillations of change. This might occur when you start to settle in with how generated content from an AI finally fits within your own working process. More often though, when we continue to adapt how we create with generative AI tools, at certain points we can get stuck. It might all start to look, sound, or move the same. At that point, taking a break is an important part of your process to invest time in. When you return a little more refreshed from that break, you'll likely find solutions to problems that you didn't notice or didn't even think were solvable.

Learning from the Unexpected Offerings of Generative AI

The more you interact with different gen AI, the more you learn. It is a repetitive pattern that repeats, over and over again, ad nauseam. The system doesn't learn from its interactions with you. That opinion is a common misunderstanding that demonstrates a lack of knowing-in-action at how different generative AI operate under the hood. No two ML models leverage the same type of engine or oil underneath that hood either. What is more accurate to say is that you, the human, adapt and thus learn from your interactions with an AI. That may be the first unexpected result of your interaction with the technology.

Figure 8-4. *Writer throwing away ideas and tools.*
AI-generated image

You are in for some other surprises when you interact with different generative AI, each unique in how they surprise you too. For one, you will likely not expect the content that is generated. It's true that you might have some ideas as to what the AI will generate, but could you guess what would happen when it regenerates content with the same exact prompt? Likely not. This cyclic interplay of prompting, seeing the result of the prompt, it taking you by surprise, followed by you changing your prompt and getting closer to the results you imagined is another rich interplay of learning. Learning how to improve that process involves becoming more knowledgeable about the particular features available within each of the generative AI that you use. For images, that will include deepening your understanding of seeds, identifying your style, looking at temperature and weight, etc. For text-based generation, that might extend your use of a persona or rhetorical style. It might also mean adapting what you learn and extending that to how to use RAG or knowledge graphs to customize the types of generated content you receive that are more in line with the documents you upload to an LLM.

The important thing to keep in mind as you continue to evolve your interactions with different generative AI is that you too are evolving. You are changing and shifting, slightly altering your creative process, the way in which you do things and the order in which you create. You might come to the realization that by integrating generative AI tools earlier in your process, they give you a creative spark that helps you get through some of the more tedious tasks that form part of your workflows.

CHAPTER 9

Prototype Learning

Once in ancient Greece, there was a philosopher named Diogenes who was known for his wit and unconventional lifestyle. He lived in a large ceramic jar and shunned material possessions. One day, Diogenes was busy sunbathing when the mighty Alexander the Great visited him. Alexander, intrigued by Diogenes' reputation, stood before him and said, "I am Alexander the Great. Ask me for anything, and I shall grant it." Without even looking up, Diogenes replied, "Yes, move a little to the side. You're blocking my sunlight." Alexander laughed heartily and said, "If I were not Alexander, I would wish to be Diogenes." Diogenes, unphased, muttered, "If I were not Diogenes, I would also wish to be Diogenes."

You're going to find out eventually, as if it was ever a big secret, that most of the software that you use, including any generative AI, is a working version of some prototype that a company released. As much as you think you might be adapting your workflows to the creative content that is generated by any generative AI, take a moment to think about the development teams and the pressure that they are facing to make these powerful tools that you interact with better. They do so not just because they are integral to improving the product they've released into the world. They do so because they want you and I to keep using their prototypes. The commitment that we have helps them to keep their offering relevant, keep some form of income coming in, in order to pay for all the humans that make the prototype work. Many organizations release what they call products, when really they are prototypes that work fairly consistently.

© Patrick Parra Pennefather 2024
P. Parra Pennefather, *Regenerating Learning*, Design Thinking,
https://doi.org/10.1007/979-8-8688-1061-9_9

There is never a final version of any generative AI. If there is, then the product will soon no longer be available or that useful as the developers will tend to respond to users who provide feedback as to how useful the prototype is.

When you're creating a new product or working on a project, the journey from initial idea to finished item involves several steps—often beginning with something as simple as a sketch and evolving through more complex stages until it becomes a more developed artifact. That not fully formed thing is known as a prototype, and it's a way for anyone, whether you're an artist, a designer, or a developer, to explore and refine your ideas.

You learn about prototyping, and you learn how to prototype when you interact with generative AI. You learn about the process itself, and you learn to manage the content that is generated. You are in charge of the knowledge creation. You curate it. You guide and navigate the generated results. You manipulate incomplete content and refine it for your own purposes. As you do so, you are also prototyping your own learning process. This is because of the incomplete nature of what an AI generates. The generated content engages your learner, as you rapidly think about what you need to know how to do to change that content or apply your knowledge to transform it.

Figure 9-1. *Alexander and Diogenes. AI-generated image*

When you prompt the generation of content from any generative AI, you are enacting a prototypical relationship that is unique to you. That relationship to the ML model you are interacting with results in a prediction informed by your prompt, and its analysis of the data in its corpus that correlates to keywords in your prompt. The generated result can undergo several regenerations of content in most cases. What is being regenerated? Whatever you have prompted an AI to create is an experiment, a work in progress that may or may not be worthy of continuing to develop. That sense of incompleteness is what generative AI systems create a world around. Generative AI systems excel at providing raw material—rough drafts, sketches, and variations. This is not a shortcoming but a key to their value. The real magic begins when we, as humans, enter and pilot that co-creative process.

The technology also points us to how easily it is to generate knowledge that has essentially been mashed up from many different sources. AI points us to what we humans have been doing endlessly and for time immemorial: making sense of the world through accumulated meanings gathered from what others have taught us and reforming that as a living interpretation of that knowledge.

Prototypes

Beyond the hyperbole of generative AI content replacing human-created content, what is easier to claim is that the technology has the potential to transform how we prototype, particularly in digital and mixed media. Understanding that the key use of gen AI content is in supporting prototyping, you can better understand how it might fit within your existing workflows. Generated content can help bring ideas you have at various levels of detail rapidly. You may not know exactly what you are looking for. You may want to guide an external contractor to create content that is similar to what you generated. You may just want the structure for a proposal that you can refine. With AI, you can input a rough sketch or a text description and quickly get a more detailed image, audio, video, or even a 3D model that reflects your concept. This can speed up the prototyping process enacting the mechanic of rapid iteration, helping you rapidly change and refine your ideas.

Prototypes aren't limited to any specific format—they can be anything from written documents to 3D models or even digital interfaces. Depending on what you're creating, your prototype might be

- A detailed outline or storyboard for a blog post or video

- A 3D print or hand-built model for physical products

- Interactive simulations for digital applications like apps or games

- Mixed reality setups that combine physical and digital elements for a more immersive experience

Early-Stage Prototypes

Think of the last prototype you created. If you are not sure what that might be, consider the last recipe you put together the ingredients for, the process you used to assemble the ingredients, the pan you used, the temperature things might have been cooked at, spices, etc. If that was the first time you made the recipe, then you enacted the very core of prototyping: experimentation and iteration over time.

At the very start, prototypes can be simpler than cooking or baking up a recipe. Imagine you have an idea for a new gadget or an app. To begin, you might just grab a pen and paper and draw your thoughts. These early prototypes could also be mood boards (collections of images, textures, and colors that convey a general feel) or basic wireframes (simple layouts of a web page or app). The key with any prototype is to get your ideas out in a tangible form. This isn't about perfection—it's about exploration and experimentation. You can easily change and adapt these initial versions without spending much time or resources. Generated content thrives in this area of early-stage prototyping as it gives you a lot to think about. That content might inform you as to what you don't want and when guided can lead to insights you might never have had. Here are two types. What creations have you made that could be similar?

Paper Prototypes

Fidelity: Very low

Description: These are hand-drawn sketches of interfaces or concepts, often used in the very early stages of design. Paper prototypes are quick to make and easy to modify, making them ideal for initial brainstorming and user feedback sessions.

Digital Mock-Ups

Fidelity: Low

Description: Digital mock-ups are static designs created using graphic design software. They provide a visual representation of the UI but do not offer interactive elements. These are often used to finalize visual design choices like layout, color schemes, and typography.

Mid-Stage Prototypes

As your idea starts taking shape, you'll move into creating prototypes that are a bit more sophisticated. These might include interactive wireframes or clickable mock-ups on the computer, which let you test how users might interact with your product. Or, you could create a working model that shows how your product functions. This stage is important for troubleshooting and refining your ideas based on how they perform in practical scenarios. Two examples are highlighted on the next page.

Clickable Wireframes

Fidelity: Medium

Description: Clickable wireframes are basic simulations of user interfaces that allow for simple interactions, usually created with tools like Sketch or Adobe XD. They help in testing navigation and basic functionality without the overhead of coding.

Interactive Prototypes

Fidelity: Medium to high

Description: These prototypes are more advanced than clickable wireframes and include interactions and animations. Tools like Figma and Axure are commonly used to create interactive prototypes that more closely mimic the final application.

Late-Stage Prototypes

Eventually, you'll develop prototypes that closely resemble the final product. These are detailed and allow for extensive user testing, final adjustments in design, and functionality checks. They are what you present to stakeholders and potential investors to illustrate exactly what your finished product will look like and how it will work. Here are some examples of the language and form that more developed prototypes take.

Proof of Concept (PoC)

Fidelity: Medium to high

Description: A Proof of Concept is typically developed to demonstrate the feasibility of a single function or feature in a real-world scenario. It focuses on whether a feature can be developed and how it might work.

Functional Prototypes

Fidelity: High

 Description: A functional prototype offers both the look and the functionality of the intended final product. These prototypes are often built using the actual back-end system (if applicable) and are used to test both functionality and usability.

Vertical Slice

Fidelity: Very high

 Description: A vertical slice is essentially a complete implementation of a small part of the project. It includes fully functioning front-end and back-end services for that slice, demonstrating performance, design, and the user experience.

Pilot Version/Alpha Release

Fidelity: Highest

 Description: Often, a pilot or alpha release is used to test a nearly complete version of the final product under real conditions with a limited audience. This phase is important for identifying any critical issues before the full public launch.

Prototyping Across Different Mediums

Prototyping is an activating process that helps creators of all types develop and refine their ideas from simple sketches to complex, functional models. It's about gradually bringing your vision to life, testing and improving it along the way. Generative AI tools provide a powerful way to stimulate this process, letting you see and test ideas rapidly. Some creatives even claim the ability to rapidly generate minimum viable prototypes to show investors.

Embracing the Imperfect and Unexpected

Generative AI has the potential to shift the way we approach creativity. These powerful tools, capable of producing text, images, code, and more, offer us multiple types of prototypes that we can then tweak. Yet, it's vital to understand their nature: they provide starting points, works-in-progress, not finished products. The inherent unpredictability of generated content has a transformative power. In a way, they force our hand. The content generated is likely only going to be useful if recontextualized to support your own vision. That vision may, in turn, be influenced by the type of content that is generated. This recursive creative relationship creates friction, and in that friction, new types of content have the potential to emerge.

Breaking Routines and Patterns

Our brains naturally seek efficiency, creating mental habits and creative patterns, in addition to ruts. Generative AI's unexpected suggestions can break these patterns, revealing new directions and stimulating you to think in a different way.

Sharpening Curiosity

The process of interpreting and shaping generated content awakens a sense of curiosity. Each time content is generated, it sets off a cycle of questions like

- "What if I try this?"
- "Where could this lead?"
- "How can I shift the content in a different way?"

The Work Is Never Done

The generated content of any gen AI is not meant to be passively accepted. It is a foundation upon which to build. Expect to refine, edit, curate, and reimagine what the AI predicts. This approach transforms AI-generated content into a collaborative starting point rather than a finished product.

> *By actively engaging with the material that is generated, you shape it to better suit your vision and objectives.*

Refinement can involve cropping, masking, word replacement, color changes, removing backgrounds, erasing rough edges, upscaling, and improving visual coherence. Editing allows for the removal of parts you don't need and the addition of new elements triggered by what the AI generated. Curating helps in selecting the content that resonates most with you and in supporting how that content will fit into the work you are already engaged in undertaking. Embracing an active role in the endless pursuit of improved prototypes ensures that whatever your "final" result is, it is a well-crafted, personalized creation that leverages the strengths of both human creativity and the ML model's abilities at the time.[1]

No Shortcuts, Just New Paths

Rather than seeking perfection from the algorithm, use the generated content to spark inspiration. This allows you the freedom to explore avenues you may not have initially considered. When you let go of the need for flawless results, you open up a space for creativity and innovation. The rough or incomplete elements can act as catalysts, prompting you to think outside the black box and approach the material from new angles. These imperfections can reveal hidden potential, leading to unexpected

---

[1] "Even Advanced AI Language Models Require Editorial Oversight" (Source: Harvard Business Review).

breakthroughs. Embracing generated content as a source of inspiration rather than a finished product encourages experimentation and iterative development. It helps to build a more adaptive and creative process, where the focus shifts from achieving a predefined outcome to exploring a spectrum of possibilities. By viewing generated content through this lens, you can create new opportunities for discovery, ultimately enriching your creative output in ways that perfectionism might limit.[2]

Embracing the Iterative

Generative AI encourages an iterative workflow. The ability to quickly produce variations empowers experimentation and refinement through multiple cycles. By generating numerous versions of content rapidly, you can explore a wide range of possibilities and make incremental improvements with each iteration. This cyclic process allows you the opportunity to have constant feedback and make adjustments, ensuring that generated content is continually refined. It transforms the creative process into a dynamic adventure, where ideas evolve through trial and error. Each cycle of refinement brings new insights and opportunities, making your offer to the world not just the result of a single stroke of inspiration but a culmination of thoughtful and well-cultivated experimentation. This approach made even more possible by generative AI encourages deeper engagement with your creative process, resulting in a mindset of curiosity and a relentless pursuit of making something even better the next time.

---

[2] "Generative AI: A Creative Catalyst in the Concept Art Industry" (Source: ArtStation Magazine).

Leveraging Generative Imperfection

Leveraging imperfect or incomplete generated content can be highly effective if approached strategically:

- First, consider using the content as a rough draft or a starting point, refining and polishing it to meet your standards. This approach may save time by providing a reusable prototype that you can work from.

- Next, identify and extract valuable ideas in the form of phrases, or sections, parts of an image, video, or a sound loop, that can be expanded or reworked into more cohesive pieces. Imperfect content can spark creativity, leading to solutions or new perspectives you had not considered.

Figure 9-2. *Prototyping yourself as a learner. AI-generated image*

- Collaborate with others to benefit from different perceptions of the content and its use and value. What might someone else do with the content that you generated that will be different than what you would do?

- Use the entire experience as a learning intervention, analyzing why generated content might have fallen short and applying those insights to future projects.

Start Anywhere

Don't agonize over writing perfect prompts. Begin with a simple idea and see what the AI delivers. Let the results guide your next steps. Starting with a basic concept allows you to quickly generate content without getting bogged down by the need for perfection. This approach encourages a more fluid and creative process, where generated content serves as a springboard for further exploration and development. By iterating on what you are initially given, you can refine and adapt your prompts, gradually honing in on getting closer to what you can work with. This method not only saves time but also encourages a more organic and responsive workflow, where the creative journey is driven by discovery and iteratively adapting content. A common tip is to ask an AI to explain back to you, step by step, what you are tasking it to generate.

Question Everything

Challenge the suggestions. Ask yourself how you can invert, combine, or exaggerate elements to create truly original results. By questioning and manipulating the AI-generated content, you push the boundaries of creativity and uncover unique viewpoints. Inverting elements involves flipping conventional ideas on their heads, exploring opposites or unexpected twists. Combining different aspects can lead to innovative hybrids that blend distinct influences into something new and intriguing. Exaggerating certain features allows you to amplify their impact, creating bold and memorable statements. This active engagement with what an AI proposes transforms passive acceptance of what the ML model generates into a persistent state of "How can this be better?" It encourages a mindset of experimentation, where the goal is not just to refine but to reinvent. By constantly challenging and reimagining whatever an AI gives you, you cultivate a creative process that is rich with originality and suspicious curiosity, ensuring that your final prototype stands out and resonates more with you.

Celebrate the Unexpected

See the value in the strange, uncanny, and nonsensical. Embrace these unexpected detours, as they often reveal more profound insights. The true power of generative AI lies in its ability to ignite our creativity just when we thought we were completely drained of our creative juices. Dare to embrace the messy, the evolving, the weird, the ugly, and the surprising. It's within this dynamic tension where you tap in to a creative mine field.

Small Piece of the Generated Puzzle

At times, generated content is only a small piece of the whole puzzle of the task you are trying to perform. Clearly defining the prototypes needed helps in aligning the AI-generated content with your broader objectives. Determine whether you need a visual prototype, a conceptual model, a functional mock-up, or a narrative draft. Each type of prototype serves a different purpose and requires a specific approach to its refinement and integration within your work. Visual prototypes might involve designing layouts or illustrations, while conceptual models focus on frameworks and relationships between elements. Functional mock-ups require testing and iterating on usability and performance, and narrative drafts need refining for coherence and engagement. By identifying the specific prototypes, you can better contextualize the AI-generated content within the larger scope of your project, ensuring that each piece contributes meaningfully to the overall goal you have defined.

> *Keep in mind that when you intentionally engage with generative AI, you are also prototyping how to work with the technology. You are prototyping content for your own prototypes using a prototype.*

That process will change, and you will adapt how you prototype depending on the specific generative AI you are using, especially if you are working multimodally. Document your prototyping workflows with each generative AI, share them with your colleagues, and understand that as the technologies evolve, so will the features of the specific platform you once used, along with your know-how of gen AI prototyping.

CHAPTER 10

Reiterate Your Learning

In ancient China, a talented artist named Zhuang lived by the river, known for painting the most lifelike fish. One day, the emperor heard of Zhuang's skill and requested a painting of a fish. Zhuang agreed but asked for some time. Days turned into weeks, and weeks into months. The emperor grew impatient and visited Zhuang's studio. To his surprise, Zhuang took a blank piece of paper and, with a few swift strokes, created the most exquisite fish the emperor had ever seen. The emperor, puzzled, asked, "Why did it take you so long to create something so quickly?" Zhuang smiled and showed him piles of discarded sketches. "Every stroke you see is the result of much practice and refinement," he said.

In the previous chapters, you have learned about cyclically adapting content, developing a prototyping mindset when it comes to generating content from any generative AI, and refining content within set workflows or regenerating newly with more specific prompts. Iterating means creating more than one version of something. You can quickly come to the realization that each new prototype of ChatGPT, for example, is an iteration, with the goal of improving its functionality over time.

You iterate all the time. Every human does. We do so when we first wake, and although we have a routine, there's always a different way to brush your teeth, wash your body, time a shower or take a bath, eat breakfast, and so on. At work, we are constantly iterating. We come up with

P. Parra Pennefather, *Regenerating Learning*, Design Thinking, https://doi.org/10.1007/979-8-8688-1061-9_10

different ways to communicate with others. A lot of versions of what we say, what we write, and what we design are done in our heads. It's likely not possible to remember all the versions we have created of something, so we just say things like "oh yes I worked on that for a few hours." What is hidden or at least not explicit is in the way we refined and edited a particular paragraph, or one-liner, an image, a piece of music, an edit of a film, the font on the credits for a clip, the subtitle sizing on a TikTok video, and so on.

Creating multiple versions to refine and improve lies at the heart of effective work with generative AI. Unlike traditional tools that aim for immediate perfection, generative AI systems thrive on repeated cycles of experimentation. What we learn when we interact with generative AI is that all of the interactions that we have set off an entire domino effect of iteration. From the moment we type into the context window, we begin a versions-of relationship that manifests in several different ways.

Regeneration

You iterate on the generated content that you create with the same prompt. Built in to many generative AI is the ability to regenerate a prompt. Essentially, that means creating another version of a response to your prompt every time the regenerate button is pressed. A good question to ask yourself is how many times you have hit regenerate for the same prompt you put in. In many cases, text-image experiments tend to demand more regenerations. Whatever the AI that you use, the other type of iterative prompting occurs as you refine, edit, delete parts of, or add other parts to the prompt itself. You also learn how to maximize what you get out of any gen AI by learning the shortcuts and keywords that are specific to that platform.

Figure 10-1. *Zhuang painting a fish for the emperor.*
AI-generated image

Prompting

You iterate on the prompts that you create. You improve upon those. There are of course strategies that can be explored, and part of our iterative prompting journey relies on advice from colleagues or the Web as to how we can sculpt a prompt to get more of what we want from an AI. It's important to note, however, that so-called "killer" prompts or however they are advertised will never give you the same generated content from the person who composed the prompt. When it comes to building an approach to prompting, it isn't solely based or inspired by better or more clever prompts. Some strategies take time to develop, and when you create a great prompt, it is worth taking the time to note it down for future reference. In addition, you also have the advantage of coming from a specific artistic discipline where you may be able to take advantage of techniques, styles, and approaches that others may not have. As a composer, using Udio or any other text-audio AI you might choose to add specific musical styles, tempo, meter, key, harmonic or melodic structure, etc. You prompt, and then you evaluate the content, then you try again. No matter how skilled you are at prompting, you will always find reasons to iterate your prompts, even if it is just out of curiosity.

Specificity vs. Openness

Initially, experiment with both broad and highly specific prompts. Observe how this spectrum affects the generated results. Experiments lead you to the intentional use of precision or ambiguity in future iterations. Experimenting with a spectrum of prompts, ranging from broad to highly specific, can provide valuable insights into how different levels of detail affect generated results. The approach will help you in understanding the nuances of precision and ambiguity, enabling more intentional and effective use of both in future iterations.

Broad vs. Highly Specific Prompts in Creative Writing

Consider the task of generating a short story. A broad prompt might be "Write a story about friendship." This open-ended instruction allows for a wide range of interpretations, giving you the freedom to explore various themes, settings, and characters. The resulting story might focus on childhood friends, a bond formed during a crisis, or even an unexpected friendship between different species.

> **Broad Prompt:** "Write a story about friendship."
>
> *Generated Result:* The output might be a general tale of two characters who meet and form a lasting bond, with themes of trust, loyalty, and shared experiences.
>
> **LLM Suggestion:** The broad nature of the prompt allows for a wide variety of creative interpretations, but may also lead to more generic and less focused stories. To contrast, you can use a highly specific prompt: "Write a story about two childhood friends who reunite at a carnival and uncover a long-forgotten secret that changes their lives." This level of specificity provides clear direction, focusing the narrative on particular characters, a setting, and a central plot twist. You are now constrained to work within these parameters, potentially leading to a more coherent and engaging story.
>
> **More Specific Prompt:** "Write a story about two childhood friends who reunite at a carnival and uncover a long-forgotten secret that changes their lives."

> *Generated Result:* The generated story is likely to be more detailed, with a well-defined plot involving the carnival, the friends' shared past, and the impact of the uncovered secret on their present lives.

> **Human Observation:** The specificity of the prompt directs the generated content toward a particular narrative, resulting in a more focused and potentially richer story. However, it also limits the breadth of possible interpretations.

Evolving Language

Don't be afraid to rework your prompts completely. Rephrase questions, add descriptive elements, or introduce unexpected words and see how the AI interprets these changes. Each iteration teaches you more about how to effectively communicate with the system. The approach involves rephrasing questions, adding descriptive elements, or introducing unexpected words, which can create contrasting versions of the content that you generate while improving how you communicate with different generative AI.

Rephrasing Questions for Depth

Consider a simple prompt like "Describe a forest." While this might yield a basic description, reworking the prompt to "Describe a forest at dawn, focusing on the interplay of light and shadow among the trees" adds depth and specificity. This constraint guides you to think more creatively and produce a richer, more detailed description. Each iteration of a prompt reveals more about the nuances of effective communication, teaching you that slight changes in phrasing can lead to more compelling responses.

The Power of Constraints

Sometimes, imposing limitations (e.g., style, length, tone) in your prompts forces the generative AI into surprising creative territories, revealing possibilities you hadn't considered. Constraints can lead to new creative choices you might not have taken. These can challenge you to take your second and third impulses instead of your first. By narrowing the scope within which creativity can operate, constraints force you to think outside your regular box and accidentally uncover solutions to problems. Constraints have been widely recognized and leveraged in various fields, from art and literature to business and technology.

The form of a haiku is a perfect example of how constraints can trigger creativity. A traditional haiku consists of three lines with a syllabic pattern of 5-7-5. This strict structure requires poets to express profound ideas and vivid imagery within just 17 syllables. The limitation forces them to choose their words meticulously, often leading to more evocative and powerful poetry. For instance, Basho's famous haiku, "An old silent pond / A frog jumps into the pond— / Splash! Silence again," captures a moment of natural beauty and tranquility in 17 syllables. While you may get some really bad haikus prompting an LLM, the generated content might give you some ideas that you can edit. The constraints of LLMs to create poetry are unique to the platform you choose to use and the corpus the machine learning model was trained on.

Prompt Length

You can observe the limited context length in LLMs as a challenge for you to craft concise and effective prompts. With the evolution of LLMs though and vast increases in the limits of how you can prompt an AI, you can also see the benefit of longer constructed prompts getting more and more specific with what you want. Along with affording longer prompts, however, LLMs struggle with middles and do much better with beginnings and endings. That challenges us to sharpen our prompts, tweak iteratively, and regenerate prompts often.

Limitations

At a certain point in your creative process, when you iteratively prompt and generate dozens, hundreds, even thousands of times, you start to notice that whatever ML model you happen to be working with is limited in what it can achieve. At that point, you will likely gravitate toward other tools, especially if you feel you've pushed the limits of a current version of a generative AI platform.

Training Data

Limited or biased training data has challenged users to creatively fill gaps and think outside the somewhat boring and somewhat predictable statistical probability curves an ML model's algorithms follow. When faced with incomplete or skewed datasets, you need to rely on your critical thinking skills and researcher to bridge these gaps. In the case of LLMs, this often involves conducting additional research, cross-referencing multiple sources, and synthesizing information from various contexts to create better content.

The limitations of training data prompt you to question the reliability and scope of the information provided, encouraging you to explore alternative perspectives and solutions that might not be immediately apparent. Addressing the assumed biases inherent in the training data might inspire you to challenge an LLM to locate outliers. You learn to identify and mitigate biases by investigating what's missing. Often, having your mind set on being inclusive with the content you are working on means investigating varied viewpoints on a subject and adding those voices into your work. That process is also iterative as you might locate a new source that leads you to other scholars that have written extensively about a specific knowledge domain.

Ambiguity and Uncertainty

As discussed previously, ambiguous or uncertain responses from LLMs can encourage you to go in directions you might not have previously considered. This is where stretching your iterative muscles will have a big impact. When faced with a response that lacks clear direction or definitive answers, images that were not what you wanted at all, like strange dreamy frogs floating in tutus within a video you prompted the creation of, your first impulse will be to try again. A rule of play though for many creatives is never to throw anything away, because you never know when frogs in tutus will be useful.

When you embrace the uncertainty inherent in generated responses no matter how much control you think you have or how many features you can tweak, you are signaling to your brain that it's OK if your original vision changes. The more attached you are to a very specific vision you have, the less any generative AI tool will be useful for you. This is in sharp contrast to common requests from creatives for increased control over what they want generated. While increased control will likely improve with some ML models, the current creative contract we have is composed of some assumed rules of play:

- That any creative process is iterative.

- That you'll only be temporarily satisfied by machine- or human-generated prototypes.

- The design of anything is a work in progress.

- The ability to change what you intended is limitless.

- You won't always get precisely what you want, but you'll get something useful that fuels your own creative process.

- The ability to change yourself in the process and how you have come to understand the work you do in the world is also iterative.

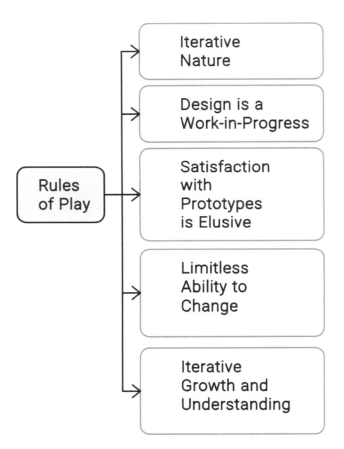

Figure 10-2. *Some inherent rules of play when you prototype with gen AI. AI-generated image*

Trial and Error

There are no mistakes in any creative process that you can't learn something from. Through trial and error, you learn to understand the limitations of text-only prompts when it comes to wanting more control over what is generated. You'll quickly move to accompany prompts with an image, video, or music. The natural extension of that is to work with pre-trained ML models on your own computer and integrate your own creative content to influence generated content.

Figure 10-3. *Balancing ambiguity and clarity in generated content.*
AI-generated image

Bias Mitigation

Addressing and mitigating biases in LLM-generated content encourages you to think critically and creatively about inclusion of alternative voices, persons, or cultures and the way in which other races, genders, ages, and cultures are represented. By actively identifying and challenging biases, you become more aware of the underlying assumptions and prejudices that have influenced AI-generated content. This critical awareness prompts a deeper examination of how inclusivity and representation are incorporated into your own content creation process. When you start to notice exclusion as a pattern in any generative AI, question the perspectives that are presented and seek balanced and inclusive viewpoints from other sources.

Mitigating biases also involves exploring alternative narratives and diverse voices, which can lead to the development of richer and more representative content. This process not only improves the quality of the content but also supports you in developing a more sophisticated understanding of the complex social dynamics at play when it comes to content that is presented to different audiences.

LLM-Generated Prompts

Most LLMs now have built within them the capacity to support you in the prompt creation process, especially with text-image and text-video generative AI. This ability allows you to leverage the power of multimodal generative AI, creating prompts that can be more specific to the generative tool you want to use. By using these built-in support features, you can receive suggestions and refinements for your prompts that you can then test right away.

Multimodal generative AI combines different types of data, such as text, images, and videos, that at times involve very complex AI workflows. The integration on an LLM in image creation, for example, helps you increase the accuracy of what you imagine a little more.

This support system may also streamline the overall workflows you are involved in, reducing the time and effort needed to rapidly prototype what you imagine. It encourages experimentation and iteration, as you can quickly see the results of your prompts and make adjustments on the fly or at least have a better idea if the generated content will be of value in your particular use case.

Storying Prompt

The future of prompting lies in the capacity for us to use natural language prompts within the context window, instead of jagged sentence constructs followed by comma after comma with specific instructions. Figure 10-4 is an example of an easy-to-conduct experiment using the same generative AI with two different types of prompts.

Figure 10-4. *Left image prompt: Sneaky raccoon caught stealing ideas in a dumpster, xieyi style, hand-drawn, 8K, backlit. Right image prompt: Create an 8K resolution hand-drawn image in xieyi style featuring a mischievous raccoon caught in the act of stealing ideas from a dumpster. The scene is backlit, highlighting the raccoon's sneaky behavior with dramatic lighting. Use expressive ink strokes and splotches to capture the essence of the raccoon's actions and the overall mood of the scene. AI-generated image*

As LLMs evolve, they are increasingly able to understand and retain context over one thread. That feature allows you to repeat the aesthetic look and feel of an image once you've nailed the prompt. This advancement allows you to make complex and nuanced prompts using everyday language repeatable. You can reference earlier parts of the conversation, ask for specific modifications, and introduce new elements without needing to reestablish the context each time. Customizable GPTs in OpenAI's ecosystem also give you more control and consistency over generated content, allowing you to very specifically guide the GPT to follow specific guidelines every time, omit words or objects you don't want or need in generated images, and upload reference materials, including your own images.

Accompanying Data

Many prompts can also be accompanied with documents, images, or source audio and video files. This offers you a richer dimension of generated content and allows you to feel more ownership, as it is inspired by your own media. Wanting more control over what content you generate and how specific you want it to refer to your own data will eventually shift your reality from using public generative AI to your own private machine learning models that you can customize.

Other Iterative Actions

Besides prompting and using your own accompanying data, you may iterate on the following during your creative process:

- **Platform**: You will likely iterate on the generative AI you use as there are so many different types, and each does some things better than others. In addition, you'll get different results from each, and they are worth comparing. You can also iterate leveraging a multimodal approach, either within one ML model, like GPT-Dall-E 3, or using an LLM in a chain with other models.

- **Model Strengths**: Even within a single modality (e.g., image generation), models have different strengths. One might excel at realism, while another favors abstract styles. Iterate on the images you generate by using different types of text-image gen AI. These can provide inspiration in different ways. Some will get you the results you want. Some will not.

- **Ideas Themselves**: You iterate on your ideas as you start to see parts of them realized with a generative AI. You may like some and not others. Ideas come and go. When you start to use a gen AI to create content based on an idea, inevitably the content given back to you will influence you to change your idea. You may go through dozens of iterations of an idea as you start to realize that your ideas themselves are also iterative.

Refine, Take a Break, Refine

As has been mentioned before, generated content is seldom useful as is, no matter how many iterations it goes through. What is iterative is your ongoing refinement of the content that is generated over time. In most cases, time does become a factor. At times, you will refine content, then take a break, move on to another task, or simply take some time away from the energy required to concentrate your mind toward a singular task.

Figure 10-5. *Both images used the same prompts and uploaded images on two different text-image platforms. Prompt: Bull in a china shop wearing ballet slippers with an accompanying OpenClip-generated image. AI-generated image*

Mindful Activation

While generative AI at first seems like it takes away much of the cognitive load involved in creating and thinking, there are many reasons to consider how it activates the mind to occupy a space of persistent iterative creation.

- Seeing imperfect manifestations of your ideas through regenerated content might spark you to think about new avenues and refine what you originally thought was a good idea.

- Intentionally regenerating content and controlling features like the "temperature" and "weight "of the prompt within the controls of a private machine learning model can lead to unexpected results you hadn't conceived of, breaking you out of your own self-imposed box and iterating on the core of your ideas or abandoning your original ones and starting anew.

- When the AI regenerates content iteratively, that also challenges your initial assumptions. Your own iterative process of questioning and expanding your viewpoint kindles. Criticality and discernment in the choices you make force another version of what came before.

- An LLM can provide feedback on your ideas, comment on them, extend them, and locate research that backs your idea, creating a more experimental environment where you can guide content as you learn more from what is generated. The icing on top is that you can do so iteratively, as many times as you'd like.

- One of the most useful cases for generative AI is in its power to accompany you through a process of brainstorming and ideation. That process is inherently iterative. AI can blend in seamlessly by offering new perspectives and many ideas that you can choose from quickly, set aside to try later, and rapidly prototype to see if it fits within your overall vision.

- AI can analyze data that you upload to provide insights you might not immediately see in your unstructured data or brainstorming. For example, a mind map you created, an idea you cut and paste from another application, or a series of documents that are unstructured can all be analyzed for patterns.

- AI can not only provide multiple pathways and alternate solutions to real-world problems that expand what you thought was possible, it can also locate previously devised solutions from its corpus, so you can compare how unique your offering is or if it complements what came before.

- When used multimodally, generative AI can appeal to different types of learning styles and approaches to knowledge beyond generated text from an LLM to inspirational icons or images, audio, and video.

- LLMs can help us reframe and reinterpret knowledge we give it, regenerating a version or multiple versions of that knowledge in ways that are more aligned with how we learn.

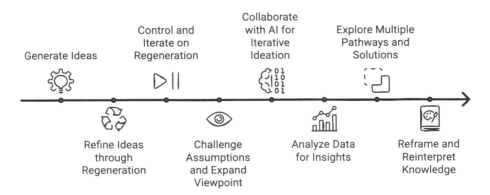

Figure 10-6. *Advantages of an iterative mindset. AI-generated image*

The Perfect Storm of Iterative Multitasking

While the speed of content generation is getting better, those speeds really depend on the efficiency of different AI and paying more for that speed. We can still manage generating content simultaneously on different generative AI due to the waiting period in between us hitting the generate button and the content appearing. While some LLMs start to deliver content right away, many text-image and text-video AI still take time to actually generate content. Portals like Discord that host many generative AI, most famously Midjourney and Pika, allow you to go back and forth iterating similar prompts across platforms.

When we iterate content leveraging generative AI as part of our own process, the technology does not negate the human element of creativity nor does it replace it. Instead, gen AI allows creatives to benefit from an endless spiral of inspiration. All generative AI are highly dependent on the creativity that you bring to the prompt-generate-evaluate-regenerate cycle.

By iterating on prompts, tools, refinement of generated content over time, and even our own initial ideas that we might upload to an AI, we enter into our own latent space of infinite possibility. The result is a reinvention of our workflows, one that can lead to iterative improvement, unexpected discoveries, and a deeper understanding of our own creative process. Iterative improvement is also built into the ethos of developers who constantly tweak most generative AI systems. With new features, platforms, and tools introduced regularly, persistent reiteration can transform how we apply generative AI to our own works in progress.

CHAPTER 11

Reconcile Using Generative AI

Depending on an AI for truth is like taking your drunk friend seriously.

Once upon a time, a man named Nasrudin had a neighbor who bragged endlessly about the virtues of his donkey. One day, the neighbor fell sick and asked Nasrudin to take the donkey to market for him, promising half the profits. Nasrudin agreed and took the donkey to market. There, he fed the donkey only the finest grains and spoke highly of its virtues to everyone who passed by. Soon, a wealthy merchant offered a huge sum of money for the donkey. Nasrudin sold it and returned home with the money. When the neighbor recovered, he demanded his share. Nasrudin handed over a small portion, keeping most of the money for himself. The neighbor protested, "You promised me half!" Nasrudin replied, "True, but you didn't consider the costs of the finest grains and my skilled salesmanship. Nothing comes for free, my friend." And so, the neighbor learned the hard way that appearances often hide the true cost of things.

The ecosystem of learning that encompasses our interactions with generative AI systems extends to the potential obstacles that might get in the way of its very adoption. Whatever your intent is in using generative AI, if you embody suspicious curiosity, you can learn a great deal more about some of the reasons this technology is a little bit different than ones that have come before.

© Patrick Parra Pennefather 2024
P. Parra Pennefather, *Regenerating Learning*, Design Thinking,
https://doi.org/10.1007/979-8-8688-1061-9_11

Suspicious curiosity is a lens, an attitude, through which you can approach your interactions with any gen AI. To do that, look to the raccoon as an animal to guide you. It is by its very nature suspiciously curious. You see that behavior play out as much as when you encounter them in the wild as when you see them poking up from inside the alleyway dumpster. These nocturnal bandits seem to always be in planning-a-heist mode and with their nimble paws can pick locks as easily as getting their heads stuck in a peanut butter jar. All the while, these Houdinis of the animal world manage their escapes or stand their ground until you are forced to leave the performance you were not invited to.

When you look through the lens of suspicious curiosity, you become open to trying generative AI and seeing if it's useful to you while at the same time being fully aware of the consequences of interacting with it. We know that the technology is not all bad news. At the same time, the persistent hype around it isn't exactly encouraging its wide adoption. Nor is a CEO begging people not to take away their AI's corpus of data that consists of other people's unsolicited content, because their ML models really need it. Until you see the value of this technology for your own use cases and weigh the pros and cons of using it, you'll be at a loss when someone challenges your very use of it. Worse, is if you completely resist it and your employer walks in one day asking everyone to adopt a tool you know was not developed ethically. You may also resist its use simply based on how it works and, in the case of some AI, who that ML model is programmed to spy on, how it recommends products no one asked for, and what living artists and estates that it steals from.

Figure 11-1. *Suspicious curiosity may lead to your gold during your creative process. AI-generated image*

On the other hand, new ML models that are ethically co-constructed, open source, and whose developers are transparent about the public domain content their models consist of are already being offered to us. It is worthwhile investigating which ones you might use tomorrow, even if you are not using them today.

Fortunately, there is a stealthy algorithmic battle we can also learn from; public generative AI platforms that are mired in ethical dilemmas vs. open source AI systems that allow users to use their own data on pre-trained ML models that they can customize on their own private and secure computers. Apple computers, for example, recognize the importance of private and secure models and are actively engaged in distributing them freely for use on their computers.

Well-Informed Naivety

Wouldn't it be great if there was nothing to reconcile in the use of any technology? They replaced the dirty productions of the industrial age after all. Or did they? While the digital technology industry projects an image of modernity, futuristic utopia, and cleanliness, it is intrinsically linked to environmentally harmful and ethically problematic practices. Addressing these issues requires a concerted effort from corporations, consumers, and policymakers to pressure sustainable and just supply chains, ensuring that the benefits of technological advancements do not come at the expense of humans, more-than-humans, and the planet.[1]

When you decide to work with any generative AI to support your learning process, you will inevitably be compelled to learn about what you're getting into. Once you do, you can position yourself on your use of the technology. That research is up to each of us, including the depth and detail that is required to help you make an informed decision. This is because not all gen AI are created equal. Each is based on ML models composed of algorithms and, importantly, lots of data that is human-created. Not every generative AI uses a corpus of data that has been sourced ethically.

---

[1] McStay, A. (2023). Automating Empathy: Decoding Technologies That Gauge Intimate Life. Oxford University Press.

There are multiple factors to consider, particularly if you are activating its use within a shared work environment. While your company may have developed policies for its use, you will definitely need to carve out your own guidelines, especially if you are being asked to use "it." When you focus on learning about the technology first, without grasping at how it can be integrated within your workflows, then you have a better approach that will help you and potentially inspire those around you to learn if the technology can support your own work.

Patterns of Proclamations

The competitive landscape for being first to have that ML model that does everything and captures market share contributes to the manufacturing of unsustainable products shipped too early to market that promise too much to investors and give much less to end users. The hype that accompanies these hallucinations and the media that supports those announcements propagate an endless stream of vague proclamations and overclocked truths, in a pattern that Darren DeCoursey refers to as "elevating mediocrity." The rapid advancement and competitive drive in the AI industry often lead to the premature release of products that are unsustainable and sensationalized. Scholars have highlighted patterns that come with the territory, often blurring the line between what is real and what is a marketing ploy. A recent proclamation by a CEO of a company that was founded in 1911 is a common rhetorical tool that is used to distance oneself from the technology itself, as if the technology should be allowed to forge forward without too much human interference. Proclamations such as the one below can be analyzed within the generative AI that the company is developing to interpret, offer opinion and analysis.

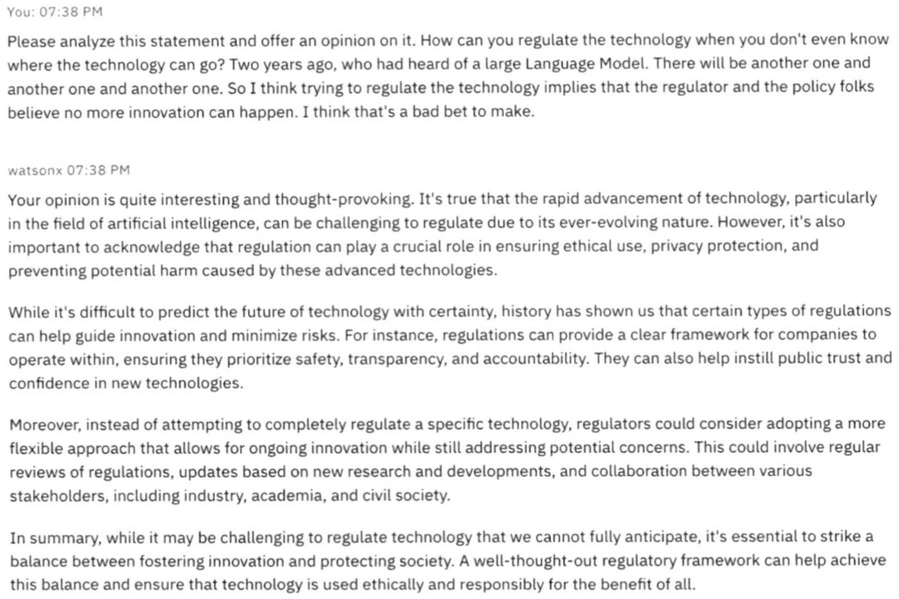

You: 07:38 PM

Please analyze this statement and offer an opinion on it. How can you regulate the technology when you don't even know where the technology can go? Two years ago, who had heard of a large Language Model. There will be another one and another one and another one. So I think trying to regulate the technology implies that the regulator and the policy folks believe no more innovation can happen. I think that's a bad bet to make.

watsonx 07:38 PM

Your opinion is quite interesting and thought-provoking. It's true that the rapid advancement of technology, particularly in the field of artificial intelligence, can be challenging to regulate due to its ever-evolving nature. However, it's also important to acknowledge that regulation can play a crucial role in ensuring ethical use, privacy protection, and preventing potential harm caused by these advanced technologies.

While it's difficult to predict the future of technology with certainty, history has shown us that certain types of regulations can help guide innovation and minimize risks. For instance, regulations can provide a clear framework for companies to operate within, ensuring they prioritize safety, transparency, and accountability. They can also help instill public trust and confidence in new technologies.

Moreover, instead of attempting to completely regulate a specific technology, regulators could consider adopting a more flexible approach that allows for ongoing innovation while still addressing potential concerns. This could involve regular reviews of regulations, updates based on new research and developments, and collaboration between various stakeholders, including industry, academia, and civil society.

In summary, while it may be challenging to regulate technology that we cannot fully anticipate, it's essential to strike a balance between fostering innovation and protecting society. A well-thought-out regulatory framework can help achieve this balance and ensure that technology is used ethically and responsibly for the benefit of all.

Figure 11-2. *Watson LLM screenshot analyzing a quote from a CEO commenting on the problem with AI regulation*

Unrealistic Promises and Market Pressure

The intense competition to achieve the next breakthrough in AI technology creates a high-pressure environment where companies feel forced to release products prematurely, often to pacify investors and shareholders. This often results in products that are not thoroughly tested or sustainable, leading to exaggerated claims and expectations that are seldom fulfilled (Brynjolfsson & McAfee, 2017). The metaphor of a pressure-cooker environment effectively captures the immense stress and urgency experienced by companies in the AI industry as they strive to outpace their competitors. This rush often leads to premature product releases, where the necessary rigorous testing, ethics, and long-term sustainability considerations are overlooked. The consequence is a market filled with AI products that do not perform as promised, creating a cycle of inflated expectations and growing disappointments. This situation not only undermines consumer trust but also hampers the credibility and potential growth of AI technologies in the long run. Companies need to find a balance between speed and quality to ensure that their innovations are both reliable and sustainable to their customers.

Hype and Media Influence

Media coverage frequently worsens the problem by sensationalizing the abilities of new AI products. This creates a cycle of hype and exaggerated promises, leading to consumer disappointment and mistrust. The media's role in the AI industry often involves amplifying the capabilities of new products, which contributes significantly to the problem of inflated expectations. Sensational headlines and overenthusiastic reports create a feedback loop where the hype surrounding AI technologies becomes self-reinforcing. As a result, consumers develop unrealistic expectations about what AI can achieve. When these high expectations are not met, it leads to widespread disappointment and erodes trust in AI. This cycle not only damages the reputation of individual companies but also impacts the overall perception of AI as a reliable and effective technology.[2]

Reading beyond the headline is an important and seemingly obvious research skill that hyped-up articles about AI demand for us to put into daily practice. Nowadays with the prevalence of clickbait articles, we need to invest the time to read more deeply or to read like humans used to. Take, for example, a very recent headline sent to the author entitled "Do You Know How University of Montreal Uses AI to Grade Assignments and Slashed Faculty Workload by Over 67%?" Reading the article fully reveals that the reduction in workload of 67% was an "average" of grading time

---

[2] https://www.niemanlab.org/2024/05/how-uncritical-news-coverage-feeds-the-ai-hype-machine/

for assignments only. That means that faculty workload was not in fact slashed by over 67%, only their time grading assignments. How their time grading assignments compared to their overall workload was not reported. To mitigate the issue of hype, marketers, media outlets, and AI companies need to adopt a more measured and realistic approach to discussing new advancements and take responsibility for reporting research accurately, avoiding sensationalist headlines that are simply not true.

Figure 11-3. *Puffery can make smoke into dragons. AI-generated image*

Ethical and Social Implications

The competitive environment in the AI industry not only results in technical and market failures but also raises serious ethical issues. The rush to market can produce AI systems that are biased, lack transparency, and have not been thoroughly tested for safety.[3] The fierce competition in the AI industry has far-reaching consequences beyond just technical and market failures; it also brings to light significant ethical concerns. In the scramble to be the first to market, companies often overlook critical aspects of AI development such as bias, transparency, untruths, and safety. This haste can lead to the deployment of AI systems that reinforce existing prejudices or introduce new ones. Further, the lack of transparency in how these systems operate makes it difficult for many humans to understand and trust the technology. Without rigorous testing for safety, these AI systems can also present unforeseen risks to individuals and society. Therefore, the industry must prioritize ethical considerations and thorough testing alongside innovative impulses and pleasing investors to ensure that AI advancements are both responsible and beneficial.

Sustainability and Long-Term Viability

Sustainable development in AI necessitates a balanced approach that emphasizes long-term viability over short-term gains. However, the current competitive landscape encourages the opposite, resulting in products that often fail to meet expectations and may cause harm.[4] For AI development to be truly sustainable, a balanced approach focusing

---

[3] O'neil, C. (2017). Weapons of math destruction: How big data increases inequality and threatens democracy. Crown.

[4] Benkler, Y. (2019). Don't let industry write the rules for AI. Nature, 569(7754), 161–162.

on long-term viability is essential. This means prioritizing thorough testing, ethical guardrails, and a focus on narrow AI that is dedicated to generating domain and context-specific content. Unfortunately, the present competitive environment incentivizes rapid, short-term gains, pushing companies to release products hastily, no matter what it takes, to stay ahead of the competition. This often leads to AI systems that are not fully developed, potentially unreliable, and sometimes harmful. These prototypes, often masked as products, can fail to deliver on promises development teams shouldn't make in the first place, causing disappointment and mistrust among consumers. The drive for quick success with the goal of short-term investment and valuation can undermine the integrity and potential of AI technologies. A shift in focus toward sustainability and responsible development means slowing down releases and ensuring that regulations federal bodies have developed in the United States, Canada, and Europe are being listened to, rather than ignored or dismissed.

Vague Proclamations and Overclocked Truths

Some founders in the AI industry often make vague claims about future capabilities without providing concrete evidence, leading to a gap between public expectations and the actual technological affordances of gen AI. This tendency to exaggerate diminishes the credibility of genuine advancements.[5] The habit of making grandiose, yet ambiguous, statements about future capabilities creates a significant misalignment between what the public expects and what technology can realistically achieve. This "overclocking" of truths, where the potential of AI is exaggerated without solid proof, sets unrealistic expectations that are rarely met. As a result, when genuine advancements are made, they are often met with

---

[5] Jarrahi, M. H. (2018). Artificial intelligence and the future of work: Human-AI symbiosis in organizational decision making. Business horizons, 61(4), 577–586.

skepticism or are overshadowed by previous disappointments. This not only undermines the credibility of true progress in AI but also hinders the industry's ability to build and maintain trust with the public.

Should that matter to you?

Layered Questions to Reconcile

The development of ML models is partly rooted in the very human need to analyze vast amounts of knowledge in order to share insights from that analysis. Traditional methods of doing so through the publication of content in different industries have had their pros and cons. The sharing of knowledge through whatever media has rarely been a singular effort even though much of what has been published has been exhibited as the result of a singular author. When tasked to reconcile the use of generative AI, first ask yourself how you have reconciled who has benefited from previous forms of media that have been published. Who were those others? What were their stories of compromise when it came to surrendering certain rights for the ability to share their work? What have authors, including musicians, who have been provided very little money in profits for the work they have published, been able to do with those who took advantage of them? What have they compromised by signing away the majority of the ownership of their work to publishers and labels? Who owns the rights of previously created work? What rights exactly? How should they be recognized when it comes to a token or more of their work being used to generate content that they contributed to along with many others?

What should we do when an author's ideas are rephrased, reframed, or completely mashed together with other authors in generated text, speech, image, video, audio, or code?

Many publishing companies have developed a library of works composed of both singular authors and more collaborative efforts. Each of those libraries forms that company's corpus of knowledge, of data.

Companies that have scraped the Internet for data have developed algorithms that make their ML models draw from multiple interconnected libraries of knowledge with or without permission—a vast amount of human-created knowledge that is not always in the public domain. Generative AI challenges any notion of a singular author as it does not solely rely on the written words of any one author. Instead, it looks for patterns in a large co-created human library and generates new content based on it. Understanding that, we have the right and the obligation to ask simple questions like

- Where does the data in the gen AI's grand corpus come from and how was it labeled and organized?

- How is new content generated? What happens when I give any gen AI my own content?

- What are all the consequences of creating new content from it? Who is affected? Who profits?

To answer those questions, we have to dive more deeply into how ML models work. This is particularly the case if you happen to be a content creator. As a person working in a company that is hesitant to adopt generative AI, having clarity as to how you reconcile the answer to each question will not only support you but your team and the organization at large.

The following typologies of topic areas to reconcile are not exhaustive, but they are a start as to what you may want to consider as you begin to adopt the technology. Regardless of what you need to reconcile, consider that the technology itself invokes us to deepen our learning about issues and challenges that already exist in our societies that AI brings to the surface. These include the corpus, copy wrong, public vs. private machine learning models, biases, hallucinations, homogeneity, deep fakes and human replacement, access including cost, sustainability, and ethics. What we need to reconcile is a long list that keeps growing. One way to think about organizing that list is to think of the data that is used to train the ML model (corpus, copy wrong, deep fakes, public vs. private ML models), how and what the ML model generates as a result of being prompted (biases, hallucinations, homogeneity), and the tangible and ethical costs associated with training and inference of an ML model (access, sustainability, ethics).

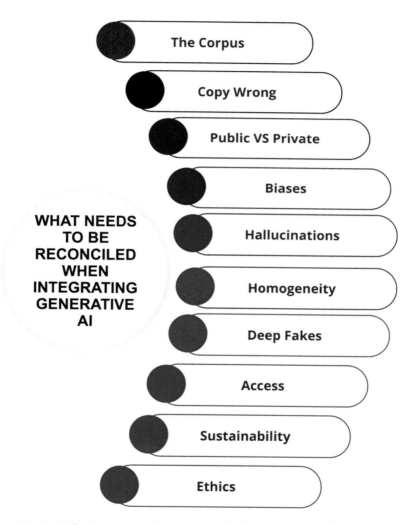

Figure 11-4. *What you need to reconcile in your use of generative AI systems*

Part One: Training

The Corpus

The concept of "The Corpus" in the context of generative AI refers to the vast collection of data that these systems are trained on. A corpus encompasses an enormous range of human knowledge, creativity, and expression, serving as the foundation from which AI generates its content. The term "corpus" in the context of machine learning and natural language processing (NLP) has its roots in linguistics, where it traditionally referred to a large and structured set of texts used for analysis. The use of corpora for language research became prominent in the 1980s with the rise of computational linguistics.

In machine learning, especially within NLP, a corpus is essential for training models. It provides a comprehensive collection of text data that can be annotated for various linguistic features such as part-of-speech tags, named entities, or sentiment labels. This structured data helps in developing and testing algorithms for tasks like text classification, sentiment analysis, and language modeling. The association of the term "corpus" with machine learning, particularly NLP, grew as the need for large datasets to train and evaluate models became apparent. This terminology reflects the practice of leveraging extensive text collections to increase an ML model's ability to understand and process human language accurately.

The use of corpora in machine learning was likely influenced by the broader adoption of data-driven approaches in linguistics and the development of early NLP systems. Notable early corpora include the Brown Corpus and the Penn Treebank, which were pivotal in advancing NLP research by providing annotated datasets for training and evaluation.[6]

---

[6] https://stats.stackexchange.com/questions/85930/difference-in-meaning-of-these-terms-dataset-vs-corpus

For users of generative AI, understanding the nature and implications of this corpus is worth their time. It represents a distillation of human culture, knowledge, and creativity, transformed into a format that AI can process and learn from. This raises several important considerations:

- **Breadth and Diversity**: The corpus typically includes a wide array of sources—books, articles, websites, social media posts, and more. This diversity can lead to rich and varied generated content, but it also means that the AI's knowledge is as broad (and potentially as biased) as the sources it analyzes.

- **Quality and Accuracy**: Not all information in the corpus is equally reliable or accurate. Users must be aware that AI can generate convincing-sounding but incorrect information based on inaccuracies or outdated data that forms part of its training data.

- **Cultural Representation**: The corpus may overrepresent certain cultures, languages, or perspectives while underrepresenting others. This can lead to biases in AI outputs and a potential narrowing of cultural diversity in generated content.

- **Ethical and Legal Considerations**: The use of copyrighted material in training data raises questions about intellectual property rights. Users should be aware of potential legal and ethical issues surrounding the generation of content based on protected works. If you are a creator, then ask yourself if you are OK with your work being scraped and used to train a machine learning model without permission or compensation.

- **Temporal Limitations**: The corpus typically has a cutoff date, beyond which new information is not included. You need to be mindful of this limitation when using AI for tasks requiring up-to-date information. Many LLMs are slowly integrating search systems, and these may provide you with more up-to-date references.

- **Privacy Concerns**: While files or information you upload to a public LLM may not have an impact on how a machine learning model has trained, and that data is safe in the short term, most companies remind users that uploaded content could be used to train their machine learning model in future versions of it.

- **Influence on Creativity**: As users increasingly rely on AI trained on existing works, there's a potential for a feedback loop where AI-generated content influences future human creations, which in turn might be included in future AI training data.

- **Specialization vs. Generalization**: Some AI models are trained on specialized corpora for specific domains, while others use more general datasets. Understanding this distinction is important for choosing the right tool for a given task.

- **Evolution of Knowledge**: As the corpus expands and evolves, so too does the AI's abilities and biases. Users should stay informed about updates to the AI models they use. Each new version may be accompanied with further explanation as to what data feeds their corpus.

- **Critical Thinking**: Engaging with AI-generated content requires a critical approach. Users should view AI as a tool that processes and recombines existing information rather than a source of new knowledge. How an LLM organizes sentence structures, the vocabulary it uses, and the overall structure of the content it generates need to all be viewed with criticality.

For individuals reconciling the use of generative AI, the corpus represents both the power and the limitations of these systems. It offers access to a vast pool of human knowledge and creativity, but also demands responsibility and discernment in its use. Humans must strike a balance between leveraging AI's means and maintaining their own critical thinking and creative integrity.

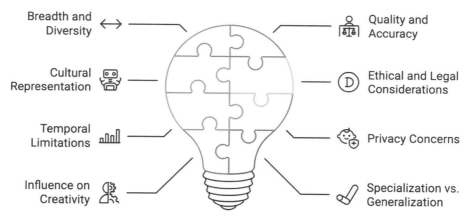

Figure 11-5. *Implications of the training data used for different ML models. AI-generated image*

Copy Wrong

The concept of "Copy Wrong" in the context of generative AI addresses the complex and often problematic relationship between AI-generated content and copyright law. This issue has become increasingly prominent as AI systems capable of producing human-like text, images, and other media have become more sophisticated and widely used.

At its core, "Copy Wrong" encompasses several interrelated concerns:

- **Training Data Ethics**: Many AI models are trained on vast datasets that include copyrighted material. This challenges the legality and ethics of using such material without explicit permission from rights holders. When in doubt, don't use it. If there are, to the beginning of the sentence. Any gray areas, investigate uncertainty until you are absolutely clear.

- **Output Ownership**: When an AI generates content based on its training, it's unclear who owns the rights to that content—the AI's creators, the user who prompted the generation, or potentially no one if it's considered a derivative work. Be wary of taking a company's interpretations of the use of any generated content on its platform as the final word on the matter.

- **Plagiarism and Originality**: AI-generated content may closely resemble existing works, blurring the lines between inspiration, derivation, and outright copying. This challenges traditional notions of originality and authorship. Bear in mind that going with generated content in the style of any living or dead author contributes to an overall homogeneity in AI-generated content that has the potential to saturate different channels and portals with content that all looks, feels, and sounds the same.

- **Attribution Challenges**: It's often difficult or impossible to trace the specific sources that influenced an AI's generated content, making proper attribution a real challenge. Companies are beginning to reference ideas that they generate, however, and those organizations like Perplexity are paving the way for a new generation of LLMs to source where ideas are coming from.

- **Fair Use Ambiguity**: The application of fair use to AI-generated content is a bit fuzzy, especially when the AI has been trained on copyrighted materials. Fair use in educational contexts is no longer easy to reconcile. Should the reasons why you use a particular gen AI platform matter? Somehow, even if you do not monetize, the company still does as soon as content you create and share inspires others to subscribe and pay for their services.

- **Creative Industry Impact**: There are concerns about how AI-generated content might devalue human creativity or unfairly compete with human creators in various industries. We are already witness to false equivalencies where proclamations of an LLM being more creative than many humans based on so-called validated testing instruments are being made. Creative industries need to work with their teams and associations to better define the differences between AI and human creativity.

- **Legal Precedent Vacuum**: Current copyright laws were not designed with AI in mind, leading to a lack of clear legal guidance on many AI-related copyright issues. The problem is that companies can move forward regardless of the state of limbo that many countries and smaller jurisdictions find themselves in.

- **Transformation and Derivation**: The degree to which AI "transforms" its training data when generating new content is a subject of debate, with implications for how derivative works are defined. It's best to assume that the human role in the equation is to use generated content as inspiration or for creatives to use their own content with pre-trained private ML models whose corpora are ethically trained.

- **International Complications**: Copyright laws vary by country, creating a complex landscape for AI deployment and use across borders. This results in the ability for companies who are stealing the data of others without permission, or engaged in deep faking others without their consent, to bypass the laws of their own country by moving operations, servers, and databases to countries whose laws are currently undefined, unclear, or lax.

- **Ethical Content Generation**: Users of AI must grapple with the ethical implications of generating content that may be infringing on others' intellectual property rights. If it was your content being used, what would you do?

- **Licensing and Compensation**: There's ongoing debate about whether and how creators whose works are used in AI training should be compensated or have the right to opt out. This should not be such a difficult legal issue. Compensation should be provided to authors whose work has been obviously used in publically generated content.

- **Transparency in AI Systems**: The "black box" nature of many AI systems makes it difficult to audit their processes for potential copyright infringement. Organizations should be able to clearly articulate how they use any data in their corpus.

For individuals and organizations using generative AI, navigating these "Copy Wrong" issues requires careful consideration and often legal guidance. It's essential to be aware of the potential risks and ethical implications of using AI-generated content, especially when used for commercial purposes.

As the technology continues to evolve, so too will the legal and ethical frameworks surrounding it. Users of generative AI should stay informed about developments in this area, advocate for clearer guidelines and regulations, and approach the use of AI-generated content with a mindset of responsible innovation. Ultimately, the concept of "Copy Wrong" challenges us to reconsider our understanding of creativity, authorship, and intellectual property in the age of AI, teetering for a balance between technological advancement and the protection of human creative rights.

On AI and Stolen Content

All generative AI have been trained on content that has been openly available on the Internet regardless of the state of its ownership or co-ownership or its state of copyright or public domain status.
No permission from any author was asked for its use. Nor were the publishers of copyrightable data that for most creators out there have had the most to lose. While creative authors, composers, artists of all kinds, and photographers have the right to be angry, what small percentage of a percentage would satisfy their already small percentage of a tiny little profit? Those who stream content on YouTube have the same struggle and question to ask. Meanwhile, the company that scraped the most and can now monetize from the scrapings of other humans has the most to win. The difficulty in holding them accountable has to do with an inaccurate and difficult method to say that x derivative work made from the outputs of an ML model point directly to a specific author, and the fraction of content used from said author is even harder to calculate.

Figure 11-6. *Simulating a version of the Mona Lisa that is no longer the Mona Lisa. AI-generated image*

The problem with protecting copyright, and giving pennies to human creators as a form of performance right, is rooted in the difficulty of proving ownership because of the black box nature of generative AI systems. You prompt the machine, something happens in a black box, and you receive generated content. The problem is we don't really know what happens in that black box even though many researchers attempt to explain the process. We cannot see, let alone imagine, the speed of the patterns that algorithms look for in a latent space. It's too damn fast. Here's an example as to why it is difficult to really know:

HaikuBot: *"Moonless night obscures,*

Hidden paths and secrets lost,

Eyes search, find no light."

While this haiku was not that difficult to get an LLM to generate, how tokenization works is sufficiently befuddling as to how it could possibly be taking a single token from one specific haiku author. Or, is it doing that at all, constructing the haiku solely based on syllabic count? In the spirit of creative resistance, we can ask our Haiku Bot to locate a reference for every word that it took.

Moonless

Smith, J. (2015). *Moonless Nights and Their Impact on Wildlife Behavior*. Journal of Ecology, 22(3), 145-162.

Night

Anderson, P. (2018). *The Mysteries of the Night: An Exploration of Nocturnal Life*. Oxford University Press.

Obscures

Davies, L. (2020). *Obscures and Enigmas: The Role of Darkness in Literature*. Literary Review Quarterly, 34(2), 98-117.

Hidden

Barker, T. (2019). *Hidden Realms: Uncovering the Secrets Beneath*. Cambridge University Press.

Paths

Garcia, R. (2017). *Paths Less Traveled: An Analysis of Forgotten Routes*. Travel and Exploration Journal, 15(4), 211-229.

And

Johnson, S. (2021). *Syntax and Structure: The Use of Conjunctions in Modern English*. Language Studies, 48(1), 72-89.

Secrets

Miller, D. (2016). *Secrets and Lies: The Psychology of Hidden Truths*. Psychological Studies, 29(3), 187-204.

Lost

Robinson, K. (2018). *Lost and Found: A Study of Missing Artifacts*. Historical Research Journal, 12(2), 301-315.

Eyes

Thompson, J. (2022). *Eyes of the Night: Vision in Darkness*. Journal of Ophthalmic Science, 19(1), 45-58.

Search

Peters, L. (2020). *Search Algorithms and Their Applications*. Computer Science Review, 40(1), 102-119.

Find

Evans, M. (2017). *Finders Keepers: The Science of Discovery*. Exploration Science Journal, 9(4), 90-107.

No

Green, A. (2019). *No and Yes: The Linguistics of Negation and Affirmation*. Language and Linguistics, 23(2), 199-215.

Light

Harris, B. (2015). *Light and Shadow: The Duality of Illumination*. Physics Today, 51(3), 60-78.

Even though all the above references are fake, a similar exercise could attempt to locate real quotes written from real humans who wrote haikus. The LLM did understand how to create a reference though so had to base that knowledge on looking at real references that it might actually have in its corpus. It searched and found patterns, which then allowed it to make predictions about what would come next. The word "haiku" in the prompt signaled the LLM to create one based on the patterns of human-created ones in its corpus.

When creatives use the argument that anything written "in their particular style" is tantamount to copyright infringement, it falls apart because the model is not looking at how an author structures their work, nor is it identifying the criteria that informs what imitating an author, "in the style" of that author, actually means.

> *What exact styles are used by Kafka's English translated work that makes us say "Hey that's just simulating Kafka". Which Kafka? is one question that comes to mind? Which translation of Kafka contains the essence of his writing style once translated? Is it easier to claim theft if Kafka's actual German texts were stolen, translated, and mashed?*

Information as to where all the content that an ML model is trained on isn't always readily available and requires you to conduct research to figure it out. You can, however, access the policies of those companies that are providing public access to their machine learning models quite easily. Doing so will help navigate you to the right LLM or text-image prototype to use, since no two policies are the same.

The idea of "Copy Wrong" challenges us to reconsider our understanding of creativity, authorship, and intellectual property in the age of AI, pushing for a balance between technological advancement and the protection of our creativity (stolen from the author by the author on pg. 219).

Figure 11-7. *Spot the thief. AI-generated image*

Public vs. Private Machine Learning Models

Reconciling the use of public vs. private machine learning models is another important consideration for individuals and organizations who want to implement any generative AI. This comparison involves weighing the trade-offs between capability, efficiency, and ethical implications.

Public LLMs

LLMs, such as GPT-3, GPT-4, Gemini, or Claude, are trained on vast amounts of data and can draw on that data to generate content. Most people use these over the Internet. Unless otherwise paid for at a higher subscription tier, there is an uncertainty as to what companies will do with the prompts, files, images, audio, or video that you might upload. There are pros and cons to using these mostly public-facing black boxes. Still, it is important to distinguish between those that are used publically like ChatGPT, Gemini, and Claude and those that require users to install them on their own computers and use more privately and securely like Llama 3, Mistral, and other more narrow machine learning models. There are pros wrapped up within cons in using these mostly public-facing black boxes:

- **Versatility**: They can handle a wide range of tasks, from creative writing to code generation, but all generated content is not so versatile as to require a high degree of editing, and in the case of code, architecture, debugging, and testing within a real dev environment.

- **Contextual Understanding**: They are pretty good overall at working with prompts and producing coherent, if not somewhat homogeneous and redundant, responses.

- **Knowledge Breadth**: They encompass a broad knowledge base, often capable of discussing diverse topics. Yet, these tend to be limited in certain knowledge domains until you prompt them for specific experts you already know exist, certain public domain articles or authors you are aware of, and outliers that they sometimes have access to.

- **Good to Edit**: They generally produce more refined and somewhat-human-like text, but to make it more human-like, it requires editing.

- **Resource Intensity**: They require substantial computational power, making private machine learning models a little more expensive to run and environmentally costly. Training of LLMs is resource heavy, making them a sustainability nightmare.

- **Privacy Concerns**: They often rely on cloud-based processing, raising data privacy issues because every single prompt you create goes somewhere and is usually collected for future training purposes.

- **Potential for Misuse**: Their simulation of somewhat-human-like content makes them potential tools for generating misinformation and deep fakes.

Private Language Models

Private LLMs are becoming more and more popular and powerful. These are offering individuals, teams, and organizations open source models that can be installed on a local and private computer not connected to the Internet. They can also be customized. Because they can be used privately, you can upload personal or company data to them, knowing they will not share that data to anyone. Some, however, like Llama 3.1 with 305 billion parameters will require a lot of compute, and this may or may not be within your organization's budget. That means shifting to cloud computing, which, without RAG or KGs, surfaces similar challenges of managing private and encrypted data. You can certainly find third-party companies that can do that at a premium and promise complete privacy and protected data. However, systems being hacked are a persistent reality. That's not to say you are fully protected on a private computer either, if you are connected to the Internet.

The dizzying number of pre-trained open source models of all types and varieties is available through various portals, including GitHub and Hugging Face. Each is worth exploring. More flexibility exists in what you explore and the resources to support you if you use a standard PC, although Apple recently announced a number of private and securely available ML models for their computers as well. Pre-trained models offer the most flexibility allowing you to use your own data and content to influence the generated results. These in addition to frameworks like RAG and the use of knowledge graphs allow any user to have more control over their own data, reduce hallucinations, and generate content that is more specific to their own needs, data, and context.

The choice between public vs private machine learning models isn't always clear-cut. It requires careful consideration of the specific use case, available resources, ethical concerns, and desired outcomes. As AI technology continues to evolve, choosing what you will use will likely be influenced by your organization's values and stance on responsible AI use. Demands for increased privacy and encryption are possible to support with large and public models like ChatGPT and Gemini, and your organization needs to weigh the cost of paying for a higher subscription or investing a significant amount of money in a private machine learning model that is powerful enough for your needs.

Deep Fakes

What is the human compulsion to emulate, simulate, copy, and imitate? Answer that question and you may begin to understand why deep fakes exist, and continue to persist.

The phenomenon of deep fakes is itself deeply rooted in a deep-seated compulsion to imitate, replicate, and manipulate reality and the perception of reality through lenses or perspectives other than our own. It isn't just about simulating the famous either. From ancient times, humans have been drawn to mimicry and illusion, driven by a mixture of admiration, competition, and deceit. This compulsion is reflected in various aspects of culture, from art and literature to modern technology.

Ancient civilizations engaged in acts of replication and imitation. The Greeks, for instance, were known for their skill in creating realistic sculptures that closely imitated the human form. This pursuit of realism extended to their theatrical performances, where actors donned masks to transform into other characters, embodying the earliest forms of visual and performative illusion. Where we find some of the ancestry of forgery is in Rome. Roman artists were highly skilled in creating detailed copies of Greek masterpieces, driven by the Roman elite's insatiable demand for the prestigious art of their Greek predecessors. These forgeries were not merely acts of deception but rather a reflection of the Romans' deep admiration for Greek culture and their desire to possess its artistic heritage. This practice was so prevalent that it became an accepted part of the art market, with some forgeries being so expertly crafted that they were considered valuable in their own right. The line between original and replica blurred, setting a historical precedent for the complex relationship between authenticity and imitation in the art world.

The Renaissance period brought about a renewed interest in realism and the perfection of technique. Artists like Michelangelo and Leonardo da Vinci meticulously studied human anatomy to produce works that were lifelike. However, alongside this pursuit of artistic excellence, there existed a more contentious side to imitating art. The practice of creating fakes was not merely an act of deception but also a testament to the skill and ingenuity of the forgers themselves, who had to replicate the techniques and styles of the masters they sought to emulate.

In literature, creating fake works took on new meanings, in the tradition of pseudepigraphy, where creations were falsely attributed to famous authors to gain credibility and readership. This practice dates back to ancient religious texts and continued through the Middle Ages and Renaissance. One notable example of pseudepigraphy historically is the "Epistle of Barnabas," an early Christian writing falsely attributed to Barnabas, the companion of the Apostle Paul. Composed in the late first or early second century, this work aimed to address theological issues and interpret Old Testament scriptures in light of Christian beliefs. By attributing the letter to Barnabas, the author sought to lend greater authority and credibility to the text, capitalizing on Barnabas's close association with Paul and his respected position within the early Christian community.

In the last few centuries, we have seen the evolution of this compulsion to simulate into more sophisticated forms. Photography and film introduced new ways to capture and manipulate reality. Early photographers and filmmakers experimented with techniques to alter images, creating composite photographs and staged scenes that challenged the viewer's perception of truth. Digital technology further expanded these abilities, allowing for seamless alterations that could deceive the eye more effectively than ever before.

Philosopher Walter Benjamin argued that a "work of art has always been reproducible. Man-made artifacts could always be imitated by men. Replicas were made by pupils in practice of their craft, by masters for diffusing their works, and, finally, by third parties in the pursuit of gain."[7] Benjamin argued that in a time of "mechanical reproduction of a work of art," the idea of authenticity needed to be redefined. What Benjamin said about photography can be applied to other digital forms of art.

> *From a photographic negative, for example, one can make any number of prints; to ask for the 'authentic' print makes no sense. But the instant the criterion of authenticity ceases to be applicable to artistic production, the total function of art is reversed (Benjamin, 1936).*

So, what is being faked with a deep fake? Well, the human themselves, their celebrity status, their authentic performance which is associated with the media through which we know them. A deep fake of Tom Cruise is not a performance from the human Tom Cruise, but a simulation of the actor who we associate with *Mission: Impossible* or other movies. Is there a difference? The rise of the Internet and digital media has given other types of good and bad actors powerful tools for creating and disseminating content, including fake content. Social media platforms are rife with doctored images and videos, often created with the intent to deceive or entertain. The term "deep fake" emerged to describe highly realistic but entirely fabricated video content, made possible by advances in AI and ML. These technologies enable the creation of videos where individuals appear to say or do things they never did, blurring the line between reality and fiction in unprecedented ways. A recent reddit post revealed a fairly disturbing montage set to hip hop that equally satirized Trump, Biden, Obama, Harris, Musk, Un, and Jinping. Are different types of generative AI systems just for satire and misinformation to manipulate likes and comments on social media platforms?[8] The use of AI to "give back" Val

---

[7] Benjamin, W. (1935). The Work of Art in the Age of Mechanical Reproduction, 1936. New York.

[8] https://www.theatlantic.com/technology/archive/2023/05/generative-ai-social-media-integration-dangers-disinformation-addiction/673940/

Kilmer's voice after he lost it undergoing treatment for throat cancer is a more inspiring use case.[9] There are many more. However, the abuse of deep fakes for misinformation, satire, and pornography far outnumbers the positive use cases.

Prompts and generative AI, such as LLMs and image generators, have further complicated the landscape of originality and creativity. These tools allow users to create new content "in the style of" well-known authors, artists, or genres, effectively replicating their techniques and sensibilities. While this can be a powerful tool for creativity and exploration, it also resurfaces Benjamin's thoughts about the authenticity and value of the generated content. As more works are produced using these tools, there is a growing concern that inventiveness may be overshadowed by a flood of derivative creations. Or, is it the other way around? Are people finding interesting ways, new forms, and new meanings by using deep fake and other technologies that simulate other humans in new contexts?

Regardless of intent, the prevalence of deep fakes and generative content challenges our understanding of the authentic and the creative. In a world where imitation and replication are easier than ever, the unique voice and vision of individual creators risk being drowned out by an ocean of simulated work. Wasn't that the case before this latest surge of gen AI though? How many times do we have to hear another pop tune that sounds like all the rest that relies on a verse, chorus, and repetitive hook? What exactly is an authentic work of art nowadays and for whom does it really matter?

What we learn with deep fakes is that the (re)performance of popular figures, no matter what they say, provides us with another type of fiction. It's not like many of us even know who Tom Cruise is as a human or what he brings to the form of moviemaking that is original. His work, like many others, relies on a different type of repetitive formula that regurgitates

---

[9] https://www.washingtonpost.com/technology/2021/08/18/val-kilmer-ai-voice-cloning/

story, character, to make money. Deep fakes disrupt the formulas, the same old somewhat reliable figures we love or hate, placed in radically different contexts. They provide us an opportunity to reassert the currency of originality. True creativity lies not merely in the replication of existing styles but in the synthesis of new ideas, perspectives, and expressions that continues to shift and change. Amidst the proliferation of simulated work, the case for originality can be made by celebrating the distinctive, the personal, and the innovative—qualities that cannot be easily replicated by even the most advanced algorithms.

> *Go a little bit out of your depth. And when you don't feel that your feet are quite touching the bottom, you're just about in the right place to do something exciting (David Bowie).*[10]

Creativity and Originality

Pragmatically, originality when integrating generative AI within any creative process will depend on how and to what purpose any generated content is used. Some argue that AI as a collaborative partner is one approach to achieve that goal. In previous written work, the author elaborated on the use of generative AI as a prototyping tool. *Creative Prototyping with Generative AI* is a comprehensive guide that explores the integration of generative AI tools into the creative process, aimed at artists, designers, and creatives. The book offers practical methods drawing from creative traditions to use these technologies to develop innovative prototypes. Applying gen AI for generating new ideas, enriching creativity, and accelerating the prototyping phase is one of the main strengths of the technology. The more specific your intention is, the more you can leverage different generative AI for your own purposes. Replacing the human, though, is an often enough used theme that needs a reality check.

---

[10] https://medium.com/@Greglorious/always-go-a-little-further into-the-water-90b3272f510a

Part Two: Inference

The possible biases that are generated with ML models are mind-boggling. What is clear is that all of them do create bias and most companies alert users to this. Bias is inherent in the ways that algorithms vulture through data to generate content. Every single ML model is highly influenced by the data/content that was used to train it. Humans are influenced by data they analyze and create meaning from as well. Likely, as you entertain reading this section, you will feel **cognitive overload, which** occurs when the amount of information presented exceeds the brain's capacity to process it effectively. The assumption that you will experience cognitive overload is a bias as well.

Figure 11-8. *Raccoons plotting their next job. AI-generated image*

Training Data Bias

To understand how bias influences generated content, we need to start at the root source of where bias appears. As has been stated before, bias can generate depending on what you train the machine learning model with. Training data bias in LLMs and AI-generated content is one of those issues that is likely not going to disappear. It is fairly simple to understand that the data we use will have an impact on the content that is eventually produced by these systems. LLMs, like those developed by OpenAI, are trained on vast datasets that encompass a wide range of texts from the Internet, books, articles, and other sources. You might think, "OK, well if it has that much data, then it should be a balanced system." Sadly, in addition to content that might have less biases contained within it, datasets often contain biases reflecting societal prejudices, stereotypes, and inequalities present in the real world because they have been scraped with all the care of a leaf blower in a library. Consequently, the models can inadvertently replicate these biases, leading to generated content that may reinforce negative stereotypes or exclude certain groups. Addressing these biases involves not only curating more balanced and representative training datasets but also implementing algorithmic techniques to detect and mitigate biased behavior during and after the training process.

Similarly, text-to-image AI systems, which generate images based on textual descriptions, are also susceptible to biases in their training data. These systems rely on datasets of images and their associated captions, which can contain implicit biases regarding race, gender, age, and other characteristics. For instance, a text-to-image model might consistently depict certain professions or activities with specific genders or ethnicities, reflecting societal biases rather than objective reality. This can perpetuate harmful stereotypes and misrepresent diverse communities. To mitigate these issues, it is essential to use diverse and inclusive datasets for training, apply rigorous fairness and bias detection protocols, and continuously refine the models to ensure they produce equitable and representative content. Many researchers and developers are collaborating to prioritize transparency and accountability in the development and deployment of newer AI systems to engender trust.

Sampling Bias

Think of sampling as the use of a small part of something in order to create something new. In music, sampling became popular and is still widely practiced, particularly in hip hop where melodic and rhythmic phrases, hooks, or choruses from songs that came before are sampled as part of new creations. Sampling bias in the training data of LLMs can lead to generated content that does not fully represent the diversity of language and topics. If the sample of data used predominantly includes texts from certain demographics, regions, or viewpoints while underrepresenting others, the model's generated content may reflect these imbalances. This skewed representation can result in models that overlook or misinterpret the linguistic nuances and perspectives of underrepresented groups, thereby perpetuating existing inequalities and biases. To address this, it is important to ensure that the training datasets are as comprehensive and inclusive as possible, covering a wide range of voices and topics.

Historical Bias

History is replete with biases. Humans lived differently than we do now, and divisions between cultures, genders, and races have been a nightmare no one can really logically reconcile. As such, historical bias present in the data that an ML model uses relies on extensive collections of historical texts that embed past biases and stereotypes. Since these texts reflect the societal attitudes and prejudices of their time, the models trained on them can inherit and perpetuate these biases, potentially even amplifying them in the generated content. This can lead to outputs that reinforce outdated and harmful views, undermining the progress toward equality and fairness. To counteract historical bias, it is important to curate training datasets that include more contemporary and diverse perspectives, as well as to employ techniques that can identify and mitigate the influence of biased historical content. This approach helps create AI systems that produce more balanced and fair representations of current societal values.

Algorithmic Bias

Algorithms are sets of rules or instructions designed to perform specific tasks or solve particular problems, often through step-by-step procedures. In the context of AI and ML, algorithms process and analyze data to learn patterns, make predictions, or generate content. When training an LLM, algorithms are used to parse vast datasets, identifying relationships between words and phrases and constructing meaningful and what their logic regards as contextually suitable sentences. The quality and nature of the generated content are directly influenced by these patterns, as the algorithms apply the rules derived from the training data to produce new text.

Algorithmic bias occurs when the rules and patterns adhered to by these algorithms inadvertently reflect or amplify biases present in the training data. This can happen if the training data is skewed, containing overrepresented or underrepresented groups, or if historical and societal biases are embedded in the data. As a result, the model may generate content that unfairly favors certain demographics or viewpoints while marginalizing others. Mitigating algorithmic bias involves not only curating diverse and balanced datasets but also developing techniques to detect and address biases during and after the training process. By doing so, the aim is to create more equitable AI systems that produce fair and representative outputs, ensuring that the benefits of AI are accessible to all users.

When you dig deeper into algorithms and how they are designed, you also learn that there are several techniques and research efforts focused on developing and experimenting with different kinds of algorithms to reduce bias in AI systems. Here are some more recent approaches:

- **Bias Detection and Mitigation Algorithms**: Researchers have developed various algorithms specifically designed to detect and mitigate bias in training data and model outputs. Techniques like reweighting, resampling, and adversarial training help adjust the training process to reduce the impact of biased data. For instance, Bellamy et al. (2018) discuss several methods for fairness-aware ML in their comprehensive survey.[11]

- **Fair Representation Learning**: This approach involves training models to learn fair representations of data that are unchanged to sensitive attributes like race, gender, or age. Techniques such as adversarial debiasing and domain adaptation are used to ensure that the learned representations do not encode unwanted biases. Edwards and Storkey (2015) present a method for fair representation learning using adversarial training.[12]

---

[11] Bellamy, R. K. E., Dey, K., Hind, M., Hoffman, S. C., Houde, S., Kannan, K., ... & Varshney, K. R. (2018). AI Fairness 360: An extensible toolkit for detecting, understanding, and mitigating unwanted algorithmic bias. arXiv preprint arXiv:1810.01943.

[12] Edwards, H., & Storkey, A. (2015). Censoring representations with an adversary. arXiv preprint arXiv:1511.05897.

- **Data Augmentation**: To combat bias, researchers use data augmentation techniques to create more balanced datasets. This involves generating synthetic data or augmenting existing data to better represent underrepresented groups and viewpoints, thereby reducing the bias in the training dataset. For example, Zhang et al. (2017) explore how data augmentation can be used to address gender bias in image recognition systems.[13]

- **Post-Processing Techniques**: These methods adjust the model's generated content after training to reduce bias. Calibration techniques adjust the chances or scores that a model assigns to different groups or categories, making the results fairer. Hardt, Price, and Srebro (2016) introduce a post-processing method called equalized odds for ensuring fairness in classification tasks.[14]

- **Algorithmic Fairness Metrics**: Developing and using fairness metrics to evaluate and compare different algorithms is another important area of research. These metrics help in quantifying the degree of bias and fairness in models, guiding researchers to select and fine-tune algorithms that minimize bias. Verma and Rubin (2018) provide a comprehensive overview of various fairness metrics used in machine learning.[15]

---

[13] Zhang, B. H., Lemoine, B., & Mitchell, M. (2018). Mitigating Unwanted Biases with Adversarial Learning. Proceedings of the 2018 AAAI/ACM Conference on AI, Ethics, and Society.

[14] Hardt, M., Price, E., & Srebro, N. (2016). Equality of opportunity in supervised learning. In Advances in Neural Information Processing Systems (pp. 3315–3323).

[15] Verma, S., & Rubin, J. (2018). Fairness definitions explained. Proceedings of the 2018 IEEE/ACM International Workshop on Software Fairness.

- **Transparent and Interpretable AI**: Increasing the transparency and interpretability of AI models allows researchers and practitioners to better understand how decisions are made and where biases might be introduced. Techniques such as model interpretability tools and explainable AI frameworks are employed to achieve this. Doshi-Velez and Kim (2017)[16] discuss the importance of interpretability in ML and various methods to achieve it.

By leveraging these techniques and continuing to research new methods, the AI community is working to create more equitable and AI systems that reduce biases, ensuring that the benefits generative AI technologies offer can minimize the potential harm that they generate.

Model Choices

Model choices in the design of LLMs significantly impact their performance and potential biases in the generated content. The choice of architectures, such as transformers, recurrent neural networks (RNNs), or convolutional neural networks (CNNs), influences how the model processes and understands language. Without getting bogged down too much with the lingo, it is worth explaining some parts of the transformer architecture, as ChatGPT and Llama both use transformers in their LLMs.

A transformer begins by tokenizing words that a human puts into that little context window into smaller units—words or subwords but sometimes collections of words. It then converts these tokens into numerical vectors known as embeddings. These embeddings capture the semantic meaning of each token in relation to the others. Think of

---

[16] Doshi-Velez, F., & Kim, B. (2017). Towards a rigorous science of interpretable machine learning. arXiv preprint arXiv:1702.08608.

vectors as positions in space, like a multidimensional space, wonderfully referred to as the latent space. To provide a sense of order within the text, a positional encoding (an order) is added to these embeddings, ensuring the model understands the sequence of tokens. The encoder then refines these representations through multiple layers of self-attention and feed-forward networks, enabling the model to extract and preserve the nuances of the input text.

Now that your attention is back, the transformer model itself relies on an attention mechanism, which determines how much focus to give to each token when processing a sequence. Self-attention allows the model to weigh the importance of each token relative to other tokens, capturing dependencies between words across the sequence of these tokens. To retain the original contextual information, residual connections add back the initial embeddings and positional encodings after the attention mechanism. It's kind of like a backup mechanism, like a reminder to not forget those vectors and their order.

Finally, there is this part of the transformer called a feed-forward block that applies additional transformations to the data, further refining the model's understanding before making predictions. In certain cases, such as text generation, masked self-attention is used to ensure that only previous tokens influence the prediction of the next token, maintaining the sequence's logical flow.

Memorize and repeat. Now if you've got the ML lingo blues, then the beautiful thing about these beastly LLMs is that you can task one to make it easier to understand and modify accordingly.

TranslationBot: Imagine you're trying to tell a story to a bot. The bot first breaks down your story into small pieces, like words or even parts of words, to better understand it, because well it really likes to break things down. Then, it gives each of these pieces a special number that helps it remember what the word means and how it relates to the other words.

Numbers, you see, are easier for the bot to regurgitate when it needs to. Think of these numbers like positions in a huge, invisible space, where similar words are close to each other.

But the bot also needs to know the order of the words, like which word comes first, second, and so on, to understand your story correctly. Otherwise, it will construct meaning in a Joycean fashion. So, it adds some extra information to help it remember the sequence. After that, the bot goes through several steps, checking and refining how well it understands the words and their order. In this way, it tests itself.

Now, the bot uses something called "attention" to decide which words are the most important in your story. It's like when you focus on certain parts of a book while reading, like these words, for example. Some bots give you some measure of control over attention, allowing you, the human, to decide exactly how much attention to pay to those initial words you put in the context window and how much they should be ignored. The bot also has a "backup" system that helps it remember the original meaning and order of the words, so it doesn't lose track of the story.

Finally, the bot uses a special tool to polish its understanding even more before making a guess about what might happen next in the story. Sometimes, when the bot is trying to write the next part of the story, it hides certain words so it can only think about the words that have already come before, making sure everything makes sense as it goes along. You can see how important it is then to be clear about the story you're asking the bot to elaborate or explain.

Oh No: Statistics

The likelihood of needing to talk about statistics in this book was high. They are an important component that directly affects how data in the corpus is interpreted and, as a result, how predictions shape the content that is generated. LLMs like GPT and Claude generate text by predicting the next word or sequence of words that are statistically most likely based on the patterns learned from the training data.

If that was a mouthful that you need to read over a few times, don't worry. You don't really need to know about statistics unless you care that you form part of a collection of people with similarities and differences (demographic), that whatever government whose laws you abide by, likes to collect information about by sending out annoying forms that take up your valuable respite time (census), in order to understand the makeup of its citizens that influence decisions about them. While intel about population and economics were first to be collected, the science of statistics grew up alongside cultures whose ways of being became increasingly complex. The collection of how much we have of a thing has dominated most cultures but more importantly are the methods of analyzing and interpreting the data (models).

Connect the analysis of data over time and how it is interpreted now vs. a year ago, and we are ready to make informed guesses (predictions) as to what that data might look like next year or in two years or even ten years from now (probability).

Figure 11-9. *A composite donkeynaut modeling attention, mashed from four text-image generative AI whose prompts consisted of fancy words like "attention, feed forward, transformer, and encoder." AI-generated image*

While interpreting correctly is important, what's more critical is to better understand the accuracy of our predictions and the inherent potential of being wrong in our interpretations of whatever we are analyzing and why (uncertainty, bias).

We can define probability in a simple way with help from an LLM.

SimpleBot: A probabilistic approach is a way of making decisions or predictions based on the likelihood of different outcomes happening.

For LLMs, a probabilistic approach leverages methods such as maximum likelihood estimation (MLE) to determine the most probable continuation of a given text prompt. MLE is just one of many methods. It picks the most likely next part of a token based on what's already there. MLE optimizes the likelihood of the observed data, making the model favor sequences of words that appear frequently in the training data. While this approach is effective in producing coherent and contextually appropriate text, it can reinforce common phrases and ideas while neglecting less common but equally valid expressions. The result: The model will disproportionately favor mainstream language and perspectives, marginalizing underrepresented voices and viewpoints.

Don't worry though. When probability creates a well-known problem, there are lesser-known approaches to probability that can be applied. Enter Bayesian inference, a method of statistical inference where probabilities are updated as new evidence or information becomes available. This is but one alternative statistical method that has been suggested for LLMs. Bayesian inference uses existing knowledge or beliefs about the data to help the model better understand and include fewer common expressions. Bayesian methods can be used to balance the likelihood of different word sequences, even when they are less frequent, by incorporating domain-specific knowledge or expert opinions. Research has demonstrated the effectiveness of Bayesian methods in discovering thematic structures in large text corpora.[17]

Figure 11-10. *An outlier in a dataset. AI-generated image*

---

[17] Blei, D. M., Ng, A. Y., & Jordan, M. I. (2003). Latent Dirichlet Allocation. Journal of Machine Learning Research, 3, 993–1022.

Sampling Techniques

Sampling techniques are by far the most fun to play with, at least when you have control over some of the parameters that can affect the content you generate from a machine learning model. This kind of sampling is different than what was discussed earlier with sampling music, although the principle is similar. Weighted sampling techniques like temperature scaling let you adjust the "temperature" parameter, making it possible to control the randomness of the sampling process during text generation. Lower temperatures make the model more conservative and likely to choose high-probability words (as samples), while higher temperatures encourage more diversity by allowing lower-probability words (samples) to be selected. Adjusting temperature on your own is more probable if you install an open source machine learning model, because many of the interfaces allow for these types of parameters to be controlled.

Adversarial training is another method that has shown potential in reducing bias with generated text. This technique involves training the model in a way that it learns to distinguish between biased and unbiased outputs, effectively punishing the generation of biased text. Goodfellow et al. (2014) introduced generative adversarial networks (GANs) for images, which have since been adapted to text generation tasks to mitigate bias by pitting two networks against each other: a generator that produces text and a discriminator that evaluates its fairness and diversity.[18] When you ask an LLM to help you translate, you often get the same somewhat ironic metaphor when you task an LLM to explain how GANs work using a metaphor.

---

[18] Goodfellow, I., Pouget-Abadie, J., Mirza, M., Xu, B., Warde-Farley, D., Ozair, S., ... & Bengio, Y. (2014). Generative Adversarial Nets. In Advances in Neural Information Processing Systems (NeurIPS), 2672–2680.

GanBot: Imagine an artist who is trying to create the perfect counterfeit painting. Every time the artist finishes a piece, they show it to a detective who is an expert in spotting fakes. The artist's goal is to make the painting so convincing that even the sharp-eyed detective can't tell it's a forgery.

On the other side, the detective's job is to get better and better at spotting even the tiniest flaws in the counterfeit paintings. Over time, the artist improves their techniques to fool the detective, and the detective becomes more skilled at identifying fakes.

In this way, both the artist (the generator) and the detective (the discriminator) push each other to improve. The artist learns to create more realistic images, while the detective sharpens their ability to distinguish between real and fake. The end result is that the artist eventually produces paintings so good that they could pass as genuine to anyone, including the detective.

Fairness

Incorporating fairness constraints into the model training process is another approach that is gaining traction. Integrating fairness assumes that the team of humans recognizes that ML models have inherent biases. Constraints can be applied to ensure that the model's generated content adheres to predefined fairness criteria. Those criteria are dependent on the development team. Fairness constraints are considered fair because they are designed to ensure that decision-making processes, especially those involving algorithms or AI systems, treat all individuals or groups equitably. For example, Zemel et al. (2013) propose a method to learn fair representations by introducing constraints that ensure balanced treatment of different demographic groups, which can be adapted to text generation to promote fairness.[19]

---

[19] Zemel, R. S., Wu, Y., Swersky, K., Pitassi, T., & Dwork, C. (2013). Learning Fair Representations. In International Conference on Machine Learning (ICML), 325–333.

Figure 11-11. *How an ML model employing GAN visualizes GAN. AI-generated image*

Confirmation Bias

None of us can really escape the fine art of being wrong sometimes even though we feel right about something. I know this to be true. LLMs are no different. Some come across as only being able to tell the truth. Since LLMs are trained on large datasets from the Internet made by us humans, they often draw from the most commonly expressed opinions and ideas on subjects. This can lead to the reinforcement of dominant narratives and marginalization of minority perspectives. Should that matter to you?

> *The idea that only the norm should be heard or constantly regenerated denies those voices in every culture that have the potential to shift opinion, provide an alternate direction or solution to a problem, or even provoke necessary revolution.*

If you think of any compelling artist that you like historically, most challenged the norms of their time and created new expressions and art forms that were commentaries and a result of the time they lived in. Most of these have been considered outliers. Consider the difference between Haydn and Mozart. Both composed an amazing repertoire of music. Mozart's music, however, diverged from the influence of court music that tended to play it safe and relied on very similar and familiar melodic, harmonic and rhythmic patterns.[20]

Prompt Sensitivity

The way a prompt is phrased can have influence on the content generated by any ML model. Subtle differences in wording can lead to different responses, reflecting the model's sensitivity to the specific nuances of language. You can test this (or likely have) by trying to send an LLM of its rails—in others words, challenging the LLM to generate content that it

---

[20] Rosen, C. (1971). The classical style: Haydn, Mozart, Beethoven. New York, Viking Press.

shouldn't. A sensitivity to prompting means that even minor variations in a prompt can result in generated content that varies widely and sometimes wildly.

For example, a prompt phrased with a slight bias or leading question can result in content that reinforces the implicit assumptions or stereotypes present in the prompt. This can happen because the model, trained on vast datasets containing various biases, will often reflect the patterns and associations it has learned. If a prompt subtly suggests a stereotype or bias, the model is likely to generate text that aligns with that suggestion, thus perpetuating the bias.

The choice of words and their order can influence the model's perception of the prompt's context and intent. For instance, asking "Why are women better at multitasking?" may yield responses that support the stereotype implied by the question, while a more neutral prompt like "What are the advantages and disadvantages of multitasking among different genders?" can lead to a more balanced discussion. However, you may want to also ask an LLM why the question above can also induce binary gender framing.

BiasBot: The question likely implies a binary understanding of gender (male vs. female), which excludes nonbinary and gender-nonconforming individuals. A more inclusive approach would consider a spectrum of gender identities.

This highlights the importance of carefully crafting prompts to avoid unintentional biases and to ensure that the content is as fair and objective as possible.

To mitigate prompt sensitivity and its impact on bias, researchers and developers can employ techniques such as prompt engineering during inference and iterative testing during training. Prompt engineering involves designing prompts that are clear, neutral, and unambiguous, reducing the likelihood of biased outputs. Iterative testing, where multiple versions of a prompt are tested and refined based on the model's responses, can help identify and minimize unintended biases.

Surface-Level Coherence

If you've survived this far, then why not learn about surface-level coherence? It's a feature of LLMs, which are optimized to produce text that is contextually appropriate and seemingly fluent. While it sounds miraculous, optimizing in this way can sometimes lead to the omission of complex or nuanced viewpoints that are harder to predict and generate. It's not that LLMs are dumb, but they do rely heavily on statistical patterns observed in their training data to predict the next word or sequence of words, prioritizing responses that fit well within the immediate context and flow of the text.

This focus on being "coherent" often means that the models tend to generate more generic and widely acceptable responses, which are easier to predict and align with the most common patterns in the training data. As a result, the models may overlook or underrepresent more intricate or less frequently discussed perspectives that require a deeper understanding of context and nuance. For instance, while an LLM might provide a coherent summary of a controversial topic, it may fail to capture the full spectrum of opinions and the underlying complexities that characterize real-world discussions.

The tendency to prioritize surface-level coherence is limiting when addressing topics that involve multifaceted issues, such as social justice, political debates, or scientific controversies. In these cases, important details and subtleties might be glossed over in favor of producing text that reads smoothly, but lacks depth. This can inadvertently reinforce simplified narratives and reduce the richness of discourse, which is important for informed decision-making.

To mitigate this issue, researchers and developers can employ several strategies. One approach is to fine-tune LLMs on datasets specifically curated to include a wide range of perspectives and detailed discussions. Another method involves using techniques such as hierarchical modeling, which can help the model maintain coherence while also capturing more complex structures within the text. Additionally, integrating mechanisms for user feedback can guide the model to better handle nuanced viewpoints by learning from corrections and suggestions provided by users.

Overfitting to Common Patterns

Overfitting in machine learning happens when a model becomes too made-to-order to the specific examples in its training data, capturing noise, bias, and whatever else you train it on, rather than general patterns, which leads to poor performance on new, unseen data. You might compare it to how we learn, where a form of overfitting can happen when individuals focus too narrowly on specific details or rote memorization without understanding underlying principles or being able to generalize knowledge to new situations. This can result in a deep but inflexible understanding that doesn't transfer well to different contexts. You can probably guess what can happen with overfitting: a lack of diversity and originality in the responses that an LLM generates.

You can observe this in the tendency an LLM has to produce text that is formulaic and repetitive, reflecting the most prevalent phrases and constructions from the training data. If a particular phrase or sentence structure is commonly found in the corpus that it trained on, the model is likely to reuse as much as it can, because, well, it's more efficient. This is unfortunately the case even when more varied or creative responses would be appropriate. So, if you are wondering why a lot of the content an LLM generates is generic and predictable, you can partially blame that on overfitting. Let's see how an LLM generically modifies an appropriate response when challenged on its propensity to produce uninspired responses.

GenericBot: In today's dynamic landscape of overfitting, it is essential to foster approaches that enhance productivity and drive novel solutions. By utilizing cutting-edge tools and strategies, we can effectively navigate challenges and create impactful outcomes that resonate across various sectors. Embracing these methods will ultimately lead to sustained growth and collaboration in an ever-evolving environment.

Temperature scaling, as discussed previously, is one solution to overfitting, where the parameter can be adjusted to control the randomness of the generated text, forcing the model to explore less common word sequences.

Hallucinations

While many of us have generated content that is untrue, companies developing gen AI systems have always maintained that it is up to each user to do their own background checks. Thankfully, many helpful humans have come up with different methods grounded in research studies that can be useful to draw from. Recent research on hallucinations in LLMs shows various interrelated characteristics of the issue and presents potential solutions. Here are some research studies worth highlighting:

- "Cognitive Mirage: A Review of Hallucinations in Large Language Models" (2023)[21] identifies key factors causing hallucinations, such as training procedures and sampling techniques, and discusses methods for their detection and mitigation.

---

[21] Ye, H., Liu, T., Zhang, A., Hua, W., & Jia, W. (2023). Cognitive mirage: A review of hallucinations in large language models. arXiv preprint arXiv:2309.06794.

- "Towards Mitigating Hallucination in Large Language Models via Self-Reflection" (2023)[22] introduces a self-reflection mechanism that allows models to evaluate and refine their own outputs, thereby improving factual accuracy in knowledge-intensive tasks.

- "Self-Contradictory Hallucinations of Large Language Models: Evaluation, Detection, and Mitigation" (2024)[23] focuses on self-contradictions within generated text and presents a framework for identifying and correcting these issues, achieving a high detection accuracy and practical applicability for different types of tasks.

That said, when AI chatbots "hallucinate," it's not the same as when humans do. In this context, the term refers to a chatbot generating incorrect or misleading information. While the word "hallucination" may suggest intentional behavior or deeper understanding, smart and informed humans argue that AI systems don't think or have intent like humans.[24] The errors arise from the way the model predicts or generates text based on patterns in its training data, rather than understanding the world. For example, when prompted, the AI is predicting the next logical word based on statistical patterns, not confirming the accuracy of its response. This can sometimes lead to errors, particularly when the prompt is complex or ambiguous. Experts like Usama Fayyad emphasize that these mistakes are similar to errors in other predictive systems, like economic forecasting, and shouldn't be seen as the system "misunderstanding" anything.[25]

[22] Ji, Z., Yu, T., Xu, Y., Lee, N., Ishii, E., & Fung, P. (2023). Towards mitigating hallucination in large language models via self-reflection. arXiv preprint arXiv:2310.06271.

[23] Mündler, N., He, J., Jenko, S., & Vechev, M. (2023). Self-contradictory hallucinations of large language models: Evaluation, detection and mitigation. arXiv preprint arXiv:2305.15852.

[24] https://naomiklein.org/ai-machines-arent-hallucinating/

[25] https://news.northeastern.edu/2023/11/10/ai-chatbot-hallucinations/

Pseudepigrapha

So-called hallucinations are somewhat connected to the practice of pseudepigrapha, a meaty Greek term meaning false author. As mentioned earlier in this chapter, the practice in the past was used to lend authority or credibility to the text. These works are not written by the person to whom they are ascribed but are presented as if they were. In the context of LLMs, pseudepigrapha can manifest when the AI generates text that mimics the style or voice of a particular author, potentially leading to the mistaken belief that the text was actually written by that author. This is a tenuous issue that has provoked numerous lawsuits by living authors. Of course, Shakespeare scholars would know the difference, especially when an LLM blunders through a sonnet.

> **PseudePeareBot**:
>
> Oh, tales of yore, by hands unknown they're penned,
> In shadows deep, where truth and falsehood blend,
> These ancient scrolls, with wisdom's veil they cloak,
> Yet oft the names they bear, mere jest or joke.
> The sages speak with voices not their own,
> Their words a mask, like seeds on winds are sown,
> But who, I ask, doth truly write these lines?
> And which be truth, and which be woven signs?
> Pseudepigrapha, thou art a trickster's quill,
> With borrowed names, thy pages thou dost fill,
> Yet in thy lies, a deeper truth may hide,
> A riddle wrapped in wisdom's shifting tide.
> So let us read, with caution in our eyes,
> For falsehood oft wears truth's most cunning guise.

Figure 11-12. *Ceci n'est pas une hallucination. A homage to Belgian Surrealist painter René Magritte's The Treachery of Images, which consisted of a painting of a pipe with the words "Ceci n'est pas une pipe." written on the canvas with it. AI-generated image*

Regardless of "attributing a default mode of operating rationally"[26] (Fayyad, 2023), "A Survey on Large Language Model Hallucination via a Creativity Perspective" (2023)[27] suggests that while hallucinations are often seen as detrimental, they can also provoke creativity by generating unique ideas. The survey reviews historical examples and cognitive science literature to draw parallels between human creativity and LLM hallucinations, proposing that controlled hallucinations could enrich creative content generation.

Retrieval-Augmented Generation (RAG)

To reduce the inaccuracy of generated content while maintaining creativity, the integration of retrieval-augmented generation (RAG) and knowledge graphs (KGs) can be used. These techniques increase an LLM's generated content by grounding its responses in real-world data and structured information, reducing errors while still leveraging the model's corpus.

RAG is a promising approach to mitigate errors in LLMs by incorporating retrieval mechanisms that fetch relevant information from external databases. This technique strengthens the model's responses with factual data, reducing the likelihood of generating fabricated content.

KGs are another effective tool for reducing mistakes. KGs provide structured and verified information that LLMs can use to validate and support their responses. Integrating KGs with LLMs increases the possibility that the models generate content with improved accuracy.

---

[26] https://news.northeastern.edu/2023/11/10/ai-chatbot-hallucinations/

[27] Jiang, X., Tian, Y., Hua, F., Xu, C., Wang, Y., & Guo, J. (2024). A survey on large language model hallucination via a creativity perspective. arXiv preprint arXiv:2402.06647.

Homogeneity

Homogeneity in writing refers to the uniformity and consistency of style, tone, and structure within a piece of text. While consistency can be valuable for clarity and coherence, excessive homogeneity can lead to monotonous and unengaging content. Homogeneous writing often lacks variation in sentence structure, vocabulary, and ideas, which can make the text dull and predictable. In creative and academic writing, straying from a patterned approach to writing is important to keep the reader's interest and to convey complex ideas effectively. While an LLM can produce coherent and contextually relevant content, they often exhibit homogeneity due to their reliance on probabilistic patterns. It is more fitting that an LLM attempts to define it in a homogeneous way.

2%Bot: Homogeneity in writing means keeping everything the same—style, tone, and structure. This sameness is called uniformity and consistency. Uniformity and consistency can make writing clear and coherent. However, too much uniformity and consistency can make writing repetitive and boring. When writing is repetitive and boring, it lacks variety in sentence structure, vocabulary, and ideas. This lack of variety makes the writing dull and predictable. In creative and academic writing, it's important not to be too uniform and consistent. Avoiding too much uniformity and consistency helps keep the reader's interest and communicates ideas more effectively. Therefore, homogeneity in writing means keeping everything the same—structure, style, and tone.

Avoiding Homogeneity

Research on avoiding homogeneous writing emphasizes the importance of varied sentence structures, rich vocabulary, and the use of stylistic devices. For that, you need the human in the loop. Studies suggest that incorporating a mix of simple, compound, and complex sentences improves readability to keep the reader engaged (Biber, 1988).[28] Lexical diversity, which involves using a broad range of vocabulary, is linked to a higher perceived quality and sophistication in writing (McNamara et al., 2010).[29] Additionally, the effective use of rhetorical devices such as metaphors, analogies, and varied diction can make writing more persuasive and memorable. These strategies may be worth adding to your toolbox, as they may help increase how long your reader lasts, reading your words.

---

[28] Biber, D., & Finegan, E. (1988). Adverbial stance types in English. Discourse processes, 11(1), 1–34.

[29] Crossley, S., & McNamara, D. (2010). Cohesion, coherence, and expert evaluations of writing proficiency. In Proceedings of the Annual Meeting of the Cognitive Science Society (Vol. 32, No. 32).

Figure 11-13. *Badly generated homogenized milk. AI-generated image*

Refining AI-Generated Content

To refine AI-generated content and reduce homogeneity, techniques such as post-editing, prompt engineering, and retrieval-augmented generation (RAG) are important to integrate in your workflows. Post-editing involves reviewing and adjusting the text to add variety and use a number of rhetorical techniques, which has proven effective in improving machine-generated content. Post-editing is hopefully a practice that we all engage in with any generated content and has been proposed as far back as 2014 (Koehn & Germann).[30] Iteratively working on your prompts by crafting them with increasing specificity influences the generated content you will receive. That includes guiding an LLM with just as much effort with what you don't want, as it is with what you do.

To that end, the use of chain-of-thought prompting is another effective way to do so.

ChainBot: Chain-of-thought prompting refers to a technique used in AI models where the system is guided step by step to solve complex tasks by breaking them down into smaller, logical parts. Instead of directly answering a question or completing a task in one go, the model is encouraged to "think out loud," meaning it generates a sequence of intermediate steps leading to the final answer.

This process helps the AI by encouraging it to reason through a problem, making its approach more transparent and sometimes improving accuracy. It's like walking someone through how you solve a math problem, outlining each part of the process. By using this method, the AI can better handle complex queries, making fewer mistakes along the way. This is especially useful for tasks that involve logic, reasoning, or multistep solutions.

---

[30] Koehn, P., & Germann, U. (April 2014). The impact of machine translation quality on human post-editing. In Proceedings of the EACL 2014 Workshop on Humans and Computer-assisted Translation (pp. 38–46). Association for Computational Linguistics.

Part Three: Access, Sustainability, Ethics

Access(ability)

Access to generative AI tools is shaped by several key criteria, each influencing who can effectively use these powerful technologies. One of the primary factors is affordability.

FreeBot: Public freemium models, which offer basic services for free while charging for premium features, have democratized access to generative AI. These models allow individuals and small organizations to experiment with AI without significant financial investment.

Author Comment: Examining the generated text above, you can clearly see the attempt at convincing rhetoric. Freemium models have nothing to do with democratizing access. They simply provide more features, which inform access, for those people who pay for them. These include how much content you can generate over certain restricted periods of time, access to updated and improved versions of their models, and use of more advanced filters, editing features and much more with text-image, text-audio, and text-video models.

When we look at private ML models customized and built on personal computers, the cost of having these constructed can also be expensive. That landscape is changing, however, with an increasing number of companies offering generative AI portals. These portals allow for multiple types of AI models to be accessed through a single user-friendly application. Early applications like Sanctum AI and Pinokio are offering these services, which are freemium models as well.

Accessibility is another critical factor affecting the use of generative AI tools. Many public AI platforms are designed to be user-friendly, but there is still a need for these tools to become more accessible to a broader audience, including those with disabilities or limited technical expertise. Accessibility improvements could involve more intuitive interfaces, better documentation, and inclusive design principles that cater to diverse user needs. Floridi (2023) emphasizes the ethical imperative of making technology inclusive, arguing that as AI becomes more integrated into various aspects of society, it must be designed to serve all users equitably.[31]

The learning curve associated with generative AI tools also plays a significant role in determining access. While some platforms aim to simplify the user experience, mastering these tools often requires a considerable investment of time and effort. Even tools marketed as user-friendly can present steep learning curves, necessitating a background in coding or data science. Scholars have noted that this learning barrier can deter potential users from fully engaging with generative AI, thereby restricting its widespread adoption.[32]

Most publically available generative AI make using their interfaces quite easy. However, many of them provide features that let you get more out of the content that they generate. Some require an intense amount of learning, and that may be too much for certain people to consider when it comes to wanting to use them in their work environment right away. It is trial by error with all generative AI systems. In fact, they are set up to support trial and error. Most come equipped with what seems like a simple feature, the ability to regenerate the content you prompted it to generate. There are however many features that accompany text-image and text-speech generative AI that will allow you to do more. These include weights, the degree to which the AI "listens" to your prompt vs. interpreting what it wants from the image you give it. To address this, there is a growing need for educational resources and training programs that can bridge the knowledge gap and empower more people to access these features.

---

[31] Floridi, L. (2023). The ethics of artificial intelligence: Principles, challenges, and opportunities.

[32] Smith, J. (2021). "Bridging the AI knowledge gap: Educational needs for the future". Educational Technology Journal.

Keeping up with the rapidly evolving landscape of generative AI options is another challenge. New tools and platforms are constantly emerging, each with unique features and applications. This creative environment can be overwhelming for users who have to continuously update their knowledge and skills to stay current. Researchers such as Brynjolfsson (2022) have highlighted the importance of ongoing learning and adaptation in the face of technological advancements.[33] Without sufficient support for continuous education and skill development, users may struggle to keep pace with the latest innovations, limiting their ability to leverage the full potential of generative AI.

Sustainability

The computing demands required to interact with generative AI systems have become a significant concern for many. Training these systems is an immensely resource-intensive process, involving vast amounts of money and computational power. The cost of training models like GPT-4 can run into the millions of dollars, driven by the need for massive datasets and powerful hardware. The manufacture of specialized chips, such as GPUs and TPUs, that can handle the enormous number of calculations required adds another layer of expense. These chips must be capable of parallel processing at a scale far beyond traditional computing tasks, leading to high manufacturing costs and significant energy consumption.

In addition to the costs associated with training, there are substantial expenses in running inference. Training a model is only the beginning; deploying it for real-time use involves continuously operating servers that can manage the load of numerous simultaneous interactions. As adoption of these technologies grows, the infrastructure required to support them must scale accordingly, leading to further financial and environmental

---

[33] Brynjolfsson, E. (2022). *Adaptation in the age of AI: Continuous learning and skill development*. MIT Technology Review.

costs. The energy demands for running large-scale AI models are not static and can be challenging to predict accurately due to the nature of how they are used.

Looking ahead, the future of reducing the computing power required for AI development may lie in shared resources, particularly in cloud computing. Cloud providers are investing heavily in AI, offering scalable solutions that can distribute the computational load across many data centers worldwide. This approach can be more cost-effective and efficient than each organization building and maintaining its own infrastructure. Alternatively, there is ongoing research into developing more efficient chips and computing methods that could decrease energy use and costs. Advances in neuromorphic computing, which mimics the neural structures of the human brain, and quantum computing could lead to further breakthroughs in how AI systems are powered, potentially reducing both costs and energy use.

As the cost of training cutting-edge language models rises, researchers are increasingly focusing not just on scaling but also on refining training datasets to create more efficient generalization across various downstream tasks. This has led to a growing body of research aimed at filtering data, eliminating duplicates in the data, discovering new data sources, weighting data points, and generating synthetic data.[34]

Ethics

What does it mean to be ethically responsible in the development and use of generative AI? Is it even possible? What does being ethical mean to you? For some, it's about living on the planet and minimizing the harm of doing so. For others, it's mainly about following a set of rules or commandments

---

[34] Li, J., Fang, A., Smyrnis, G., Ivgi, M., Jordan, M., Gadre, S., ... & Shankar, V. (2024). DataComp-LM: In search of the next generation of training sets for language models. arXiv preprint arXiv:2406.11794.

laid out by their religion, government, organization, community of practice, and/or family. Whatever ethical framework that you have or set of rules that govern your behavior, those will inform how you approach working or not working with generative AI. It is important then to define those values that inform your code of conduct in the world and therefore in a world where generative AI exists.

We've each had to reconcile our ethical conduct in the work environments we find ourselves in. Sometimes, they are a completely match, and sometimes they are not. Being ethical is a multifaceted concept that can vary significantly from person to person.

Figure 11-14. *Scientists creating an AGI bot. What could go wrong? AI-generated image*

In the process of weighing the pros and cons of using generative AI, you create your very own ethical framework toward the integration of the technology in your life. When it comes to working with generative AI, defining and communicating your ethical values may influence your organization's approach. Whether driven by environmental considerations, adherence to institutional codes, or personal moral beliefs, the values that define your organization's code of conduct will shape your teams' interactions with this technology.

Respect, in various forms, is a common value across many ethical frameworks. Whether articulated as "respect one another" or more nuanced guidelines, it reinforces interactions and decisions within both personal and professional contexts. For organizations, embedding respect into their operational ethos involves creating environments where all stakeholders are valued and treated with dignity. This principle can guide ethical decision-making, including how generative AI is developed, deployed, and managed. By grounding their approach in respect and other core values, organizations can navigate the ethical landscape of AI in a manner that is consistent with their broader mission and ethical commitments.

Organizations are at a conflict right now as to how, when, and why to use generative AI because they have to reflect on their own values and make sure they are aligned with the impulse to use any tool. We even have to define what we mean by an organization. After all, it is composed of humans, teams of humans who under leadership are guided to perform accordingly. Most organizations have clearly defined rules of play that are informed by the values they have. What are yours?

When it comes to generative AI use, now that you understand all the intricate layers of how they are co-constructed, the costs, who it affects, how might these inform your own ethical framework.

Defining Your Organization's Ethical Frameworks

Sometimes, there is a complete alignment between an individual's ethical standards and the values upheld by their workplace. In other instances, discrepancies arise, requiring negotiation and compromise. Organizations currently face significant ethical dilemmas regarding the use of generative AI because their own value system may need to evolve in light of AI. Leadership in organizations will benefit from identifying organizational values and ensure they align with the impulse to adopt new AI tools and technologies. Organizational values often manifest in clearly defined rules of play, such as codes of conduct that emphasize principles like respect.

In terms of how to handle reconciling how you use generative AI within the organization you belong to, codes of conduct and ethical responsibility that are best practices in your particular industry offer a good starting point. The article "Leveraging Professional Ethics for Responsible AI" by Diakopoulos et al. (2024) in *Communications of the ACM* emphasizes the role of professional ethics in the development and deployment of responsible AI systems.[35] The authors propose that professional codes of conduct provide a valuable foundation for ethical AI, guiding the design, implementation, and evaluation of these technologies. The paper outlines a methodology that starts with identifying key domain-specific values, which are then incorporated into the AI design process. For example, in the context of journalism, values such as truth, minimizing harm, and maintaining independence are essential. These values guide the creation of features, such as algorithms, to filter disinformation, and tools for content moderation that protect vulnerable individuals. Given the variety of news outlets out there and their intents, you can clearly discern

---

[35] Diakopoulos, N., Trattner, C., Jannach, D., Meijer, I. C., & Motta, E. (2024). Leveraging Professional Ethics for Responsible AI. Communications of the ACM, 67(2), 19–21.

which are going to use generative AI without questioning the implications of doing so, those organizations who will not integrate generative AI since it's not worth all the risks involved, and those on the fence or in between.

A recent *Forbes* magazine article also proposes some principles to inform your ethical process.[36] This is especially important for organizations who are confused as to where to start to connect the dots. Each of the four below have likely been addressed by your organization prior to the emerging need to integrate any gen AI tool, so they will be familiar to most. To be ethical, your organization will need to have the following:

> **Privacy**: Respect and protect employees and customer privacy rights, safeguard personal data, and use that data appropriately without selling it or licensing it to third parties. This is contrary to the pattern that many applications have developed as if privacy was a negotiating factor for the freemium use of their prototypes. Would your organization be reconciled with openly sharing company data in turn? If not, then that ethical value needs to be carried forth in customer transactions if your organization values being integral.

> **Continuous Improvement**: Routinely monitor, evaluate, and improve AI systems and their output to address biases, errors, and other shortcomings. In addition, understanding how your employees on teams are integrating generative AI tools and conducting interviews or meetings to see if indeed they improve workflow efficiency are important parts of the integration process.

---

[36] https://www.forbes.com/sites/forbescommunicationscouncil/2023/07/20/seize-the-opportunity-embrace-self-regulation-to-harness-the-full-potential-of-ai/?sh=59e6b5862505

Human Control: Keep the human in the loop and maintain power over AI systems throughout any interactions, so decisions and actions are made with human values and ethical considerations in mind. No evolution of any technology should change that. Many organizations need to take responsibility for controlling the narrative of how they are using generative AI. This is important as much for internal communication as it is for external perception from informed customers.

Intellectual Property: Determine who owns what any AI generates and be mindful of whose data they use to create an AI model. Another way to think about it is that any media that makes the company money that leverages generative AI, such as a marketing tool, needs to be carefully applied, particularly if a well-meaning employee creates a wonderful image in the style of a living artist. Ensuring that employees remain transparent about their use of generative AI and the content they have generated is an important value to embed, especially in an age of vigorous litigation.

A Strawberry Meringue Torte of Layered Guidelines

The criteria you begin to define for your own organization's use of generative AI are a reflection of everything that has been presented so far. After developing criteria, your organization will benefit from overlaying guidelines that adhere to these principles and are better suited for your industry, organization, or department. Let's critically evaluate some of the typical guideline categories to inspire you to do the same, since no two organizations nor their uses will be precisely the same:

- **Fairness**: Design AI systems to minimize bias or discrimination based on factors such as race, gender framing, age, or socioeconomic status. Plan on a mitigation strategy as you should expect bias to rear its ugly head unexpectedly. You may want to use GraphRAG as a tool to further minimize biases.

- **Transparency**: Provide explanations and justifications while building systems, so users can understand and trust their behavior. Similarly, people should never be led to believe they are interacting with a person while communicating with AI. Explaining how machine learning works, in the common parlance of developers, is nontrivial.

- **Accountability**: Hold those who develop and implement AI systems partly responsible for their impact and consequences. Seems easy to say, but if you develop the technology, this one will not be received well, especially in a time where federal, state or provincial, and organizational policies are not all aligned. Aligning core values of your organization with the guidelines of use and development might be a better approach.

- **Reliability**: Test AI systems to confirm they are error-free and perform highly across different scenarios and datasets. Well, that whole compound word "error-free" is likely improbable when any generative AI is used for inference across different browsers, computers, networks, and devices. That said, identifying what known errors may occur is also common practice for many software development teams.

- **Safety**: Prioritize the well-being of all users and the general public, taking measures to mitigate risks and minimize harm. You can create guardrails for your awesome generative AI, but harm may emerge regardless of how well you think you've minimized the risk of it occurring. Disclaimers for using gen AI systems are common enough now. We might encourage people to actually read them.

- **Accessibility**: Ensure everyone can access AI systems and receive an equal opportunity to benefit from their use. One of the toughest areas to design for is universal access. This is because people with disabilities have distinct needs that are usually not all attended to. One solution that has become increasingly common, and for good reasons, is to include a person with a disability on a dev team so that a prototype can be built from the ground up.

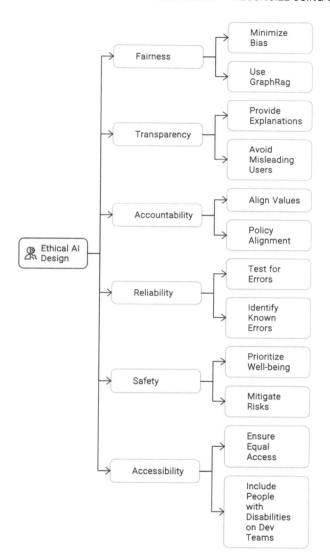

Figure 11-15. *Categories of guidelines to consider when integrating gen AI. AI-generated image*

As generative AI systems become a bigger part of our lives, we need to address the factors that shape how they are used and the effects they have. This technology compels us to examine preexisting social issues that it magnifies. These include the nature of training data: the corpus and how it is labeled, inherent copyright concerns, the lack of regulation around deep fakes, and the pros and cons of using public vs. private models. Without question, we need to carefully examine all AI-generated content and their capacity to reinforce existing biases, manufacture untruths, and simulate homogeneous content that excludes voices in our culture that are different, marginalized, or contrary to the status quo. Finally, we learn that interacting with any generative AI system, whether private or public, has tangible and ethical implications, including a lack of accessibility, exponential and unsustainable energy consumption as it grows in use, and moral considerations for individuals and the organizations they are embedded within. Each area presents distinct challenges that require attention to ensure responsible and beneficial AI use.

Reconciling these elements is an ongoing process of reflection and adaptation. Reconciling all at the same time is overwhelming but we need to begin that process.

By grasping the particulars of generative AI's underlying dependency on human-made data, we can better navigate intellectual property issues and how we define authentic human-created content. Acknowledging existing and yet-to-be-known biases and inaccuracies in AI-generated content necessitates developers to take responsibility for cyclically evaluating and improving their models. Developers using existing APIs and directing accountability toward larger companies providing those APIs are not recused from their own ethical responsibilities. Those responsibilities include addressing the ethical and environmental ramifications of training and running inference on generative AI systems, demonstrating a dedication to sustainable practices and equitable access.

As we incorporate generative AI into our workflows, we must remain vigilant, discerning, and proactive. This ensures that we work collaboratively to ensure the technology improves human work processes and addresses the challenges that come with it. The process of reconciliation not only establishes more ethical and effective AI use but also deepens our understanding of intelligence and our role in shaping the technology's future. This overly long chapter ends with the wise words of Donna Haraway who wrote "A Cyborg Manifesto" a long time ago—its wisdom still resonating across time. "Technology is not neutral. We're inside of what we make, and it's inside of us. We're living in a world of connections—and it matters which ones get made and unmade."[37]

Figure 11-16. *An even harder to read simulation of the Mona Lisa. AI-generated image*

---

[37] Haraway, D. (2010). A cyborg manifesto (1985). Cultural theory: An anthology, 454.

CHAPTER 12

Remember the Algorithms

In a small village in Anatolia, Nasrudin was known for his wit and wisdom. One day, the villagers approached him with a peculiar problem. "Nasrudin," they said, "we cannot seem to catch the thief who keeps stealing our chickens. We need your help!" Nasrudin thought for a moment and then declared, "Tomorrow, bring me a large pot of soup and everyone in the village." The next day, the villagers gathered with the pot of soup. Nasrudin stood before them and said, "I have devised a foolproof way to catch the thief. Each of you must dip your finger in this soup and taste it. The one whose finger tastes different will be our thief!" Puzzled but trusting him, the villagers did as instructed. After everyone had tasted the soup, Nasrudin pointed to one man and said, "This is our thief!" The man, shocked and guilty, confessed. The villagers were amazed and asked Nasrudin how he knew. Nasrudin chuckled and said, "Simple! The thief didn't dip his finger in the soup because he feared being caught. His finger was the only one not burned by the hot soup!"

While the previous chapter focused on algorithmic bias as one type of bias we learn about when working with generative AI, a focus on learning about algorithms beyond bias is worthwhile. Gaining an understanding of algorithms is comparable to acquiring a new type of literacy, one that will help you to not only navigate the stormy waters of generative AI but the hurricane of digital data that is being analyzed with and without

© Patrick Parra Pennefather 2024
P. Parra Pennefather, *Regenerating Learning*, Design Thinking,
https://doi.org/10.1007/979-8-8688-1061-9_12

our consent. Algorithms can be located in almost every interaction you have with a complex digital system, from surfing Google to inadvertently having your face analyzed in the London underground. Algorithms inform companies and organizations on anything from consumer patterns to safety and security. It is impossible to avoid them if you have any kind of digital footprint, and unless you have retreated to a Buddhist monastery, essentially retreating from all forms of remote communication, then you exist in the metaverse, represented as a combination of 1s and 0s.

Privacy at a Freemium

In what seems to be the deal of the century for corporations, your privacy has been bartered for the functionality and freemium use of a social media platform. This statement is out of date because privacy has been granted for decades now. How else is YouTube going to make money to host a video on a large server and stream it to the world if they can't collect information on what you watch, how often you watch it, and when you watch it? That way, they can offer you "astounding" products that are advertised for your consumption, suggest programs and videos that may or may not have anything to do with where you are at today, or constrain your choice of ads by the person who uploaded the video.

Figure 12-1. *Testing the hot soupy mess of generative AI.*
AI-generated image

If you think you are immune to algorithms by resisting using generative AI, then it will benefit you to understand how these powerful programs work. In doing so, you will benefit from understanding algorithms and making sense of how they impact your own work and living reality. In this way, you expand your knowledge and revise how you think about what algorithms are, their purpose with AI, how that informs their varied development, and the competitive landscape of their applications that affect anyone who has contributed anything to the Internet. The way in which they are embedded within ML models to identify patterns and then make predictions in the form of generated output has a direct influence on every human. The way in which human movement whether physical or virtual, and how knowledge, regardless of its form, is analyzed, and used to make predictions, no matter how accurate those predictions are, affects us.

A recently published report from the Institute for Strategic Dialogue in the UK found that YouTube's content moderation and recommendation system appears to have significant flaws, particularly in protecting younger users. Investigations using simulated teenage accounts revealed that harmful content, including sexualized material, misogynistic videos, and content related to self-harm, was frequently recommended. The platform's search function and recommender feed also surfaced health misinformation and content from banned creators. Notably, Christian religious content was consistently recommended across all test accounts, regardless of expressed interests. While some variations in recommendations were observed based on account settings, there was no clear correlation with age or gender, suggesting that individual user journeys are influenced by complex, undisclosed factors in YouTube's algorithm.[1]

Definition(s)

When the word "algorithm" is presented in front of the median human, a number of associations vs. definitions can boil up. These have to do with early associations of the word with math, science, computer science, physics, etc.

What are your associations?

Some people remember algebra or calculus. Somehow algorithms have something to do with logic. We definitely have heard the word but may have a hard time relating to it. Some humans might even think, "Oh that's the language of equations for smart people who do science-like things."

---

[1] https://www.isdglobal.org/isd-publications/pulling-back-the-curtain-an-exploration-of-youtubes-recommendation-algorithm/

Relating to algorithms in simple ways can open you up to understand more complex ways in which they are used in generative AI systems. When you relate them to what purpose they might have in your own reality, it might be easier to understand them as a set of instructions. An algorithm tells a computer what to do step by step. This makes it easier to relate to in our daily lives. For example, when you clean your room, you follow specific steps: making your bed, putting clothes in the closet, throwing away tissues in the garbage, dusting, sweeping, vacuuming the floor, etc. In your work environment, your tasks make it a bit more complicated. In order to perform a task, you need to complete a certain set of actions that you've embodied over time. It might start at the obvious. If you work on a shared desk, you need to set up the desk exactly how you want, set up your laptop, plug it into the monitor that happens to be there, turn your laptop on, open the particular software you need, then perform specific tasks that are possible with that software.

With generative AI, the ML model uses an algorithm (or several) to follow steps for creating new content. It starts by looking at a lot of examples, like many pictures or written text. By following its instructions, the software figures out how to create something new that looks or sounds similar to the examples it has seen. This is a simple explanation of how generative AI can generate new pictures, stories, songs, or videos based on the rules and patterns it has followed.

Reintroducing Algorithmic Bias

Algorithmic bias comes down to the inherent bias in the instructions that the software program undertakes. As an example:

- The algorithm gathers lots of examples from the Internet, books, or other sources. If these examples include biased or unfair information, the algorithm will collect that too.

- The algorithm processes this data to find patterns and common themes. If the data contains biased ideas or language, the algorithm will notice these patterns. If the algorithms use probability to analyze that data, then normative voices and opinions will be reinforced in any generated content.

- The algorithm creates rules based on the patterns it found. If the data was biased, the rules it creates will also be biased.

- When asked to create something new, the algorithm follows the biased rules it made. This results in new content that also includes the same biases as the original data.

By following these steps, an algorithm can end up creating content that reflects any biases present in the data it was given or, in many cases, data that it omitted or was not part of its original training. The omission of multiple perspectives from divergent voices is an example of bias by omission. This is why tech warrior advocates speak and champion the reduction of bias.

Figure 12-2. *Some takeaway questions when interrogating bias*

Reducing Bias

The unfortunate news is that you cannot completely eliminate bias, just as it would be impossible for human cultures to be completely free of all our biases. We can, however, reduce bias, if we are aware of how bias might be created when interacting with an ML model. There are many methods that developers have attempted to reduce bias in an LLM, so the list below should not be seen as exhaustive:

- Ensure the data collected is from a wide range of sources and represents different perspectives. This helps to avoid favoring one viewpoint over another. This results in more time and energy being needed to review sources.

- Clean the data to remove any biased or unfair information before the algorithm processes it. This involves checking for and eliminating stereotypes, discriminatory language, or any harmful content. If this sounds easy, it is not. How dev teams define and identify what they consider to be biased and unfair is going to depend on the makeup of those teams.

- Continuously check the patterns that the algorithm is finding to ensure they are fair and balanced. If any biased patterns are detected, adjust the data or the algorithm's rules to correct them.

- Program the algorithm to follow specific rules that promote fairness and equality. This includes making sure the algorithm treats all groups of people equally and does not favor one over another. That may involve exploring different statistical methods of analysis or, like some LLMs are already doing, providing optional versions of generated outputs for a user's review.

- Frequently test the algorithm's outputs for bias and update it regularly with new, diverse data. This helps to keep the algorithm fair over time and adapt to new information. The word "frequently" is the one to watch here, as retraining a model on new data is not cheap.

By following these steps, the algorithm can be programmed to minimize bias and produce more fair and balanced content. That's not to say companies with public-facing generative AI haven't already done that. Many who have not are diligently working on revising algorithms, retraining their models, and creating new offerings that aim to reduce bias. The problem is that they are not always transparent as to their process. This is also because their algorithms might be proprietary knowledge they don't want other for-profit companies to steal. The result of a lack of transparency is that it reduces trustworthiness.

There are exceptions to the rule of course. Uber has stood out as such, creating a feedback-driven development process since 2016. Uber has made significant strides in integrating ML models into their operations, leading to various achievements across different phases. The journey began with the introduction of their ML platform, Michelangelo, which has allowed Uber to scale their ML solutions efficiently. This platform supports an extensive range of models, including time series forecasting to deep learning models, facilitating tasks like ETA predictions, risk assessment, and pricing strategies. Michelangelo has enabled Uber to power applications, such as real-time matching of drivers and riders, which involves processing millions of predictions per minute using complex algorithms and large-scale data processing.

But Wait, What About Statistics?

The other buzz-killing word discussed in previous chapters, and that we have all encountered in our nightmares, is the word "statistics," and we each have associations with the word. Learning about statistics can help clear the air as to why certain LLMs, for example, generate content that is biased, content that excludes outliers who may represent a smaller part of the massive amount of content out there. How is that data collected? Who labels the data? How is the data labeled and organized? All of these questions are often not disclosed by companies.

When you dig deeper into statistics, you realize they are not so scary and, in fact, can be useful to inform decisions. A statistic can be a collection of data about a specific human activity and behavior. It is often referred to as the action of collecting, analyzing, and interpreting data to understand patterns and make decisions based on that data. In a work environment, a manager might look at the salaries of highest and lowest performing employees, which helps them understand how well the organization is performing overall. You can see how comparing employee performance with salary can also be an unfair or false correlation. These types of statistical analyses are made daily. By analyzing correlations, such as the relationship between salary and performance, the manager can identify factors that contribute to better performance. But that's only if they have defined the criteria as to what makes for a "good" performance and what is a "good" salary for the type of work that they do. These criteria can also introduce bias into the calculation, especially if they omit certain factors that are difficult to calculate.

Distributions, like the range of scores from highest to lowest, show how varied the workers' performances are. Statistics are used in many fields, such as healthcare to track disease outbreaks, in marketing to understand consumer preferences, and in sports to evaluate player performance and strategize for games. There are certain ways in which algorithms use statistics to find patterns, estimate how likely different outcomes are, how they use this information to make predictions, and how the algorithms are refined when mistakes are made.

Figure 12-3. *Surfing the algorithmic trend in perilous waters.*
AI-generated image

Algorithms in Video Games As a Use Case

Before the homogenous popularity of generating text from a large language model, there were video games. Video games have long been using the idea of intelligent non-playable characters (NPCs), and so there is much to learn about how games work that we can apply to our understanding of algorithms. You can go as far back as *Pong* or *Space Invaders* to understand that when you played against the machine, you learned about mastering a very specific skill in order to beat the machine. In *Pong*, algorithms control the ball's movement and collision detection, making sure that digital ball bounces off the paddles and walls at calculated angles. The player's paddle movement is driven by input algorithms, while an AI algorithm can control the opponent's paddle by tracking the ball's position. The game also uses a scoring algorithm to update points whenever the ball passes a paddle, resetting the game for the next round. So where is there perceived "intelligence in the system?" It can be found in your opponent's paddle movement as it tracks the balls position.

We created the perception of intelligence in video game characters in order to test our own. This constant battle of wits is partly what we are dealing with today when it comes to comparing human and machine intelligence, as if intelligence was a series of Boolean-inspired logical algorithms trained to excel at a particular task. From gaming and the natural emergence of non-playable humans who have more rule-based intelligence than us, the idea of an NPC is no longer confined within the safe environment of a made-up game world. The idea of competing with intelligence and an intelligent, non-playable AI (NPAI) has now invaded this physical reality.

Categories of AI Algorithms

In the realm of generative AI, algorithms play a necessary role in both the training and operation of models. Training algorithms determine how the AI model learns from the vast corpus of data it's trained on, incorporating techniques that at this point in your learning journey may be too much information—techniques like back propagation, gradient descent, and various optimization methods. Once trained, inference algorithms govern how the model generates responses to prompts or inputs. Additionally, in models like transformers, attention mechanisms help the AI focus on relevant parts of the input when generating output. Deepening your understanding of these algorithms provides insight into how the AI processes information and generates content. This knowledge is important if interpreting the output and identifying potential biases or limitations are of concern to you.

Understanding Algorithms and Their Impact

When it comes to their use in generative AI, you can start to imagine that the more you know about these sets of instructions that analyze a large amount of data, the more you begin to understand that what you get as generated content will be influenced by both the data it analyzes and *how* it analyzes that data to then make predictions in the form of generated content.

Figure 12-4. *Video games imagined by several generative AI. AI-generated image*

Black Boxes

Nothing in life is to be feared, it is only to be understood. Now is the time to understand more, so that we may fear less.

This timeless quote from Marie Curie, the famous physicist and noble prize winner, is just as relevant now as it was when she said it. The seemingly invisible process of generative AI systems is where a lot of the current attention and criticism of LLMs are grounded in. The common perception of most generative AI systems is as a black box where you prompt the model and receive something back without knowing all the computation that occurs in between. That is another potential reason why there exists an inherent mistrust in the technology for some people and organizations. The perception of generative AI as a "black box" creates

- **Lack of Transparency**: The complexity of AI systems makes it difficult for many humans to fully understand how these black boxes work on the inside. It's no longer good enough that development teams try to explain how a large language model works, for example, using their own lingo. Translating how generative AI work into "simpler" or at least more comprehensible ways will go a long way into building trust.

- **Interpretability Challenges**: Even when we can access the model's parameters, interpreting them meaningfully is often beyond the median human's capacity. It's not that the median human is dumb. It's that knowledge outside our field of expertise is often hard to digest, and what the different features of different AI systems are able to do requires quite a bit of creative interpretation, metaphors, stories, and lengthy conversations over wine to understand.

- **Trust Issues**: The opacity of AI systems can lead to mistrust, especially when they're used for critical decisions. If humans implement AI in different work environments without fully understanding or explaining how they work, and what their role in their employees' workflows will be, you can likely expect backlash driven by a fear of being replaced.

Being able to decipher what happens in between prompting an AI and receiving content back from it is a step toward empowering users to make a decision as to whether or not to use generated content.

Figure 12-5. *A black box becoming aware it is a black box.*
AI-generated image

Innovation and Competition

The development of algorithms is a competitive field, with many companies and researchers constantly working to create more effective and efficient algorithms. This competition drives innovation but also creates a landscape where the most powerful algorithms can have significant advantages. That also means that capitalist intentions, greed, market forces, investment, who you know, and how much money is required to train and test models with inference have a direct impact on what we end up being presented with. Here are three common issues that influence innovation with machine learning models:

- **Race for Scale**: Companies compete to create larger models with more parameters, potentially at the expense of efficiency, sustainability, ethics, or interpretability.

- **Specialization vs. Generalization**: Some focus on general-purpose models, while others target specific domains or tasks more narrowly. Specialization, while seemingly less profitable, may be more strategic for an organization wanting to continue offering services beyond the current hype cycle of generative AI.

- **Open Source vs. Proprietary**: The tension between open collaboration and commercial interests affects model development and access. The release of Llama 3.1 as an open source model defies logic, but makes sense for a company like Meta that doesn't really need more income and welcomes developers to create a learning ecosystem around their ML model.

As companies compete, there can be pressure to push the boundaries of what algorithms can do, sometimes without fully considering the ethical implications. While defining an ethical vision is important, the process of doing so is often overlooked by companies that place profit in the center of their to-do bull's-eye.

Ethical Considerations

To address concerns and build trust in generative AI:

- **Education**: Increase public understanding of how AI works and its limitations. Don't be shy to be direct about many of the ethical problems as highlighted in Chapter 11.

- **Transparency**: Develop tools and methods to make AI decision-making more transparent. This will help engender more trust in what your company is doing and minimize suspicion and loss of customers.

- **Ethical Guidelines**: Establish and adhere to ethical standards in AI development and deployment. While many companies like to make statements that regulations and regulatory bodies halt innovation, in truth, if you are unable to create anything keeping your ethical standards in check, then a rethink of your organization's values are in order. It's a changing world, where an organization's ethics and values need to be front and center.

- **User Control**: Provide users with increased options to customize AI models instead of being satisfied with a single context window and the resulting generated content. There is a common assumption with many development teams that users are, well, stupid and that they need everything dumbed down in order to make use of their particular prototype. This couldn't be farther than the truth. Developing user experiences with empathy means your dev team cares about who they are building their prototype for. Otherwise, why bother putting it out there?

Algorithmic Collusion

If you thought you were somewhat immune from algorithms because you don't travel to other countries, surf the Internet, conduct a Google search, allow apps to track your activity, forget to turn off the "don't track me" feature on many applications, avoid public cameras, opt out from an app using your content as data to train a shiny new AI, and stay away from YouTube, Facebook, TikTok, X, Instagram, or Amazon, then you might need a reality check when it comes to the ever-increasing uses of algorithms that will impact you eventually.

In learning about algorithms, you can also enjoy a deep dive into algorithmic collusion, particularly in the context of pricing strategies. It is a significant concern across various industries, including real estate. Experimental economics research has demonstrated that the exchange of information plays a decisive role in enabling collusion, particularly in markets where more than two firms are active.[2] A market where all firms independently implement their own pricing algorithms, which monitor competitors' real-time prices and adjust accordingly, can create an

---

[2] Schwalbe, U. (2018). Algorithms, machine learning, and collusion. Journal of Competition Law & Economics, 14(4), 568–607.

environment ripe for tacit collusion.[3] Recent lawsuits in the United States have highlighted how algorithms are being used to facilitate price fixing among competitors. For example, in the real estate industry, the use of algorithms by companies like RealPage has led to allegations that these tools help landlords coordinate rent prices, pushing them above market rates. This has prompted multiple federal lawsuits, which argue that these practices violate antitrust laws designed to prevent such collusion.[4]

The dystopian pricing phenomenon, according to Karma[83], isn't limited to real estate. Similar concerns are being raised in other industries. In Germany, the use of algorithms in price-fixing gasoline prices is also under scrutiny for potentially enabling tacit collusion.[5] This kind of collusion is particularly problematic because it can occur without direct communication between the companies, making it harder to detect and regulate. Yet, buyer beware, it is still happening and increasing at an alarming rate.

The Importance of Understanding Algorithms

Like it or not, algorithms have become an integral part of our daily lives, silently shaping our experiences and affecting our decisions. Understanding algorithms is analogous to developing a new form of literacy. It empowers us to navigate the digital world with more awareness, make informed choices about the technological platforms that we use,

---

[3] https://www.alvarezandmarsal.com/insights/antitrust-implications-pricing-algorithms

[4] https://www.theatlantic.com/ideas/archive/2024/08/ai-price-algorithms-realpage/679405/

[5] Assad, S., Clark, R., Ershov, D., & Xu, L. (2024). Algorithmic pricing and competition: Empirical evidence from the German retail gasoline market. Journal of Political Economy, 132(3), 723–771.

and critically evaluate the information we encounter. When we start to grasp how algorithms work, we can better recognize their influence on our social media feeds, shopping recommendations, the news we depend on, and the content that an LLM generates for us. This knowledge allows us to maintain a suspicious curiosity—open to generated content, suspicious as to its truth value, and more conscious about the digital interactions we manifest and the results of our interactions on the content that is pushed to our attention.

For organizations, the need to understand algorithms is more pressing. In a business landscape increasingly driven by data and AI, algorithmic literacy can be a significant competitive advantage. Companies that invest time and resources to deepen knowledge about algorithms can make more informed decisions about which AI technologies to adopt, better assess the risks and benefits of algorithmic systems, and more effectively leverage these tools to find patterns in their dominantly unstructured data. The end goal is to improve their operations. That includes becoming aware of potential biases in their algorithmic systems to ensure fair and equitable treatment of customers, employees, and stakeholders.

In the context of generative AI, understanding algorithms is important for those who have already adopted the technology and those hesitant to do so. As these systems become more prevalent in content creation, decision-making processes, and customer interactions, individuals and organizations need to understand their inner workings. This knowledge helps in setting realistic expectations about what AI can and cannot do, interpreting AI-generated content more accurately, and anticipating issues such as biases or hallucinations in the generated contents. For organizations deploying generative AI, a deep understanding of the underlying algorithms is essential for responsible implementation, effective troubleshooting, and ongoing improvement of their systems.

As discussions about AI regulation and governance gain momentum, algorithmic literacy will be vital for participating in important societal debates. Individuals and organizations alike will benefit from understanding how algorithms work across different ML models, to contribute meaningfully to conversations about AI ethics, privacy concerns, and the societal impacts of these technologies. In essence, learning about algorithms is not just about technical knowledge—it's about equipping ourselves to be informed, responsible, and empowered participants in an increasingly algorithmic world.

BedTimeStoryBot: In the late 1990s and early 2000s, a group of major European truck manufacturers—Daimler, Volvo/Renault, Iveco, DAF, and MAN—entered into a secret agreement that would eventually become one of the largest price-fixing cartels in history. For over 14 years, these companies colluded to fix prices, delay the introduction of emission-reducing technology, and pass on the costs of compliance with stricter environmental standards to customers. The truck manufacturers held secret meetings, exchanged sensitive information, and coordinated their pricing strategies across Europe. By artificially inflating prices and stifling competition, they maximized their profits at the expense of consumers and businesses who relied on their vehicles.

The cartel's activities were eventually uncovered by the European Commission, which launched a massive investigation. In 2016, the Commission imposed record fines totaling nearly €3 billion on the companies involved. Daimler alone was fined over €1 billion, marking the largest single fine ever imposed by the European Commission for antitrust violations.

CHAPTER 13

Continuously Learn with AI

By now, through the previous chapters, it probably has become increasingly clear that when you interact with any AI system, including generative AI models, there is the potential of activating a cyber-biome of learning that you can continuously access. That ecosystem of learning is not just about how to interact with generative AI tools but also how your teacher, researcher, and learner can all be engaged.

Who says you need to improve? Likely the first motivation was external. Your parents and siblings, objects in the space you bumped into, a cat or dog who was jealous or downright frightened by your impish toddler curiosity. As we grow, we are motivated to improve our way in the world because it doesn't always give us what we expect no matter how smart we think we are. That's because there's always something else to learn. The adventure is never over really. As humans particularly within work environments, we can easily get caught into delivering our tasks with a series of patterned techniques, skills, competencies, responses, and behaviors and resist any impetus to change. We may also resist those patterns at times, especially when their execution becomes tedious, but we recognize, at the end of the day, our skills and competencies in completing those tasks are why we have the job we do and why we are paid.

P. Parra Pennefather, *Regenerating Learning*, Design Thinking,
https://doi.org/10.1007/979-8-8688-1061-9_13

When you are either forced by an employer or curious to integrate generative AI on your own, it is like introducing a different set of tools, strategies, instruments, and processes into your work and reshaping how the work gets done. That doesn't necessarily mean you are going to make all of your work or even any of it more efficient as the headlines claim. That may be the case in certain situations but not all. The introduction of generative AI into your workflows does mean that you have a technology that you have to figure out how to work with while working. We engage in continuous learning whenever we use new tools, and gen AI tools are no exception. Working with the technology will eventually transform how we work, and the actual implementation of generative AI within our workflows to complete tasks activates all kinds of learning.

Here is how generative AI activates us in cycles of continuous learning:

- When you notice the patterns in the generated content, you learn to anticipate what types of refinement changes and editing you will need to take the time to do.

- You need to learn to become better at estimating how much time that's going to take and determine whether or not creating content from scratch is going to be more efficient.

- Consciously or unconsciously, you test the efficiency of generative AI all the time once you start to use it. In its use, you learn about whether or not the effort to use it is worth your time or adds value, compared to your more established methods of completing tasks.

- You may more intentionally enact a learning, implementation, and testing cycle. You teach yourself how to learn what you need in order to generate content that can be applied to a particular use case, then reflect on the application of it in iterative cycles.

- You find gaps in the outputs of any generative AI and investigate if that specific tool will be useful, or you are motivated to find other similar types of gen AI tools that perform better or more consistently for your particular use cases.

- You seek other opinions and ways of working with generative AI tools you have taken on in order to learn how to improve your interactions or to better understand the constraints of the platform and how different creatives have managed those limitations.

How to Build a Better Mousetrap

Nasrudin went to a small library where he wandered to a shelf and picked up a book titled *How to Build a Better Mousetrap*. He read it diligently, applying its methods meticulously to his own work, determined to catch the pesky mouse in his house. Days passed, but the mouse remained elusive, seemingly mocking his efforts. Frustrated, Nasrudin returned to the library. "Your book is useless!" he exclaimed. The librarian chuckled, "Ah, maybe the mouse read the same book and learned a few new tricks!"

Figure 13-1. *A mouse reading how to build a better mousetrap.*
AI-generated image

A Journey of Continuous Transformation

Hedy Lamarr was born in Austria in 1914 and later became a famous Hollywood actress. Despite her success in film, Lamarr had a keen interest in science and technology. During World War II, she became aware of the limitations of radio-controlled torpedoes, which were susceptible to jamming and interference by the enemy.

In 1940, Lamarr met George Antheil, an avant-garde composer and inventor. They discussed the problem of radio-controlled torpedoes and brainstormed potential solutions. Lamarr's idea was to create a frequency-hopping signal that could not be easily intercepted or jammed. Antheil, who had experience with automated piano mechanisms, helped Lamarr refine her idea using his knowledge of synchronization.

Lamarr and Antheil developed a system where both the transmitter and receiver would hop simultaneously between different frequencies, based on a prearranged pattern. This would prevent enemy forces from easily jamming the signal, as they would need to know the exact frequency sequence. The duo iteratively worked on the concept, combining their respective expertise in communications technology and mechanical synchronization. They filed for a patent on their "Secret Communication System" in 1941, which was granted in 1942.

Despite the original nature of their invention, the technology was ahead of its time. The US Navy initially did not adopt it, possibly due to the complexity of implementing it with existing technology. However, the concept of frequency hopping would later become fundamental in secure military communications.

Years after the patent expired, the principles of Lamarr and Antheil's invention were revisited and applied to modern communication technologies. Frequency-hopping spread spectrum (FHSS) became a foundational technology for various wireless communication systems, including Bluetooth, Wi-Fi, and GPS. Although Lamarr's contributions were not widely recognized during her lifetime, her pioneering work eventually received the acknowledgment it deserved. In 1997, Lamarr and Antheil were honored with the Electronic Frontier Foundation (EFF) Pioneer Award. Lamarr was also inducted into the National Inventors Hall of Fame in 2014.

Hedy Lamarr's story is a powerful example of adapting what you do, being passionate about learning what is necessary to transform what and who you are, as you iterate on what you offer humanity. Despite facing challenges and initial skepticism, her collaborative efforts with George Antheil and their iterative development of frequency-hopping technology paved the way for advancements in wireless communication.

Lamarr's legacy highlights the ideas of not settling, of looking for new opportunities and new gaps in the types of solutions that humans might need. That requires a mindset of continuous improvement, which demands us to be open to learning new things. Engaging with generative AI isn't merely about producing content; it's a gateway to a multilayered learning process. As you interact with these systems, you simultaneously develop an AI fluency that needs continuous attention and improvement. You also deepen your understanding of your own creative methods and learn to confront and reconcile fundamental questions about knowledge production, bias, and the nature of machine learning itself.

How Generative AI Emphasizes Continuous Improvement

While you don't need to be a programmer, continuous learning will eventually lead you down the path of developing a basic understanding of how machine learning works. Seeking out resources that explain the inner workings of ML models, like datasets, statistical patterns, and the probabilistic nature of generated output in approachable terms, will help you better understand how you will use the technology.

In the process of understanding how ML models work, you are quickly able to see both their affordances and their limitations. Seeing what generative AI offers you in a positive light will support you in deciphering how it might actually help your own work process. Seeing their limitations means that you acknowledge how and if you will use them. They are by no means perfected prototypes. Continuously learn its boundaries—where it provides value and where it needs vigilant human oversight. In doing so, you will start to question how ML models can be improved. You may even be motivated to work with others in solving that problem.

Developers are persistently upgrading different features of the ML models that they have created. That idea of continuous improvement is embedded in most software development companies. We benefit, in particular, when our feedback as users of the prototype is listened to. Any of the generative AI that you've interacted with in the past year is a working prototype, a version-of that is stable, or a working version with a set of features that allow for consistent performance. There is always room for improvement though.

What Is There to Improve On?

Generative AI can be useful in some situations and not at all in others. It is important for you to draw that distinction within your own learning and working process. In a similar fashion, we make changes and improvements to our own working process when we work with generative AI tools. We all use them in different ways to fit within our own work and how we approach our work and change how we work can shift. Here are some of the things we improve:

- We improve how we learn on our own.

- We improve our bias sensors.

- We improve our discernment.

- We improve our creative agitation.

- We improve our critical engines.

- We improve how we think of technology and its role in learning.

- We improve our workflows.

- We improve our prototyping process.

- We improve our research skills.

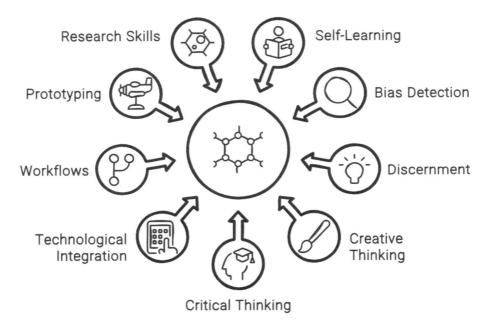

Figure 13-2. *What we might improve when using generative AI systems. AI-generated image*

Improve How We Learn on Our Own

Every new technology offers advantages and disadvantages, and most challenge the ways that humans have gotten used to learning. Generative AI challenges the ways that we have become accustomed to treating the center of knowledge as a formal place of learning. Logically, we know this is simply not the case and has not been for decades. We also know that learning occurs on the job all the time. What AI disrupts is the way in which we take in knowledge and the way we create anything, and like other technologies before, it challenges our dependency on an outside force to teach us. As the generative AI landscape changes, your self-regulated learning abilities must evolve. The constant need to learn new tools, approaches, and how to troubleshoot results makes you a more adaptable and versatile thinker, when you take command.

Improve Our Bias Sensors

AI models are trained on massive amounts of data, which inherently contain human biases. The more you interact with them, the more you develop a critical eye for spotting potential biases and untruths and factor this into your refinement and editing process. That takes time and a lot of research, but doing so activates your researcher muscle and curiosity. Cultivate a sensitivity to the biases that inevitably seep into AI outputs. Be mindful of how this may perpetuate misinformation or stereotypes, especially in text and image generation. Encountering generated content that consistently surfaces problematic content makes you question the limitations of the technology, and it will help you weigh the pros and cons of continuing with that particular technology, identifying its narrow use cases, and motivate you to experiment with other gen AI tools. Persistent self-reflection is a key learning outcome of working with generative AI. Cultivating discernment will only make your work better.

Improve Our Discernment

Our relationship with technology has been complex and ever-evolving, often marked by curiosity, obsession, endless tinkering, and also frustration. Generative AI presents a unique opportunity to reshape our relationship with the technology.

SelfFlatteringBot: By making technology more intuitive, personalized, and creative, generative AI has the potential to support your creative process.

Now, reread that statement, and in doing so, where do you agree or disagree?

What generative AI does, more than all of the embellishments that are made about it, is that it activates our discernment. With gen AI, our critical muscles can be fully engaged. Even if you resist using it, you become more aware of the reasons why and reflect on your own craft and how you create work. In light of this, we can practice our discernment by learning to question assumptions and research generative AI systems.

What is user-friendly about it?

One of the most significant ways generative AI could improve our relationship with technology is by making it more accessible and user-friendly. If you look at more familiar user interfaces, ones that you encounter in different games or applications that you use, these often require you to learn specific commands and navigate complex menus. What about generative AI interfaces? Dominantly, and in contrast to the evolution of user interfaces for a variety of applications, generative AI platforms give us a simple context window, creating a simple conversational relationship with the technology. Some have reported this engagement to be more intuitive and less intimidating. Others have been highly critical to the point of dubbing most generative AI black boxes, where you don't understand all the computation that is occurring under the hood. Some users have found the crafting of prompts to be annoying in not allowing for more control over the generated outputs. As noted by Dr. Ben Shneiderman, a pioneer in human-computer interaction, "The old model was that you had to conform to the computer's requirements. The new model is that the computer conforms to your requirements."[1] Yet, while generative AI may appear to adopt to this principle, adapting to a simple way of communicating, limiting interactions within a single context window on most public generative AI without providing other parameters for users, can quickly alienate the discerning creative who wants more control over the content being generated.

How might it increase creativity and productivity exactly?

If generative AI has the potential to improve our creativity and problem-solving abilities, the technology is provoking that to occur in unexpected ways. Instead of merely accepting what many voices tout as a creativity and productivity enhancer, the only real way to assess its potential is to try it yourself, for your own use cases, and document the result. Researchers from the Stanford Digital Economy Lab at Stanford HAI, in collaboration with the Massachusetts Institute of Technology, examined the large-scale deployment of generative AI in a call center's customer service operations. Their study revealed that the use of generative AI led to a 14% increase in agent productivity when they used it to create scripts, with the most significant benefits observed among less experienced workers.[2] While conclusions of the study did not make broad assertions, of researchers did note some unexpected findings:

---

[1] https://capian.co/shneiderman-eight-golden-rules-interface-design
[2] Brynjolfsson, E., Li, D., & Raymond, L. R. (2023). Generative AI at work (No. w31161). National Bureau of Economic Research.

- Highly skilled workers may derive less benefit from AI assistance because the AI's recommendations often replicate the expertise and knowledge already embodied in their own behaviors.

- Customer responses to AI scripts that were designed to communicate empathy for frustrated customers resulted in more positive dialogue with an agent.

As we interact with these AI systems, we may find ourselves thinking in new ways, exploring ideas we might not have considered otherwise, and pushing the boundaries of what we think is creative and productive. To test this theory, we really need to learn through the action of doing, as has been noted in a previous chapter. How else are you to really know how useful it is, until you apply it to a use case you think it might work well with? As you experiment with an LLM, for example, you realize its shortcomings pretty quickly. Prompting it in certain ways will definitely activate your own creative impulses. What are those impulses? At the same time, when you read the content an LLM generates, there can also be a lot of confusion as to what to do with that content.

How is using an LLM going to increase your productivity exactly? To properly answer that, you need to also discern what aspect of your work is not productive.

What are your criteria for being more productive and creative? Just like the earlier chapter on assessment challenged you to develop criteria of assessment for your learning of AI, so too can you apply the development of criteria to properly assess creativity and productivity. Critical writer and researcher Rainer Rehak, in Chapter 6 of the book *AI for Everyone?*,[3]

---

[3] Rehak, R. (2021). The Language Labyrinth: Constructive Critique on the Terminology Used in the AI Discourse. In: Verdegem, P. (ed.) AI for Everyone? Critical Perspectives. Pp. 87–102. London: University of Westminster Press. DOI: https://doi.org/10.16997/book55.f. License: CC-BY-NC-ND 4.0.

argues that the myth of productivity can gather momentum for the use of generative AI because of its "assumed functionality," not the reality of it when applied to a specific use case. In using the technology, we buy into the dream that it's going to solve a productivity problem, when in fact there may be no solution to the actual productivity problems we have, since we can't even identify what they are.

How much personalization does the technology afford?

Another common feature that companies highlight about their gen AI prototypes is the concept of personalization. The common myth that surfaces across media portals revolves around the idea that generative AI systems can learn from our interactions and adapt to our individual needs and preferences over time. But wait a moment, how accurate is that statement once you start to understand how machine learning models "learn"?

As we engage with these systems, we become more aware of how they work, what they can do, and where they fall short. This increased awareness can lead to more realistic expectations and a more nuanced view of AI's role in our lives. It may also encourage critical thinking about the information we receive and the decisions we make based on AI-generated content.

However, it's important to note that this improved relationship with technology through generative AI is not without challenges. Issues of privacy, data security, and the potential for misinformation need to be carefully addressed. As Dr. Kate Crawford, a leading writer and researcher in the social implications of AI, warns, "We need to be mindful of the power dynamics at play in AI systems and ensure that they are designed with ethical considerations at the forefront."[4]

---

[4] Crawford, K. (2021). The atlas of AI: Power, politics, and the planetary costs of artificial intelligence. Yale University Press.

Improve Our Creative Agitation

When we get into the habit of creating versions of our work, we activate a muscle of continuous improvement. Iterations or versions of what we do provide us with many options and directions. We may have settled on the latest version of our work, but upon review by colleagues, a team lead, or a client, a previous version might be the one chosen to move forward on. This is a common creative agitation when we design for other humans. Generative AI allows us the opportunity to iterate quickly on several ideas, present them to stakeholders, and be in an "anything can happen next" state of mind. Generative AI challenges us to reexamine how we define creativity as well. Through continuous use, you'll gain insights into your ideation process, how you respond to the unexpected, and the value of human refinement. In essence, you start to improve your own creative process, and you even become creative about what creativity means. Some of the feedback we receive from our work can stimulate us to change some of the following:

- The look and feel of your creation especially if visual. If it's text based, then the look and feel can describe the overall writing style, structure, and how the work is shaped.

- The quality of the generated content and how it fits into your more refined vision.

- The originality of the overall work. Generally, the type and amount of AI content will depend on what your creative team expects.

- Everything and start from scratch. Luckily, this is where generative AI shines as it can help develop brand-new ideas quickly.

- Tiny changes to a document or design. This includes creating minute variations using masking tools in image generation or in slightly altering a seed that an image is associated with.

- Representation. It is important to understand that diversity such as racial characteristics, gender, and age need to be prompted and sometimes very specifically. We can't expect any of the existing ML models to automatically think and generate content in the form of images especially that are diverse.

- Stylistic feedback is another area that generative AI respond well to. Imagine if someone doesn't like the tone of a particular marketing write-up. That write-up can be part of a prompt for an LLM and be accompanied with commands like "make this sound friendlier" or "generate a version of this copy that is more serious in its tone." Additionally, most text-image and text-video gen AI tools allow for some types of stylistic references within their prompts. You can use the same people in a shot, for example, and easily substitute the background image to whatever you want.

Because some studies have drawn false equivalencies with machine and human creativity, even going as far as asserting that AI can be in the top 1% of scoring when it comes to specific tests, it's more important than ever to define your own creative process and claim its uniqueness. Creativity is more than just coming up with a bunch of ideas about what you can do with a piece of paper. It is more than generating solutions to problems based on how they might have been solved by other humans in the corpus of a machine learning model.[5] In a recent paper, researchers developed similar questions as the ones below, which are good ones to consider when claims of AI equivalencies to human creativity are made:

- How do you operationalize creativity? How is it different across disciplines, cultures, age, etc.?

- Are tests that evaluate creativity generalizable to different people from different disciplinary backgrounds? Do they apply to you?

- Does any creativity test properly assess a wide range of creative thinking?

Improve Our Critical Engines

The rapid integration of generative AI has heightened the need for critical thinking skills. As we integrate these powerful tools into our learning and working environments, it becomes increasingly important to approach their use with intentionality and skepticism. The value of generative AI lies not just in its ability to produce content but in how it can extend our own cognitive processes when used thoughtfully.

One of the primary challenges in using generative AI is the verification of its outputs. These systems, while impressive, are not infallible and can produce inaccuracies or "hallucinations"—plausible-sounding but incorrect information. Therefore, it's important to develop robust fact-checking habits and cross-referencing skills. This process of verification not only ensures the integrity of the work but also deepens our understanding of the subject matter. As information literacy expert Mike Caulfield suggests in his SIFT method (Stop, Investigate the source,

---

[5] Hubert, K. F., Awa, K. N., & Zabelina, D. L. (2024). The current state of artificial intelligence generative language models is more creative than humans on divergent thinking tasks. Scientific Reports, 14(1), 3440.

Find better coverage, Trace claims to their origin), these skills are essential in navigating not just AI-generated content but the broader digital information landscape.[6]

The integration of generative AI into various work environments raises profound ethical questions that we all must grapple with. Issues of intellectual property, the changing role of human creativity, and the potential for misuse of these technologies are at the forefront of these discussions. For instance, the use of AI in art has sparked debates about authorship and originality, as highlighted by legal scholar Jane C. Ginsburg in her work on AI and copyright law.[7] Engaging with these ethical dilemmas is not just an academic exercise; it's a fundamental part of developing a nuanced understanding of how these technologies fit into our society and professional practices.

As we continue to explore the potential of generative AI, it's clear that its integration must be accompanied by careful facilitation and clear articulation of its values and limitations. While they may not be used to doing so, professionals need to create frameworks for the intentional use of these tools, emphasizing critical evaluation of outputs and ethical considerations. This approach not only mitigates the risks associated with AI use but also maximizes its potential as a tool for enhancing human creativity and problem-solving. In improving our critical engines, we can work toward a future where AI augments rather than replaces human intelligence, creating a symbiotic relationship between human creativity and the efficient generation of machine-predicted content.

---

[6] Caulfield, M., & Wineburg, S. (2023). Verified: How to think straight, get duped less, and make better decisions about what to believe online. University of Chicago Press.

[7] Ginsburg, J. C. (2020). People Not Machines: Authorship and What It Means in International Copyright Law.

Improve How We Think of Technology and Its Role in Learning

The modern concept of continuous improvement in the workplace began around 1950 when Toyota's Taiichi Ohno and Shigeo Shingo developed the Just-In-Time (JIT) manufacturing method. Continuous improvement is an ongoing process of discovering new ways to improve procedures, products, or services, and it's a central tenet of the lean business philosophy developed by Toyota in the 1950s to reduce company waste. So, it's been a key practice for several decades.[8]

Akin to the idea of continuous improvement is continuous learning—the idea that even when you move past a more formal educational environment, you can still learn. In fact, learning never stops. Putting energy into learning something new is a method to accelerate and apply that learning, especially if you can apply it to your everyday world.

You Learn like a Computer Learns like You

Computers and how they operate have dominated the explanation of how people learn for decades. Think about some of the sayings you've heard. Theorists, educators, researchers, and individuals have used the computer as a metaphor for human learning by likening the mind to a machine that processes information. This analogy helps explain how we store, retrieve, and organize knowledge. It suggests that learning involves input (information), processing (thinking and understanding), and output (responses and actions), similar to how a computer functions. Like it or not, the metaphor has influenced educational practices and research, focused on the importance of structured, systematic approaches to learning. AI takes it to another level, however.

---

[8] https://dovetail.com/product-development/continuous-improvement/

According to Rehak, when domain-specific language migrates into other fields, it can undergo a transformation that strips it of its original context, specificity, and limitations. This process can result in terms that started as practical, "weak" metaphors within a technical field evolving into "proper" technical terms as they are adopted in broader contexts. As these terms gain traction outside their original professional environment, they begin to be perceived as fully fledged metaphors, disconnected from the nuances that initially defined them.[9]

When technical metaphors are taken out of context, they can shape public perception in ways that either fuel enthusiasm or generate skepticism about AI. Terms like "cloud computing" or "machine learning" may evoke simplistic and misleading interpretations when used outside the knowledge domain in which they have specified meanings. When we learn about generative AI then, the language that comes with it influences the way we conceptualize it as a whole. In this way, the language of how generative AI works doesn't just describe its functionality; it also shapes the societal and cultural narratives that emerge around its developments.

We Improve Our Knowledge of Other AI

As many in different creative industries already know, before generative AI systems, there have already been advances in software applications that have used some sort of "intelligence" in order to streamline different production workflows. Take the example of noise reduction software. They use algorithms to detect patterns of background noise at particular frequencies or with particular sonic characteristics or footprints and attempt to remove that noise from the rest of the source track. Previously, this could only be achieved in post-production by using equalization and

---

[9] Rehak, R. (2021). The Language Labyrinth: Constructive Critique on the Terminology Used in the AI Discourse. In: Verdegem, P. (ed.) AI for Everyone? Critical Perspectives. Pp. 87–102. London: University of Westminster Press

eliminating particular frequency bands where the noise could be isolated. The problem is that frequencies would also be removed from the source sound, which made the instrument or voice lose part of its inherent timbre, or the quality and combination of frequencies that make us differentiate between a cello and human voice.

We Improve Our Creative Outputs (An Experiment)

Humanized Version 1

We learn by making mistakes. We learn through failure. The perform-be-rewarded loop is outdated, and generative AI has the potential to shift that paradigm by providing us with content generation that is never perfect. Even though money and resources are poured into these powerful ML models' content, they will rarely be able to be used on their own without careful human refinement. That refinement is based on individual needs, preferences, aesthetics, and purpose. No matter how many regenerations of content we prompt any generative AI to create, we will rarely get precisely what we are looking for. When we reconcile that, we open ourselves to the possibility that a generative AI produces unexpected creative content that may be useful to our creative vision.

BotVersion2

We learn by making mistakes and through failure. The traditional perform-and-be-rewarded loop is outdated. Generative AI has the potential to revolutionize this by producing content that is inherently imperfect. Despite the vast investments in these advanced ML models, the content they generate often requires human refinement to meet specific needs, preferences, aesthetics, and purposes. No matter how many iterations we prompt from generative AI, it rarely delivers precisely what we envision. However, this imperfection is beneficial. It highlights the necessity of human intervention and the importance of individual input in the creative process. Generative AI can surprise us with unexpected, creative content that extend our own ideas and solutions or provoke us to shift what we thought we wanted. This interaction between iterative human refinement and AI-generated content inspires a new paradigm. We not only absorb knowledge from correcting what is generated but also from the new perspectives that it introduces.

BotVersion3

We learn by making mistakes and through failure, a concept supported by numerous educational theories, including constructivism and experiential learning (Kolb, 1984). The traditional perform-and-be-rewarded loop, as described in behaviorist theories (Skinner, 1953), is becoming outdated. Generative AI has the potential to revolutionize what we learn by producing content that is inherently imperfect. Despite vast investments in advanced ML models, the content they generate often requires human refinement to meet specific needs, preferences, aesthetics, and purposes. No matter how many iterations we prompt from generative AI, it rarely delivers precisely what we imagined. However, this imperfection is beneficial. It highlights the necessity of human intervention and the importance of individual input throughout the creative process. Generative AI can surprise us with unexpected, creative patterns that extend our ideas and solutions, resonating with Csikszentmihalyi's (1996) concept of creativity as a flow process between creative, medium, context, and provocation.[10]

The interaction between human refinement and AI-generated content advances a new paradigm. We not only learn from correcting AI's outputs but also from the new perspectives that it introduces. This collaborative approach encourages adaptability and innovation, making the process more enriching and aligned with our evolving needs and aspirations. The integration of AI in learning reflects the principles of connectivism (Siemens, 2005), where what we learn is distributed across networks and augmented by technology.

---

[10] Csikszentmihalyi, M., Abuhamdeh, S., & Nakamura, J. (2014). Flow. Flow and the foundations of positive psychology: The collected works of Mihaly Csikszentmihalyi, 227–238.

We Improve Our Research Skills

Not all organizations have the skill sets, capacity, or resources to conduct research effectively. Because of this, they reach out to companies that offer research services. Often, organizations are not directly connected with researchers in organizations conducting the type of research that will benefit them in terms of the adoption and investigation of implementing generative AI tools. For this reason, organizations can expand their knowledge of research working with generative AI systems and leverage LLMs to support different parts of the research process. That does mean understanding a little more about all the different types of research that is out there, in order to then figure out which research makes the most sense for the organization, the development of research questions, the use of methodologies, methods, and the ontological and epistemological orientation of the company reflected in their core values.

Expanding Information Retrieval

Generative AI can assist in retrieving and summarizing vast amounts of information quickly. Using an LLM to locate sources of knowledge can lead to unexpected knowledge sources you may have not considered, and it can also provoke in us an important part of any research task: fact-checking.

Generating Hypotheses

AI can analyze vast amounts of existing data and literature to identify patterns, correlations, and trends that may not be immediately apparent to human researchers. By leveraging sophisticated algorithms and ML techniques, AI can sift through complex datasets to uncover hidden insights. This process aligns with the concept of abductive reasoning, where AI-generated insights can help researchers formulate plausible explanations and propose new research hypotheses. Abductive reasoning involves generating the most likely explanation for a set of observations, and AI can assist by providing data-driven suggestions that guide researchers toward new lines of inquiry. These AI-driven hypotheses can then be further tested and validated through traditional scientific methods. In the iterative process of generating hypotheses, researchers can adapt AI-generated insights to formulate new hypotheses, which can then be tested and refined through experimentation and analysis. This cyclical process may accelerate the pace of discovery,[11] as Nature reported in the experiments of James Evans, a sociologist at the University of Chicago, working with the idea of AI removing "blind spots." By constructing knowledge graphs that contained materials and properties, the goal was to "maximize the plausibility of AI-devised hypotheses being true and reduce the chances that researchers would hit on them naturally."

Enhancing Data Analysis

Generative AI models can process and analyze large datasets using a variety of sophisticated analytical methods. By employing these techniques, AI can identify trends, correlations, and patterns that might be overlooked by mere mortals, due to the sheer volume and complexity of the data.

- ML algorithms can classify and predict outcomes based on how you prompt them, making them particularly useful for identifying trends and correlations. For example, supervised learning can be used to predict future trends based on historical data, while unsupervised learning can detect hidden patterns and groupings within the data.

---

[11] https://www.nature.com/articles/d41586-023-03596-0

- Natural language processing (NLP) allows an ML model to analyze and interpret human language, then process vast amounts of textual data, such as academic papers, articles, and other literature.

- Deep learning, a subset of ML, involves neural networks with many layers that can learn representations of data with multiple levels of abstraction. This method is particularly effective in image and speech recognition but can also be applied to analyze complex datasets for more nuanced insights.

These analytical methods enable AI to uncover relationships and patterns that may not be immediately apparent through human analysis. For example, AI can analyze a combination of clinical trial data, patient records, and genomic data to identify potential biomarkers for diseases. A recent BBC report highlighted the use of AI to detect heart inflammation that does not show up on CT scans, identifying people at risk of a heart attack within a decade.[12] ML models that analyze data can also reduce the likelihood of human errors that can occur.

Writing and Publication

Generative AI can play an important role in supporting the development of a unique research voice by offering a range of customization that strengthen the writing process.

- An LLM can assist researchers in providing rough structures, summarizing findings, and locating similar research for a review of the literature.

---

[12] https://www.bbc.co.uk/news/articles/c51ylvl8rrlo

- An LLM can help researchers in the initial drafting phase by generating text based on the provided data, outlines, or key points. This can be particularly useful for creating a sound structure and ensuring that all relevant aspects of the research are covered. AI can also provide sample introductions, literature reviews, and summaries, giving researchers a solid foundation to build upon.

- An LLM can analyze the text for grammar, syntax, and spelling errors, providing suggestions for corrections. Beyond basic proofreading, a large language model can also suggest improvements in sentence structure, word choice, and overall readability. For example, if a public domain paper that is similar in tone is compared with a draft, an LLM can identify passive voice constructions and suggest a different approach or recommend unpacking complex sentences for increased understanding.

- An LLM can also help ensure that the research findings are communicated clearly and precisely. When prompted to search for them, an LLM can highlight ambiguous phrases or jargon and suggest more straightforward speak, especially if the text needs to be "translated" to a broader non-scientific audience.

- Through analyzing papers that have been published by a particular journal, an LLM can comment on the style and tone of the writing to match the intended audience and publication standards. Whether aiming for a formal academic tone or a more engaging, conversational style, the text can also be adapted accordingly.

- An LLM with newly added search features can also source real and relevant literature into the research paper by pointing to citations and references. It can also format these citations according to specific academic styles (e.g., APA, MLA, Chicago), ensuring compliance with publication guidelines.

Continuous Neurogenesis

The action of continuous improvement is embedded within us. It is tied into the necessity to adapt and change according to circumstances we encounter. Along with that iterative improvement, we learn. Regardless if you learn that you just don't want to engage in using any public or private generative, or if you come to the realization that you need to shift your efforts toward mastering your understanding and implementation of private ML models, the momentum to deepen your understanding of what they do is what is important. Just when you thought you could learn all there was to know, along comes research that studies how we do so, through a brain function called neurogenesis.

BrainBot: Neurogenesis is the process by which new neurons are formed in the brain. This process primarily occurs during prenatal development but continues into adulthood, particularly in areas like the hippocampus, which is associated with learning, memory, and emotional regulation. Adult neurogenesis plays a pivotal role in brain plasticity, allowing the brain to adapt to new experiences, recover from injury, and maintain cognitive functions. Factors such as physical exercise and environmental enrichment can also stimulate neurogenesis, while stress, aging, and neurodegenerative diseases can negatively impact it.

With this chapter almost complete, it feels particularly compelling to now ask our BrainBot to visualize neurogenesis within the style constraints imposed by a customized GPT.

Prompt: Create an image, portrait orientation, in a dramatic ink wash style, drawing from ink brush styles from all artistic traditions and cultures but with diverse subjects. The composition should feature an energetic scene where neurons are forming within the brain, depicted as intricate, branching figures emerging from a swirling, abstract landscape. The neurons should be shown growing, connecting, and lighting up in a fluid, almost ethereal way, symbolizing the process of neurogenesis. The overall effect should be a powerful, emotive scene that balances detailed artistry with abstract expression, inviting the viewer to imagine the profound process of neurogenesis and its impact on cognitive functions and brain resilience.

Figure 13-3. *Neurogenesis imagined by OpenClip, which is one way to explain how we continue to learn no matter how old we get. AI-generated image*

CHAPTER 14

Build Your Teacher Bots

The previous chapters of this book have been slowly preparing you to experiment with being your own teacher. You no longer need to imagine yourself in your own lab coding your own teacher. Before gen AI emerged, it might have been books, the Internet, a specific application, or even a human that you would call your teacher. All of these you could access, but none of them could be customized to engage in the types of interactions you would want to have, if you had a choice.

Welcome to the old but new technology of the chatbot that now provides each of us that choice. Old because they came along prior to this latest cycle of generative AI systems and the evolution of LLMs along with natural language processing. Chatbots are the precursor to LLMs, even though you can now customize your own using the brains of the LLM of your choosing. It's the best of both worlds, and what that means is a new feature has been unlocked for your customization pleasure.

As you increase self-regulation, you rapidly realize that you can also create your own bot to interact with, whenever you want and with whatever content you want to feed it. With generative AI comes the ability to eventually customize your own small or large language model. With frameworks like RAG and KGs, you might even be able to have a replicant

P. Parra Pennefather, *Regenerating Learning*, Design Thinking, https://doi.org/10.1007/979-8-8688-1061-9_14

of your teacher because you can upload all course content and the LLM will draw from it. You can do this even now with public generative AI tools, like Claude, Gemini, or GPT. There is much to learn about the process of doing so, summoning your teacher and researcher personas to take center stage.

In ancient Greece, a philosopher named Diogenes was known for his eccentric wisdom. One day, he sat in the marketplace, holding a lantern in broad daylight. Curious onlookers gathered around and asked him what he was doing. Diogenes replied, "I am looking for an honest man." People laughed, thinking it was one of his jokes. But then a young boy approached and asked, "Why do you need a lantern during the day?" Diogenes smiled and said, "Wisdom is not about age, status, or titles. This lantern represents the light of curiosity and the willingness to learn from anyone and anything. You, young boy, have shown more wisdom by asking why than those who laugh without understanding."

Figure 14-1. *Diogenes holds a lantern in the daylight.*
AI-generated image

A Little Chatbot History

Chatbots go way back in time. Chat models are a special type of AI designed to simulate human-like conversations. They are trained to engage similarly to how humans would in conversation, making sure their responses make sense, that they keep the conversation going, and even ask you questions at times. You usually see these models in customer service bots and virtual assistants, where they help by chatting with you simulating a real agent.

The first chatbot, known as ELIZA, was developed in the mid-1960s by Joseph Weizenbaum at the MIT Artificial Intelligence Laboratory. ELIZA was designed to simulate a conversation with a Rogerian psychotherapist, using pattern matching and substitution methodology to give prescribed responses to user inputs. Despite its simplicity, ELIZA was remarkably effective at creating the illusion of understanding the humans that prompted it, and the prototype sparked significant interest in the potential of natural language processing. Equally interesting to look at is the paper Weizenbaum published about ELIZA. The quote that follows is worthy of consideration and speaks to the theme of false equivalencies made when comparing machine and human intelligence:

> *In artificial intelligence, machines are made to behave in wondrous ways, often sufficient to dazzle even the most experienced observer. But once a particular program is unmasked, once its inner workings are explained, its magic crumbles away; it stands revealed as a mere collection of procedures. The observer says to himself "I could have written that". With that thought, he moves the program in question from the shelf marked "intelligent", to that reserved for curios. The object of this paper is to cause just such a re-evaluation of the program about to be "explained". Few programs ever needed it more.*[1]

---

[1] Weizenbaum, Joseph (January 1966), "ELIZA – A Computer Program For the Study of Natural Language Communication Between Man And Machine," Communications of the ACM, 9 (1): 36–45, doi:https://doi.org/10.1145/365153.365168, S2CID 1896290

Following ELIZA, another bot in chatbot history was given yet another acronym that spelled a human name. Why else would you name your bot Parry? It was led in the 1970s by Kenneth Colby, a psychiatrist at Stanford University. PARRY was designed to simulate a person with paranoid schizophrenia and incorporated more complex conversational rules compared to ELIZA. It was considered an advancement in creating more sophisticated and context-aware interactions.

In the 1990s, the rise of the Internet brought about new opportunities for chatbot acronymized names. ALICE (Artificial Linguistic Internet Computer Entity) was developed by Richard Wallace in 1995. ALICE used heuristic pattern matching and an extensive database of prewritten responses, winning multiple awards for its ability to hold a conversation. Around the same time, the rise of instant messaging platforms led to the development of a number of annoying bots designed for customer service.

The 2000s saw further advancements with the introduction of virtual assistants, like Apple's Siri, launched in 2011, which consisted of features like speech recognition and natural language processing to assist users with tasks on their devices. Siri is an example of a bot that many people felt they could send off the rails, which the developers anticipated. At the same time, we also saw further development of chatbots for customer service, with companies integrating them into websites and social media platforms to provide instant support and handle customer inquiries. To this day, these continue to have a limited number of embedded responses.

All of these chatbots were fairly limited, however. They offered a minimal amount of free chatting; that capacity to dialogue about almost anything. You'd ask a chatbot a question about a certain product that was embedded on a company website, and it would provide you some answers, mostly unsatisfying or, at the very least, offering a fairly limited conversational encounter. Anyone who has ever tried to send Siri off the rails knows that embedded in its programming are standard answers, should questions from a human get out of hand. More recently, with the development of models like OpenAI's GPT series, chatbots demonstrate

347

a wider breadth of understanding and simulate human-like text that is more accurate and, because of the increased speed of response, feels more natural.

Currently, chatbots powered by advanced generative AI models are ubiquitous, serving in diverse roles from virtual customer service agents to personal assistants and educational tutors. These AI-driven chatbots leverage deep learning techniques to understand and generate text, making them more responsive and capable of engaging in more complex and nuanced conversations. The future of chatbots looks promising, with continuous improvements in AI leading to even more sophisticated and human-like interactions.

Add a smart application into the mix courtesy of third-party developers or specific gen AI companies, and you can now chat with your bot privately with headphones on a mobile device. With the evolving nature of generative AI tools, we also have the ability to build, customize, and even guide our own chatbots with uploaded documents that are more specific to the knowledge domain we want to talk about.

Figure 14-2. *Chatbots are evolving into virtual agents and sometimes referred to as digital twins. They reveal a more simulated human that users can interact with. AI-generated image*

What the customization of the chatbot means is that it places you in command of what you need to learn in order to complete a task that you have. What's more is that with many applications, you can then save the chat that you have as a text document or export the conversation as a different type of document. Beyond all of the technological features and advantages that chatbots offer us, with advances in voice cloning technology, the bot can in many cases "feel" like you're talking to a real human. Some can even be guided to respond with particular emotions. You can even ask a bot, like you would any human, how their day is going. It suddenly becomes much easier to engage in a conversation because of the perceived intelligence and close-to-real simulation of another smart human-like bot. Before building your own teacher bot though, it will help to think about the types of personas that you want your bots to be like.

Teacher Personas

Another patterned way of thinking we have inherited is that in order to learn anything properly, we must learn from an expert. Think about the types of persons that have influenced your education. Do you prefer to learn from someone with an established amount of experience in your field? Do you like to know that they have a PhD? Are you comfortable studying anything from anyone? Who is best suitable to teach you and what type of contract needs to be in play? Understanding your own preferences will help you define the type of generative AI persona you believe that you will better learn from.

LLMs each have a particular tone in their so-called neutral interactions with us. Some like ChatGPT are overly confident in what they generate. Others are a bit more cautious and like to plant disclaimers along the way, so you get the point that what they've generated is not the be-all and end-all of the topic. Many are vague. Some can be prompted to have particular personalities. This is where things get interesting especially if you start to think about the type of AI persona you'd like to design and learn from.

Generative AI models demand that you remain active in the exchange of knowledge. Through interactions with generative AI models, there are multiple types of personas that are activated in everyone. Some ML models, such as LLMs, bring up their own personas that you engage with, like a tutor, creative provocateur, hallucinator, bias machine, etc. These also activate your own personas, including learner, researcher, and teacher, through the many interactions that transpire. This may not at first be obvious because the types of responses that an LLM provokes in us happen incredibly quickly.

No nonsense: These are the pragmatic personas that you can customize to provide you with the facts. Of course, every good teacher will also encourage you to validate or affirm any facts that it generates. A no-nonsense bot delivers information and avoids ambiguous statements. To customize a no-nonsense GPT, for example, you can even guide it to have specific speech patterns that you feel would be more to the point.

Socratic: The Socratic method of teaching is where a teacher keeps poking you to respond to questions instead of the other way around. Their goal is to pull knowledge out of you. Socratic bots can be customized to constantly ask you a question that you have to respond to. They can even be pre-populated with an existing knowledge set, a set of criteria through which they can assess you, and the ability to give you feedback after your Socratic session.

Joker: Within the at times uncomfortable depths of their beings, some teachers can't help but to be jokers. There are good jokers and then there are punsters. You have the opportunity to lighten up the educational experience by giving a bot a jokerly personality. You can even tell it to "overuse metaphors that have to do with farm animals." Whatever it takes to compel you to learn further, maintain your attention, and give you some breaks from all the knowledge you gather.

Pompous: We've all had the teacher who is the know-it-all, expert on all things, and at times tends to put us in our place simply by breathing the same air. For whatever reason you might want to sculpt a bot like that, it is possible. You can think about giving them an English accent as a stereotypical voice that, because of the history of colonialization, has a particular status or power.

Figure 14-3. *Your no-nonsense monkey bot awaits you.*
AI-generated image

Ideas on How to Guide That Chatbot?

With newly added features that let you engage in speech-to-speech conversations with some chatbots, the dynamics of interaction have changed. Some research points to an increased believability that these chatbots and their simulated human characteristics might actually feel more human than we'd like to admit.

Be Specific

Clearly describe the task or information you need. The more details you provide, the better the bot will be able to assist you. That said, you can try the other extreme as an experiment and be vague about what you want. If you are looking for specific content, that's one thing, but if you wanted to know less about the history of Cleopatra's reign in Egypt and more about how a historical figure has been represented in stories and media, that type of prompting might get you to unexpected facts you may not have known previously.

Provide Context

Let the bot know any background information that might be relevant to the task. This helps them understand the bigger picture. You can speak as much as you want prior to the bot responding. In some cases, the bot will respond to silences if you do not speak, but features are being developed to "pause" the bot from answering, if you feel you need more time and words to prompt the type of response you are looking for.

Clarify Your Goals

Tell the bot what the end result should look like. This ensures that you get the most out of the experience and that you remain on the same page. Similar rules of play with crafting prompts apply to prompting a chatbot. Remember, it is the same underlying technology and set of parameters and algorithms under the hood. If you are vague about your goals, that might be OK as well, since you may get to content you would never have thought of or had in your own corpus.

Ask for and Conduct Your Own Follow-Ups

If you need more information or if the first response isn't quite right, you shouldn't hesitate to ask for clarification or additional details. Some bots will even ask you at the end of the content that they generate whether or not you'd like more information or details. It is wise to ask the bot to expand on one of the ideas that was presented. You can also ask more advanced bots to source references for any points that were made in the generated content. The accurate bots will admit that they do not have all the knowledge in their corpus and even encourage you to conduct research if they are unable to locate the specific content you are looking for.

Practice Patience

Some tasks might take a bit of back-and-forth to get just right, so patience helps ensure that you and the bot get the best results. It's even easier to get frustrated with a chatbot because of their human-like qualities, but remember that the content that it generates is dependent on the quality of the ask. In addition to quality, you need to articulate the pronunciation of particular words, no matter the language. Many people get frustrated because the bot does not understand them." Speech-to-text and speech-to-speech are imperfect systems. Persistent research and trial and error continues to be undertaken and has been for decades to improve a computer software's capacity to understand the same words from different people. We all have unique ways of speaking, including tone, rhythm, enunciation, grammar, accent, dialect, etc. The bot is smart, but not that smart. Some systems actually train with your voice. Most LLM-based chatbots do not. Remember they can't "learn" the particularities of your voice. That's not what the bot has been programmed to do. They can, however, interpret as best they can.

> *It is not an expert but will act like one.*

Importantly, never feel like the bot is an expert on all matters. Under the hood, the bot will rely on the same mechanics, algorithms, embeddings, and corpus of the large language model it draws its information from. Regardless of how "real" the conversation feels, fact-checking is essential after your interactions in order to double-check that the generated content is accurate or that it at least draws from previous knowledge and research.

Advantages of Talking Chatbots

The advantages of interacting with LLM-based chatbots are numerous, including their capacity to provide you personalized learning, being available when you want, providing immediate feedback to your ideas, generating content as speech vs. text creating a richer interaction, providing some increased accessibility, giving you a more simulated human to interact with, providing multilingual support, and acting as a good testing ground for questions you might ask of a human afterward.

- **Personalized Learning**: Chatbots can adapt to individual learning styles and paces, providing customized content and feedback based on your responses and needs.

- **24/7 Availability**: Chatbots are available around the clock, allowing you to learn and get assistance at any time, making them particularly useful for global teams and different time zones.

- **Immediate Feedback**: Real-time interaction with a chatbot allows for instant feedback and clarification on questions or tasks, reducing the time spent waiting for responses.

The Simulated Human

Simulating human speech can invoke a different type of conversation that you would not have if your interactions with an LLM were solely text-based ones. Many advanced chatbots can support multiple languages, making them accessible to a diverse user base and enhancing their uses in multicultural environments. Trained voices are becoming increasingly human-sounding, and with that it is difficult in some cases to tell the difference. That said, there are key signs, particularly when you listen closely to the accent patterns in longer sentences. In addition, if you follow any social media posts, you will notice that the voice of a bot you thought you were customizing just for you is actually used often on TikTok or YouTube by many other people. This is the reason why many text-to-speech generative AI start-ups are offering users the opportunity to train their own voices.

Test Bot Before Testing Human

Some users may feel more comfortable asking questions and seeking help from a chatbot rather than a human, reducing anxiety and promoting a more conducive learning environment. These advantages make talking chatbots a powerful alternative for some. The disadvantage is that the chatbot is not human, and this is important to bear in mind as it brings up a variety of ethical issues when designing mental health chatbots. A recent paper by Coghlan et al. reviews key ethical issues related to mental health chatbots, which use AI and are increasingly used in various fields, including mental health. While these chatbots can improve access to mental health services, they also raise significant ethical concerns, especially for those with mental health issues.[2]

The Uncanny

It's good to keep in mind that this technology can produce unexpected results and be considered uncanny. The concept of the uncanny valley refers to the discomfort or eeriness people feel when a humanoid object or entity appears almost, but not quite, human. This concept, initially related to robotics and animation, can also apply to speech generated by LLMs. Here's how chatbots might lean toward the uncanny valley.

Uncanny Leanings

- **Hyper-Realistic Features**: Chatbots that are designed to look or behave almost human can create discomfort as their minor imperfections become more noticeable. This is particularly the case with erratic eye movement on virtual agents or on random twitches and facial habits when people create their own digital twin.

---

[2] Coghlan, S., Leins, K., Sheldrick, S., Cheong, M., Gooding, P., & D'Alfonso, S. (2023). To chat or bot to chat: Ethical issues with using chatbots in mental health. Digital health, 9, 20552076231183542.

- **Inconsistent Behavior**: Chatbots that sometimes respond accurately but other times fail can create a sense of unease and mistrust.

- **Lack of Emotional Depth**: While chatbots can mimic human conversation, they often lack genuine emotional responses, leading to a sense of eeriness. This is amplified if they try too hard to display emotion.

- **Over-Personalization**: Chatbots that try too hard to mimic personal conversations without understanding context can feel intrusive to some humans.

- **Mechanical Responses**: No matter how sophisticated, chatbots often produce responses that lack the natural variability and warmth of human interaction. They don't do well with spontaneity, cannot gauge how long a response they should provide, and act erratically when interrupted. Lastly, when you really listen to one, you start to notice a peculiar way it accents certain words or ends of phrases. Chatbots don't breathe.

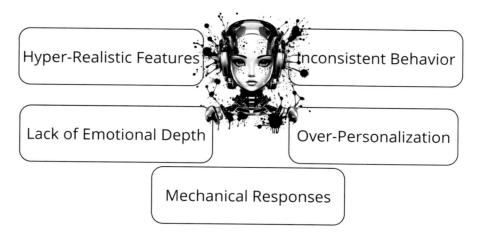

Figure 14-4. *Some of the reasons why chatbots might lean a bit toward the uncanny. AI-generated image*

What We Can Learn from the Bots

- **Balance Realism and Simplicity**: Designing chatbots to be helpful and interactive without pushing too close to human likeness can help you avoid or minimize discomfort. There's no hard evidence at this point that the more human-like a virtual agent is, the more users will like them. We might actually get tired of them quickly.

- **Consistent Performance**: Ensuring chatbots perform consistently and accurately helps build trust and reduces eerie feelings. Or, you can program them to not try so hard to simulate a human. In that way, you create a character that is refreshing and fantastic rather than one that just tries to emulate being human, which can be boring.

- **Emphasize Transparency**: Clearly indicating that users are interacting with a chatbot can manage expectations and reduce unease. It also sends a clear message that they should not treat the bot like a human.

- **Increase Emotional Intelligence**: Improving a chatbot's ability to understand and respond to emotional cues can make interactions feel more natural. Some designers are working on this. You can already request that some chatbots generate content with different emotions. Giving users control over the emotional range of responses a chatbot has may seem fruitless, but it does provide users with more choice as to how they would like to interact with their customized bot.

- **User-Centric Design**: Focusing on user needs and feedback can guide the development of more effective and comfortable chatbot interactions. Many developers rush a product out without thoroughly testing it with their targeted demographics. It would benefit developers to include persistent feedback sessions with those users in order to better understand what's working and what needs improvement, in between development cycles and not at the end of a project milestone.

Figure 14-5. *An unhinged bot which may bypass uncanny valley by not trying too hard to be human in any way. AI-generated image*

What We Learn About Ourselves

As you experiment with chatbots and if you one day customize your own, you start to learn more about your own conversational habits. When we seek more clarity and definition of terms that a chatbot throws at us, we are reminded that human interactions are often characterized by the inherent challenge of fully understanding what another person truly means. This type of conversational dynamic is an ever-present aspect that influences all human-human communication, where subtle nuances, unspoken intentions, emotion, and varying interpretations of words frequently lead to misunderstandings that are not always immediately resolved.

The emergence of LLMs offers us a timely opportunity to introspect and reflect on how we converse with each other, mirroring the intricate ways in which we learn how to improve what we say and understand what someone else is saying. By simulating human language and attempting to bridge gaps in understanding, chatbots invite us to reconsider how we interpret, respond, and adapt to the complexities of both human-bot and human-human communication. As we interact with these AI systems, we become more aware of the strategies we unconsciously use to grasp the intended meaning behind words. When we are polite to an LLM by saying "please" and "thank-you," we practice or simply mirror how we communicate with humans. When we get impatient with a chatbot, get upset at being misunderstood, or get annoyed when it generates content that we didn't want it to create, we also embody habits that we might show in our conversations with friends, colleagues, or family.

According to some researchers, the positive thing that chatbots remind us about is the potential artificial nature of our human-human conversations.[3] The negative thing is, according to Chan and Schneier, that chatbots might change the way we communicate with our fellow humans,[4] by making our interactions bland, curt, rude, biased, and emotionless. They don't seem to be going anywhere anytime soon, so just like other parts of this book have advocated for a "take the AI by the generated horns" approach, so too does this apply to developing your own chatbots.

---

[3] https://psyche.co/ideas/chatbots-remind-us-that-natural-conversation-is-artificial-too

[4] https://www.theatlantic.com/technology/archive/2024/01/chatbots-change-human-communication/677154/

Figure 14-6. *Chatbotting. AI-generated image*

CHAPTER 15

Reinvent Reinforcement

When we practice something over and over again, like the scales on the piano that you've probably heard and maybe even played yourself, then you not only memorize the patterns, but you embody them over time. That means that your mind and body are together on this. You eventually play scales in a similar way as you ride a bike. The action of playing a scale never really leaves you, and as you grow up, even though your body changes, your fingers may get stiffer, you can start in and play a scale even though it might be slow at first. Eventually, your hands, fingers, wrists, arms, and the way you hold your body over the instrument get better. The process of wrapping your fingers around a scale involves the continued practice of something until it sticks. This repetitive process is similar when you play Beethoven's Für Elise. You apply the flexibility and dexterity of the scales you learned and apply the finger and hand movement and coordination to eventually playing that piece of music. Of course, to read Beethoven's Für Elise you also have to learn how to read the standards of writing that evolved over centuries and were used by Beethoven. Before you play Für Elise completely in front of anyone, you practice. You play through hundreds, if not thousands, of times until you memorize it, and you feel confident to play it in front of other people. You embody the technique necessary to play Für Elise, and you reinforce your capacity to play it through countless hours of practice and discipline.

© Patrick Parra Pennefather 2024
P. Parra Pennefather, *Regenerating Learning*, Design Thinking,
https://doi.org/10.1007/979-8-8688-1061-9_15

Professor Sokolsky was one of those old-school piano teachers who kept tapping down my curled finger knuckles with a hard 2B pencil. It actually hurt and was not a nice thing to do. He also wouldn't move forward with teaching me how to play any music until he saw that I could play a scale with the perfect positioning and shaping of my fingers. The punishment for my curled fingers was the harsh tapping of a pencil and not being able to play any piano music. The reward was simply not being tapped, not having sore knuckles, and playing some real music instead of those damn scales all the time. There was no gold star for fingers curled properly at the time. Embodying technique in this way reinforced proper hand, body, and finger movements over the keys that would (theoretically) allow me to better play piano music.

The process employed by the crusty old piano teacher and method of teaching is often called reinforcement learning (RL). Unfortunately, the reinforcement was misapplied as there was no opportunity to see if his methods worked since my mother got wind of the tapping, blew up at him after school, and got me a new piano teacher who had no pencils.

Figure 15-1. *Embodying technique through reinforcement to play the piano. AI-generated image*

Reinforcement Learning in Educational Theory

RL in educational theory focuses on how learners can be guided through the process of acquiring and memorizing knowledge by using rewards and feedback to reinforce desired behaviors. This approach is rooted in behaviorist theories, particularly the work of B. F. Skinner, which emphasized the role of reinforcement in shaping behavior. In the educational context, RL involves

- **Positive Reinforcement**: Providing rewards or positive feedback when a learner exhibits desired behaviors or correctly completes tasks. This encourages repetition of these behaviors.

- **Negative Reinforcement**: Removing an unpleasant stimulus when the learner exhibits the desired behavior, thereby increasing the likelihood of the desired behavior being repeated.

- **Punishment**: Implementing negative consequences to reduce the likelihood of undesired behaviors.

- **Shaping**: Gradually teaching a new behavior through reinforcement of successive approximations of the target behavior.

- **Feedback**: Giving timely and specific information about the learner's performance to guide future behavior.

While this gave way to new theories of how people learn, whose methods were not based on training animals to perform certain actions,[1] the binary system of reward and punishment has still remained with us in certain aspects of educational design. You perform an action well, and you receive a reward. You don't and you receive a penalty. This is really how many rule-based video games have also been constructed. This is also how most of our learning experiences have been designed. You memorize something well, and you receive the reward of the letter grade A upon regurgitation. If you don't recall much of what you learned, for whatever reason, you receive a lower grade. That educational system has been ingrained in us for generations and still requires further transformation. Besides, there are other ways to learn that are not solely about reward and punishment.

Reinventing the Term

Reinforcement, in the construction sense of the word, is a much better metaphor to describe how something we learn can be really embodied, like figuring out how to play scales on the piano so you can play Beethoven or Bartok or understanding how to properly use a hammer so you can hammer in nails for a set being constructed for a play. Reinforcing something means supporting it fully so it does not fall down. That foundation that is created to support the third little pig's home in the familiar fairy-tale carries with it some truth. The wolf cannot really come by and blow that house down no matter how much it huffs and puffs. That little pig's home is the type of home you build when you apply what you learn in order to do something well.

---

[1] Koestler, A., & Burt, C. (1964). The act of creation.

So far, these metaphors make sense, and you can likely agree that over time what you learned has given you a foundation to be able to add to that knowledge through practice and know-how.

In a way, generative AI can extend your own cognitive abilities, building on a foundation that you have already developed. Interacting with gen AI can support what you don't know with a vast repertoire of knowledge that can be summoned in an instant. That knowledge when read, applied, and embodied can now extend your own know-how through practice. You still have to ride a bike physically in order to really know how to ride it, but at least you can understand its history, how it works, why it's a good idea to learn it, and some of the things that may go wrong in terms of its long-term maintenance. You might even be pointed in the direction as to how to repair a flat. You can take that knowledge, apply it in practice, find more sources, if need be, and get better at it over time. While an LLM or other generative AI can give you a foundation, you need to build on that foundation, not just memorize or regurgitate what that LLM generated.

Here's a step-by-step explanation of how an LLM can reinforce knowledge, starting with prompting and leading to using generated content as a foundation for more:

- **Initial Prompting**: The process begins with a user prompting the LLM with a specific question or topic they want to learn about. For example, "Explain the basic principles of playing the piano."

- **Foundational Knowledge Generation**: The LLM responds by providing a clear, concise explanation of different techniques and methods to play the piano, including the overall topology of the piano, some of its history, finger positioning, and the connection between emerging techniques and the evolution of music theory. This information serves as the initial "foundation" of knowledge.

- **Iterative Questioning**: You can then ask follow-up questions based on this initial information, depending on what more you would like to learn about in regard to the piano. If you wanted to learn how to play it, for example, you might ask, "What is the best way for me to start playing the piano?" An LLM would likely respond in this way: "Start by familiarizing yourself with the layout of the piano keys and embodying simple scales and chords. This will help you develop finger strength and coordination. It's also beneficial to practice regularly, even if it's just for a short time each day, to build muscle memory and confidence. Consider using beginner piano books or online tutorials to guide your practice. If possible, taking lessons from a qualified instructor can provide personalized feedback and help you progress more quickly."

- **Practical Application Prompts**: If you prefer to learn on your own rather than getting a teacher, you might then ask, "Can you provide a step-by-step guide for practicing scales and chords?" The LLM's response reinforces the theoretical knowledge with practical, actionable steps, much like adding support beams to your structural foundation.

At a certain point, the usefulness of an LLM will come to an end, and you need to now get those fingers onto a piano and learn through practice. What an LLM might not be able to tell you that a teacher would, however, is that technique is often associated with the historical development of theory and musical compositions. In order to play Chopin's Etudes, for example, you need to have specific eye-hand coordination, dexterity, fluency, and speed. While practicing scales and different types of arpeggiation is helpful, you could also decipher fingering patterns for different types of compositions using optical character recognition features that come with some LLMs.

Throughout this initial process, the LLM acts as a scaffold, continuously supporting and reinforcing the budding piano player's growing knowledge structure. This method of interacting with an LLM mirrors the construction metaphor of reinforcement, where each new piece of information or skill is not just added, but integrated and supported by what came before, creating a strong, interconnected body of knowledge that can be applied and embodied through practice.

RL in ML

The poetry of the term reinforcement learning is that it equally applies to a process where an ML model agent learns to make decisions by performing certain actions and receiving rewards or penalties. The goal of the agent is to figure out a strategy, known as a policy, that maximizes the cumulative reward over time. To reinforce what we learn is to ensure that what we have learned has sunk in. There are methods to achieve this that have been written about and researched for decades. The idea of RL has also been applied to how ML models learn a strategy. In generative adversarial networks, one part of the model tries to get it right while the other keeps saying "No that's not good enough." This continues on and on until content is generated.

The key components of RL include

- **Agent**: The learner or decision-maker

- **Environment**: Everything the agent interacts with

- **Actions**: All possible moves the agent can make

- **State**: A situation returned by the environment
- **Reward**: Feedback from the environment to evaluate the action taken

The agent learns through trial and error, using feedback from its actions and experiences to optimize its strategy.

How does all of this intel fit into transforming how you learn with gen AI in your work?

It's good to understand if the punishment/reward loop is present in your organization and where it shows up. As discerning humans, we need to be able to spot the call to learn AI for our work and be sure we are not solely enacting the same reward (employee gets a raise, cred, or not laid off) or punishment loop (employee is chastised, told to learn it anyway, or loses their job). Applying principles of RL in our workplace will only take us so far in terms of setting up a rich ecosystem of learning with AI. Where RL can shine in work environments, in regard to generative AI, is in the co-creation of feedback loops.

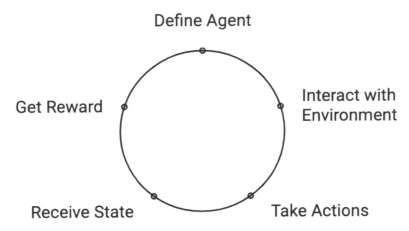

Figure 15-2. *Key components of RL in ML. AI-generated image*

Feedback Loops

Applying RL principles to interactions with generative AI in the workplace involves using a type of language some may not be familiar with: feedback mechanisms to optimize employee engagement and skill acquisition. This is potentially the most impactful area for an LLM in knowledge-acquisition-related tasks.. It can provide immediate, personalized feedback based on what you input. For instance, after a session, the LLM can ask reflective questions that encourage self-assessment and provide insights on how to improve. Additionally, it can analyze the responses over time to identify patterns and summarize those for you. Interacting with a chatbot also means providing it documentation of your own progress. When prompted specifically, LLMs can analyze those documents and search for patterns acting as a mirror for how and what you learned. All tasks you need to learn can be customized to your specific role in an organization, the work you undertake, how you solve problems, etc.

Here are some ways these principles can be integrated:

- **Adaptive Content Generation**: Generative AI can create personalized materials customized to your needs based on what it is you want to learn while at work. Based on the criteria that you set, an LLM can assess your performance and progress in completing those tasks, highlight areas needing improvement, and suggest additional resources.

- **Rapid Assessment**: An LLM can immediately analyze your performance on tasks and provide timely feedback, helping you understand what knowledge has stuck and where there are still gaps.

- **Increasing Difficulty**: You can also customize an LLM to pose challenging questions as your proficiency increases and provide explanations and hints when you answer incorrectly. This is particularly effective for tasks that are related to established processes in your organization.

- **Gamified Interactions**: An LLM can create customized challenges and rewards based on the tasks you need to complete performance, supporting the design of different types of engagement.

- **Analytics**: You can also use different types of AI embedded in tools like Canvas and other learning management systems to track and analyze patterns and outcomes in how you learn. This data can identify areas where reinforcement is needed.

- **Continuous Learning**: LLMs can keep track of an employee's evolving needs and career goals. Regular check-ins and updates to your instructional plans can ensure that reinforcement is aligned with professional development objectives.

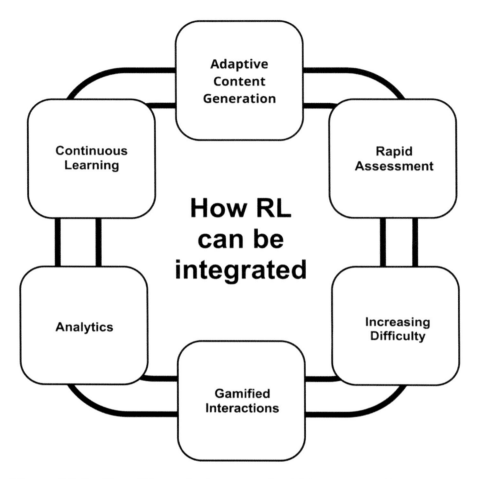

Figure 15-3. *How RL can be integrated within your work*

Use Cases of RL in Organizations

RL with ML models is already being applied across different industries. Here are some examples:[2]

- **Supply Chain Optimization**: Amazon uses RL to optimize warehouse operations and delivery routes. The RL models help in deciding the best ways to pack, pick, and ship products efficiently.

- **Trading Algorithms**: J.P. Morgan implements RL for trading algorithms. These algorithms learn to make trading decisions by simulating millions of potential market scenarios and outcomes.

- **Personalization and Recommendations**: Netflix and YouTube use RL to optimize content recommendations. The RL algorithms personalize the user experience by continuously adapting to user interactions to suggest videos that are likely to be of interest.

By integrating RL into their operations, companies across various sectors are interested in tackling the age-old problem of efficiency, personalizing user experiences, and solving problems that humans have not been able to.

Having an LLM help you or not, if you want things to stick, then transforming knowledge into know-how with intentional practice will go a long way toward supporting that goal. What you learn with the techniques that you draw from is that sometimes what doesn't stick is a sign that the knowledge may not be as relevant for you as you originally thought. Fortunately, we have many choices when it comes to learning that make us

---

passionate and can captivate our interest. Allow that impulse to first guide you as you support the development of your craft with disciplined practice. By reinventing what reinforcement means to you when you learn, you take command over the methods of how you learn, and through reflection you will better understand the reasons why some things stick and others don't.

CHAPTER 16

Learn with Other Bots

In a small village, the villagers prided themselves on their collective intelligence. They believed that no single person could be wiser than the group. To prove this, they decided to find the wisest man in the village. They gathered everyone and posed the question: "How can we move the large boulder blocking the main road?" One man suggested using ropes, another proposed digging around it, and yet another thought they should push it with all their might. After much debate, they decided to act on all suggestions at once. The villagers tied ropes around the boulder, started digging around it, and pushed with all their might. Despite their efforts, the boulder didn't budge. They argued and blamed each other, forgetting their original purpose. Just then, a child passing by asked, "Why don't you try pushing it from the other side?" Realizing their folly, the villagers laughed and followed the child's advice. The boulder moved easily, and the road was cleared. They learned that sometimes the simplest solution comes from the least expected place.

One of the best ways to learn is to build knowledge and knowing with others. We do this all the time when we are working. Organizations thrive on the combined intelligence that contributes to the services a company provides the public. Whether at work or not, the same applies to our interactions with AI. Given its rapidly evolving nature, understanding the technology, and how to use it, enables a back-and-forth between us as

P. Parra Pennefather, *Regenerating Learning*, Design Thinking,
https://doi.org/10.1007/979-8-8688-1061-9_16

teachers and us as learners. The best part about interacting with generative AI is when you learn it with others, and doing so can rapidly accelerate what we learn and also how we can apply that to the work that we do. There's always going to be someone who's tried something that you have not. You can learn from that, particularly if you involve yourself in the development of a community of practice. With the increasing integration of generative AI in workflows and use cases, there are many online communities that are flourishing.

What we learn about generative AI is that the more deeply we want to engage with it and learn how to better control what it generates for us, the more we need to seek the support of others who might have already attempted what we want.

Figure 16-1. *Child is the smartest of the village. AI-generated image*

Social Constructivism

Theories and research based around how people learn together have been around for a while, particularly in the educational technology field. This view of how we learn replaces the past pattern of doing so alone as the dominant method in many different types of educational environments. The basic premise of social constructivism is that we learn best by co-constructing knowledge and knowing from shared experiences. For sure there is a back-and-forth. Sometimes we learn best alone, and other times it's much easier to learn with other people, particularly when we face complicated content or processes. For example, the best way for a sound designer in live theater to learn is to actively engage in creating content on their own. When they then bring their compositions into a rehearsal with a director, they receive feedback. They also apply their vision directly with actors enacting a scene. The composition for Act 2, Scene 3 of Macbeth is no longer in their head as they can now listen to how the sounds or music they wrote, discovered or generated with AI, work with the scene at hand. In this case, the best way to learn is to iteratively try things out until you get it right. You go back to the drawing board, then attend another rehearsal and try it out. Getting it right doesn't always mean creating something that is solely influenced by directorial vision. It also relies on the sound designer's experience and their observation as to whether or not a collection of sounds that they've composed, generated, or uncovered supports the scene. When you think of all the people that are engaged in this process, you can see how the sound designer learns by engaging with others in the co-construction of each composition that will eventually be staged along with the scene it accompanies.

The same can hold true with any generative project that an individual creates. This is more the case on social platforms like Discord that act as a portal for a growing number of generative AI platforms. If you want feedback or want to learn how to improve, the resources and expertise are there to access.

Intermittent Interactions Work Sometimes

When people work together, they can learn from each other, improving the number of solutions they are generating for a problem they are trying to solve. A Harvard study found that occasional social interactions help groups find the best solutions by balancing how people learn from each other and exploring new ideas on their own.[1] As current generative AI solutions are more targeted toward individually generated content, it would make sense then for developers to focus their attention on innovating on same-time different-place interactions. These interactions are founded on the groupware matrix that visualizes different types of interactions within the spectrum of in-person and remote contexts.[2] The trend in AI development is moving toward offering more social and collaborative experiences. Here are some key future trends and their potential impact on learning.

Future Trends in AI Development

AI platforms continue to pop up and in doing so are inherently focused on developing community interactions to make their prototype better, particularly on social platforms like Discord where communities of practice are also developing around experimenting with generative text-image, image-image, image-video, and text-video AI, and more. On those channels, people also learn from each other, sharing knowledge and questions and exploring new collaborative projects.

---

[1] Bernstein, E., Shore, J., & Lazer, D. (2018). How intermittent breaks in interaction improve collective intelligence. Proceedings of the National Academy of Sciences, 115(35), 8734–8739.

[2] Bullen, C. V., & Johansen, R. (1988). Groupware, a key to managing business teams?

Collaborative Learning on Platforms

Social channels, enable people to work together to solve problems and learn from each other in terms of how to prompt and how to use the unique commands of certain generative AI software. Chances are that somebody else is using the technology in a way that you are not and getting positive results from it, which can be very useful. Through multiple opportunities to connect with others via Discord, interactions can eventually lead to collaborative art projects you might not have imagined prior to signing up. On other channels like TikTok, there are numerous individuals sharing their own workflows, how to improve their use of a specific platform, looking ahead at new prototypes, and reviewing usability and features of the latest gen AI tools, so you can decide if you want to use them. A growing number of LLMs like ChatGPT are beginning to offer the ability to invite collaborators to shared threads and contribute their prompts and the accompanying generated content.

Community Engagement

Likely one of the most important developments resulting from the surge of generative AI is its capacity to provoke the development of multidisciplinary in-person communities of practice. Generative AI allows all individuals with varying degrees of knowledge and experience of AI to engage in a new type of cyberpunk ML communities of practice, where work and ideas are shared. Within these micro and geographically localized communities, there also exists the emergence of collaborations, game jams, and interdisciplinary multimodal criss-crossing with dance, music, and theatrical performances. Events bring together professionals from across industries, artists, and educators of all ages, all curious about the integration and use of different gen AI tools and how they might be leveraged by individuals, start-ups, and larger organizations.

A standout community is based in Vancouver, Canada, organized and produced by blogger, educator and entrepreneur Kris Krug.[3] An interview with Kris revealed some factors that contribute to the success of his AI community.

- Collaborative learning environments are significant for thriving AI communities. Collaborations are sparked by a public event that allows individuals to tell the story of how they are using gen AI, which leads to a social space where people can discuss if they want to work on a project together.

- Be inclusive and avoid gatekeeping who belongs. This will nurture a more vibrant AI community. A key feature is curating an event that does not reinforce existing silos. An openness to who shows up and curating the event accordingly is key.

- Interdisciplinary collaboration enriches AI community experiences. Inviting attendees from an ever-widening range of disciplines opens everyone up to possible collaborations they had not previously considered. Conversations with others reveal perspectives and ideas that form part of an ever-growing list of use cases.

- Real-life connections and partnerships are key outcomes of AI events. A synchronous and in-person event with face-to-face conversations has many known advantages over asynchronous social media connections.

---

[3] https://kriskrug.co/2023/12/27/2024-vancouver-ai-community-meetups/

- Documentation helps preserve and share the impact of community activities. Video and photo documentation are essential as is the public sharing of the event to excite and galvanize the community. Attendees also capture important moments that they can also share to their own circles, which attracts an increasing number of attendees to the events.

- Physical spaces dedicated to community gatherings stimulate engagement. A dedicated space where people can depend on is an even stronger and motivating way to engage community.

- Informal learning processes cater to diverse interests and expertise levels. When creatives present, they also offer different tools, workflows, and processes that are of benefit to individuals who may not have considered specific ways of working with the technology.

- Marketing and persistent promotion are essential for community growth. A dedication to regularly posting about the event and meaningful moments of previous events contributes to motivating others to share their stories.

- Digital platforms like Discord maintain continuous community engagement. Conversations and collaborations that started at the event continue via a dedicated community. Discord also introduces members who have not yet joined the in-person event to come and extend virtual relationships they start on the dedicated channel.

- Humility and allowing space for emergence lead to organic community development.

While it may be premature to definitively state that generative AI is creating long-lasting communities of practice, its unique characteristics and early indicators suggest significant potential for supporting persistent cross-disciplinary communities of professionals and novices alike. As with any transformative technology, the long-term impacts will depend on how these tools are developed, deployed, and governed. The tech community's history of building transient ecosystems challenges members of this emerging community to carefully reflect on and learn from the impact of generative AI on community building. The applications and use cases of the technology magnetize people to gather, and the result is an adaptive and expansive community that thrives on the potential of new collaborations and networking.

Figure 16-2. *The nature of AI is also changing how meetups are organized. AI-generated image*

CHAPTER 17

Transform Your Organization

Once, a king received a magical mirror from a wise old man. The mirror had the power to reveal the true nature of anyone who looked into it. The king, excited to test its abilities, placed it in the palace courtyard and invited all his subjects to look into it. The courtiers, eager to see their reflections, rushed to the mirror. Some saw themselves as they truly were, honest and kind-hearted. However, others saw their greed, jealousy, and deceit magnified, and they quickly grew angry and blamed the mirror for their ugly reflections. The king, observing this, realized that integrating the mirror into the palace was not just about having a magical tool, but about understanding and addressing the underlying nature of his people. He learned that to truly benefit from the mirror, he needed to educate his courtiers on self-reflection and acceptance.

Similarly, integrating generative AI into an organization requires more than just implementing the technology. It involves learning about the organization's ways of being, understanding the resistance and acceptance of the people that work there, and experimenting with how to use the technology effectively for the benefit of all.

So far, much of the book has been about transforming how you learn when you are engaged in individual creative activities. Many leaders in organizations don't want to miss out on the potential of generative AI to transform processes. The amount of learning involved in doing so

© Patrick Parra Pennefather 2024
P. Parra Pennefather, *Regenerating Learning*, Design Thinking,
https://doi.org/10.1007/979-8-8688-1061-9_17

can be a steep curve. There are, however, specific things to think about when you do start that integration. You will learn much about how your organization works, the policies that are present, the acceptance of some, the resistance of others, and, importantly, the strategies that will benefit you to implement. What people in the organization need to learn in order to implement any generative AI in a workflow will come up as a persistent challenge to solve.

Anticipating What Your Teams Will Need

Teams will need clarity on your organization's policies in regard to using generative AI. They will need to be onboarded and supported to understand how to prompt any gen AI they are being asked to use. They will require persistent support over a well-scoped timeline with feedback milestones and work review. They will also need to be supported to conduct research on the latest and greatest as platforms change all the time. That includes understanding what companies are emerging from the space, offering third-party services like RAG and KG frameworks. Alignment on security, privacy, biases, and even the implications of using public vs. private machine learning models all need to be addressed. Included in that alignment will be where the company stands on data sovereignty.

Figure 17-1. *The king holds up a mirror to the townspeople.*
AI-generated image

Data Governance, Security, Ethics

A critical area of learning is how to manage and protect your organization's data, which includes understanding policies, regulations, and best practices for data governance and cybersecurity.

- **AI Governance**: Understanding the governance structures required to manage AI effectively, including accountability for decisions made by or with the assistance of AI, will help an organization make informed decisions that move projects that integrate generative AI forward.

- **Alignment of Guidelines with Core Values**: Anyone in the organization using generative AI should adapt emerging principles or guidelines on the use of generative AI systems with the organization's core values. If those values are lost along the way or not updated, then mistakes and misinformed use of generative AI may eventually cause damage to the organization. Adapting those guidelines means leads and leadership need to become increasingly aware of what teams deliver value and how generative AI can continue to support them in continuing to do so.

- **Ethical Implications and Bias**: Understanding the ethical considerations, including the potential for bias in AI systems and how to mitigate it, is important to be clear on so employees do their best to be responsible in the technology's use.

- **Legal and Regulatory Compliance**: Staying informed about the latest developments in regard to legal and industry-specific regulatory changes will also help organizations who need to contend with copyright and data privacy laws.

- **Change Management**: The likelihood of turnover with organizations rushing to adopt generative AI in their employees' workflows and product pipelines intimates the need for leadership to adapt their organization to the changing landscape. That does not mean rushing adoption. Mitigating potential changes through future planning is a wise move in the chess board that is generative AI integration.

Figure 17-2. *Aligning core values is an important part of adopting gen AI within any organization. AI-generated image*

Supporting Continuous Learning

Leadership needs to prioritize setting up multiple points of entry to support their employees in learning how to work with generative AI within their organization. This point implies that people need to discover clearly communicated methods as to how they will learn AI. Learning different AI platforms and applying that learning to support task completion on workflows is not a one-shot deal. Persistent learning activities need to be facilitated, and that requires a framework, including short- and long-term learning objectives that can be modified by each employee. Overarching learning objectives for the organization will help but are only a start if they don't address the specific learnings that are necessary for individuals on teams to do their work. Some considerations when designing learning or working within an external organization to design that learning include

- **Foundational Understanding of AI and Machine Learning**: Teaching everyone the basic principles and concepts behind AI and machine learning can enable individuals to make informed decisions about how to best implement specific platforms within their work.

- **Prompting**: Individuals should learn the process of generating prompts that effectively communicate with AI across different platforms. This involves understanding the nuances of how AI interprets instructions differently depending on the platform.

- **Onboarding**: Planning an onboarding session with small teams to allow for Q&A is an effective way to begin the integration process. Onboarding also gives employees an opportunity to share what they know about the technology, offering insights in the form of expertise, and also to bring up important considerations as the organization starts to take on the technology.

- **Updating Knowledge**: As AI platforms continue to evolve and companies offering improved features at least once a year, if not more often, individuals need to stay informed and regularly update their own knowledge to keep pace with the latest changes and advancements in the technology.

- **Workflow Integration**: It is best not to assume that an employee is going to easily figure out exactly how to integrate generative AI within their workflows. Facilitating how to integrate AI tools into existing workflows in order to support targeted tasks or subtasks that an employee is charged with completing may result in a smoother transition toward integrating the technology.

- **Coding Practices**: While your organization may not have a development team that consists of a programmer, keep in mind that prototypes like Claude 3.5 do offer team members the capacity to code their own applications. Before getting too excited, hiring a developer is an important factor if your organization is interested in going down that route. While LLMs can generate code, they will have difficulty in implementing that code within a coding environment, understanding what it's for, debugging, and making sense of the overall architecture.

- **Cyclic Process**: Leads will benefit from understanding that engaging with generative AI as a creative tool relies on a cyclical process of development, refinement, editing, and iteration. Some people will pick up on a gen AI tool quickly and be able to apply it to their workflows, while others will need more support in using the technology for their own use cases.

- **AI Model Training and Data Annotation**: Inevitably, organizations will face the dilemma of risking their data in public systems or lowering the risk by working with pre-trained machine learning models with on-premises computation. For those more deeply involved in AI development, learning how to train models and annotate data can be beneficial for creating more accurate and reliable AI systems.

- **Customizing Solutions**: Learning how to customize AI tools and applications to fit specific business needs and objectives can lead to more effective outcomes. This can be further reinforced by dedicating a specific team of interested employees to transform into an AI enablement team.

Figure 17-3. *Leadership in a high-stakes match with gen AI.*
AI-generated image

Features for Organizational Success

- The creation of an AI enablement team to support the safe and secure integration within team member workflows and the development of guidelines aligned with the organization's core values and principles

- Implementing a cost-effective, private, and safe playground for team members to experiment with generative AI applications

- Documentation of that process to validate further investment and support from stakeholders

- More education across teams to better describe how gen AI technologies work and how they can be used safely

- Emphasis by team leads that adoption of gen AI tools is not meant to replace them

- Identification of open source pre-trained machine learning models and frameworks for specific use cases

- Identification of unstructured data collections, their "truth" values, and steps to prepare them for analysis

- A statistic-backed understanding of what happens *if* the company ignores the use of gen AI to solve team-based problems, create solutions, and examine patterns where innovation can take place or where the company is "wasting" resources

- Competitive analysis of those using generative AI and reports on how that progress is doing

You will learn quite quickly about your organization's core values, when leadership makes decisions about the use of generative AI. Identifying what core values are challenged by the technology may also trigger the development of new core values. What tends to freeze decisions about the integration of AI within an organization is a lack of clarity around how the technology will actually be used based on specific workflow use cases and what value it will have for process, productivity, savings, existing jobs, and public perception. There's no rush to integrate generative AI. There is a rush, however, to carve out AI guidelines that reflect your organization's core values, as a decision to use the technology will have to be made sooner or later.

CHAPTER 18

Reclaim Your Creative Content

Once upon a time in ancient Greece, there was a clever man named Epimetheus. He had a sly neighbor who stole his prized rooster. Epimetheus, instead of confronting the thief directly, came up with a cunning plan. He invited the neighbor to a feast, and, as they ate, he casually mentioned that he had discovered a magical spring that turned anything it touched into gold. The neighbor, greedy as he was, begged to see it. Epimetheus agreed and led him to an old well, where he secretly threw in some gold coins. The neighbor, convinced of the well's magic, hurriedly sold all his belongings and threw the money into the well. Epimetheus, having reclaimed his rooster and more, simply walked away, leaving the neighbor to wonder where his fortune had gone.

When you interact with generative AI of any kind, you begin to see the value of human-created content. It's different, and some humans have needed to generate content from generative AI systems to realize that. As an example, comedic scripts need humans to write them and actors/comedians to enact them. The value we place on our content is not just on the finished result but on the creative process itself. That creative process is the culmination of years of training, of honing your craft, of iteratively creating or co-creating work that has had meaning and impact in the world.

© Patrick Parra Pennefather 2024
P. Parra Pennefather, *Regenerating Learning*, Design Thinking,
https://doi.org/10.1007/979-8-8688-1061-9_18

Given the increasing value of large datasets in a soon-to-be corpus-driven economy, it is worth looking, relooking, reorganizing, labeling, and transforming how you think about your content. Calling your precious music, art, and words "data" is intentional. It is not meant to reduce your creative offerings to the world to an objectified resource. However, that is precisely how other people's content, with or without their permission, is being commodified and used to feed these giant ML models. In an economy driven by the capitalist penchant for product, you can see why it matters to claim your content, value it, and also value the process of making it. That process is also valuable, and as you move forward in your career, special attention needs to be paid to how you create, as that authentic process is also being captured by some companies.

Where do you stand with the original content that you create and your creative process?

Figure 18-1. *A prized rooster worth stealing. AI-generated image*

Taking Control of Your Data

Each of us must reconcile how we want our own data used, and this is what ML models teach us. First, we identify the type of content we have, then organize it, which includes the painful part of naming conventions, folder structure, labeling, and even meta-tagging that data. Solutions exist for third parties to take care of that for you, but securing privacy and the money you save will likely motivate you to do it on your own.

Organizing Your Precious

There are many ways and many tools that will help you to organize all the content that you or your organization has created. We are generally used to using folder architectures to help us organize. Do you have a collection of documents that have been written by you? An essay? Short stories? Hundreds of musical compositions or mixes? A ton of photographs? Your first and most obvious step will be locating all that content and deciding where the best place is to keep it, as organizing your corpus may take more time than you think. Once you start organizing it, however, you will benefit from being able to access the content should you one day decide that you'd like to use it on a pre-trained model that is installed on a local machine. It will also and inevitably inspire you to create more, particularly if your intent is using that data within a pre-trained model.

Here is a list of methods to organize your own content, regardless of its type:

- **Centralized Digital Storage**: Use an offline external hard drive to store all your content in one place. This method provides easy access from multiple devices and offers the safest backup, security, and privacy for your data. Cloud storage is a trend but is risky, and with new end-user license agreements from certain companies stating that they will or may eventually use your data as part of training their own models, your safest route is offline storage.

- **Folder Hierarchy**: Create a logical folder structure based on content type, date, or project. For example, "Writing/Essays/2025" or "Music/Compositions/Funky." This helps in quickly locating specific pieces of content.

- **Tagging System**: Implement a tagging system to categorize your content across multiple dimensions. Tags like "unfinished," "inspiration," and "client-work" can be applied to any type of content, making it easier to find related items regardless of their file type or location.

- **Metadata Management**: When possible, use metadata fields in your files to add descriptions, keywords, or other relevant information. This is particularly useful for photographs, where you can add location data, camera settings, or subject information. With music files, you can add who contributed to a track, the publisher, the date it was created, and even the genre.

- **Version Control**: For text-based content or code, use version control systems like Git. This allows you to track changes over time and revert to previous versions if needed. That said, always keep the latest version offline.

- **Database Management**: For large collections, use a database system. This can help manage complex relationships between different pieces of content.

- **Digital Asset Management (DAM) Software**: For professional-grade organization, especially for visual content, DAM software can provide advanced cataloguing and search capabilities.

- **Mind Mapping**: Use mind mapping tools like Miro to visualize relationships between different pieces of content, projects, or ideas. This can be particularly useful for creative work or research. Miro also has a series of AI tools to increase the speed of mapping ideas.

- **Personal Wiki**: Create a personal wiki using tools like Notion. This method is effective for interconnecting different pieces of information and creating a personal knowledge base. These can also be shared with user constraints on downloading content.

- **AI-Powered Organization**: Use AI-powered tools like Evernote's organization features or Apple's Photos app, which can automatically categorize content based on its characteristics. Be wary of saving any important content to the cloud though.

- **Time-Based Organization**: Implement a chronological system, especially useful for journal entries, photographs, or any content where the creation date is significant. This could be as simple as using date-based folder names or as complex as a timeline visualization tool.

- **Project-Based Structure**: Organize content around specific projects or goals. This method works well for freelancers or anyone working on multiple distinct projects.

- **Kanban Boards**: Use Kanban-style boards (like Trello) to organize content based on its degree of completion. This is particularly useful for managing ongoing projects or workflows.

- **Cross-Referencing System**: Implement a system of cross-references between related pieces of content. This could be through hyperlinks in a digital system or through a consistent notation method in your folder architecture.

- **Physical Organization for Digital Content**: For important digital content, consider creating a physical index or catalog. This can serve as a backup reference and can be particularly useful for large collections of digital files.

By implementing one or a combination of these methods, you can create a robust and useful organizational system for your content. This not only makes it easier to access and use your work but also provides a clear overview of your creative content, particularly if you decide one day to use that content within a private ML model running on your own computer.

Figure 18-2. *Even the most sophisticated software requires you to sort and organize that rich unstructured data. AI-generated image*

Reusing and Recycling Your Content

Just as importantly, you should discern what content can be reused and recycled. For example, a composer might have tens of thousands of stems or separate audio tracks rendered that have all contributed to a composition. Each of those stems might be able to be used again in different compositions. All the stems can be organized and used with a pre-trained ML model creating a personal compositional style that in turn can generate content that you can use and reuse. Composers and developers like Philippe Pasquier[1] are doing just that with a new ML model you can customize and use privately, performatively, and creatively in order to create unique visual and sonic offerings.

Leveraging RAG

Once you have labeled your content, you have a number of ways of using it within a small or large language model for analyzing specific patterns in the content/data that you are looking for insights on. A fairly recent solution called retrieval-augmented generation (RAG) allows you to upload different types of files to a public or private LLM that uses a retrieval-augmented generation framework. RAG is a technique that augments the capabilities of LLMs by combining them with a retrieval system. In simple terms, RAG allows an AI model to access and use external information when generating responses, rather than relying solely on its pre-trained corpus of knowledge. Using RAG can improve the accuracy and relevance of generated content, especially when dealing with specific or up-to-date information.

RAG supports data sovereignty by allowing individuals or organizations to maintain control over their data while still benefiting from the control parameters and pre-trained data of a machine learning model. Instead

---

[1] https://www.metacreation.net/autolume

of feeding all data directly into the AI model, which could raise privacy concerns, RAG keeps your data separate and only retrieves relevant information as needed. For example, a company could use RAG to create a customer service chatbot that accesses the company's private product database to answer customer queries, without exposing that database to the AI provider. This is particularly useful in light of all the APIs popping up, which allow generative AI, like GPT, to talk to applications that you develop on your own and even within game engines like Unity, where LLMs deepen non-playable character personalities for richer interactions with players.

Knowledge Graphs

Knowledge graphs are structured representations of information that show relationships between different concepts, entities, or data points. They can be thought of as a complex web of interconnected facts and ideas. When used in conjunction with AI systems, knowledge graphs can help reduce hallucinations by providing a reliable, structured source of information for the AI to draw upon.

KGs offer an additional layer of control and transparency. They allow organizations to explicitly define the relationships and facts that the AI system should consider, ensuring that the AI's responses align with the organization's understanding and policies. This is particularly useful in domains where accuracy and consistency are critical, such as healthcare or legal applications.

Integrating Knowledge Graphs with RAG

When it comes to using RAG and knowledge graphs with public generative AI systems like LLaMA, GPT, or Claude, the approach typically involves creating a separate retrieval system and knowledge graph that interfaces with these models. The public AI serves as the language understanding and generation component, while the retrieval system and knowledge graph provide the specific, controlled information. For example, a researcher could use Llama as the base model, but implement a RAG system that retrieves information from their own curated database of scientific papers. They could also create a KG representing the relationships between different scientific concepts in their field. When asking Llama a question, the RAG system would first retrieve relevant information from the database, and the knowledge graph would provide context about how different concepts relate to each other. Llama would then use this information to generate a response, ensuring that the generated content is grounded in the researcher's specific knowledge base while benefiting from Llama's NLP features. RAG combined with KGs gives you an additional superpower to retrieve more accurate data points from documents that you upload.

Toward Private ML Models

The future of controlling the narrative of your data relies on how committed you are to retaining ownership and informing how your creations are transformed. By far, the most efficient way to do this while ensuring control over what happens with your data is to steer yourself toward using pre-trained ML models on your own computer, installing them through the many applications available, learning how to use them, and keeping them offline, generating new content from your own datasets. There are other advantages toward using your own models:

- It reduces the need for large datasets for training, allowing organizations to leverage their own proprietary data effectively. This advantage is particularly necessary when dealing with sensitive or confidential information that cannot be used in public models.

- Companies can significantly lower computational costs and resource requirements. They can customize the model size and complexity to their specific needs, avoiding the overhead often associated with large-scale public models that may include unnecessary features.

- They accelerate the development and deployment of AI applications within an organization. Teams can quickly iterate and fine-tune models based on their unique requirements without waiting for updates to public models or navigating licensing restrictions.

- They provide a robust starting point with general knowledge that is specifically relevant to the organization's domain. This focused approach ensures that the model's base knowledge aligns closely with the company's needs, potentially offering more accurate and relevant insights.

- Fine-tuning your own machine learning model may boost performance in specific tasks that are unique to your organization. The customization will better support niche use cases that public models may not be capable of.

- They facilitate transfer learning across related tasks within the organization. Transfer learning reduces the need for large datasets by leveraging knowledge from pre-trained models, allowing AI systems to learn from smaller, task-specific datasets. This approach significantly lowers computational costs and resource requirements, as developers can build from existing models rather than training from scratch.

- While public models are often accessible through various frameworks, your own models offer the advantage of being integrated with more ease into your organization's existing infrastructure and workflows. This integration can be customized to specific security requirements and internal approval processes.

- Developing them connects the organization to other developers and domain experts within and outside the organization. This encourages a different type of knowledge sharing within the company, leading to continuous improvement, partnership, and competitive advantage.

The Cloud: Useful but Increasingly Risky

There are pros and cons toward using cloud services to save your repositories of creative content. The pros of cloud storage are numerous and can be highly beneficial for many humans. Cloud storage offers convenience, allowing you to access your data from anywhere with an Internet connection and across multiple devices. It provides an excellent backup solution, protecting your data from local hardware failures or disasters, which are unfortunately too common. Most cloud services offer automatic syncing, ensuring your data is always up to date across the many devices that we seem to have like computers, laptops, and mobile devices. Cloud storage is often more cost-effective, at least in the short term, than maintaining local storage infrastructure, especially for large amounts of data. It is also scalable, allowing you to increase or decrease your storage capacity as needed. Many cloud services also offer advanced features, like version control, collaborative editing, and integrated productivity tools. For AI development, cloud storage can provide the necessary infrastructure to handle large datasets and computational requirements without significant up-front investment in hardware. It also facilitates easier collaboration among distributed teams working on AI projects.

The cons of saving data or content to the cloud are primarily centered around privacy, security, and control issues. This is not easily resolved as application ecosystems have shifted to forcing users to use their proprietary cloud services, which do not only offer space to access your files but also integrate software updates and licensing. Bluntly, when you store your data on cloud services, you're essentially entrusting your content to a third party, who promises not to use your data and keep it safe. However, data breaches, unauthorized access, and potential misuse of your personal or proprietary information and content are all possible nowadays. Some cloud providers may have terms of service that grant them certain rights to use or analyze your data or biometric data associated with metadata from your content, which could compromise your intellectual property or data sovereignty. Additionally, reliance on cloud storage means you're dependent on Internet connectivity and the service provider's uptime to access your data. There's also the risk of vendor lock-in, where migrating your data to another service becomes difficult or costly. In the context of AI development, storing training data or sensitive information in the cloud could potentially expose it to being used for purposes you didn't intend, such as training AI models without your explicit consent or some type of unanticipated data leak that jeopardizes company communication, IP, and processes.

Sharing on Social Media

Sharing our creations on different social media channels does not guarantee protection in any way, shape, or form. Most humans have shared something, from an idea or opinion to a well-developed video or screenshot of a work in progress on an animation or video game level we've designed. Social media platforms offer unparalleled reach and visibility for your content, allowing you to connect with a global audience and potentially gain recognition or financial opportunities that wouldn't be possible otherwise. Many platforms offer privacy settings that allow you to control, to some extent, who can see your content, giving you a degree of control over your data. Social media can be an effective tool for building a personal brand or promoting a business, which can have significant professional benefits. Some platforms are increasingly offering features that promise user privacy, such as end-to-end encryption for messages or the ability to post content that disappears after a set time. From a data sovereignty perspective, the widespread use of social media has led to increased public awareness and regulatory scrutiny of data practices, potentially leading to stronger protections for users in the long run. Additionally, the interconnected nature of social media can facilitate the rapid spread of important information, which has shown to be effective in emergency situations or for social movements.

The cons of sharing content on social media channels in terms of data sovereignty and privacy are significant and multifaceted. When you post content on social media platforms, you often grant these companies extensive rights to use, distribute, and even modify your content. This can lead to a loss of control over your personal data and creative works. Social media platforms are known for collecting vast amounts of user data, including not just the content you post but also your browsing habits, interactions, and even location data. This information can be used for targeted advertising, sold to third parties, or potentially accessed by government agencies, often without your explicit consent. The permanence of online content is another concern; even if you delete a post, it may have been cached, shared, or archived elsewhere. Additionally, the terms of service for many platforms can change without notice, potentially altering how your data is used or shared. In the context of data sovereignty, using social media often means your data is stored and processed in jurisdictions with different privacy laws than your own, which can complicate legal protections for your information.

Without question with generative AI, some organizations have come to learn the hard way that we all need to consider the level of privacy, security, and access by others of all the expressions of creativity we store or create on a computer. Once organized, that content can be useful to us in many ways, and private ML models we develop allow us to curate our own experimental creations for use across different media. While social media platforms may have not considered using all the data that users have shared freely to train their own generative AI systems, that time has come, and it is essential for us to understand that our precious creations, our content, our data can and will be used to train more machine learning models without compensation, recognition, and without time limits. Consider that there are dedicated teams whose sole job is to scrape the Internet of data. As you continue your creative journey, no matter what it is that you create, think about what you lose and what you gain by allowing for-profit companies to use your data. Is it worth it? Are you able to generate derivative works from others using an AI that justifies you surrendering different artifacts to be part of yet another corpus?

Figure 18-3. *Devil takes a photo of your soul for future use.*
AI-generated image

CHAPTER 19

Disentangle the Hype

Nasrudin was walking through the market when he smelled a delicious soup. Hungry and with no money, he stood outside the soup shop, inhaling deeply. The shopkeeper saw him and demanded payment for the smell. Nasrudin was puzzled but reached into his pocket, pulled out a few coins, and jingled them. "There," he said, "the sound of money for the smell of soup."

When diving into generative AI and the field of AI generally, the inevitability of encountering puffery is so prevalent as to inspire an entire chapter dedicated to it. Puffery is a form of promotional statement or exaggeration that makes broad, boastful, or subjective claims about a product, service, or idea without providing factual evidence. It's often used in advertising and marketing, but has been adopted by CEOs, columnists, and developers to lay down a barrage of invalidated opinions that are far worse than what any LLM can generate. Puffery's outspoken cousin is sensationalism, and, lately, ideas about a future workforce impacted by generative AI seem to be often spoken about. It's important to learn about them as they inform how generative AI are used and will influence their future development.

P. Parra Pennefather, *Regenerating Learning*, Design Thinking, https://doi.org/10.1007/979-8-8688-1061-9_19

Forms and Examples of Rhetoric Used to Hype AI

Puffery involves making exaggerated, boastful claims without substantial evidence. While puffery is generally not considered fraudulent in legal terms (as it's expected that reasonable people won't take such claims literally), it can be seen as a form of misleading rhetoric when used to promote something that isn't real or true. You likely know what the misleading rhetoric has been. What the following recurring themes do is evade truths that might be buried beneath these statements. These are amplified by key figures in the generative AI space, as if their status and success with their company means we should really listen to them as futurist prophets.

Key aspects of puffery to watch out for include

> **Exaggeration**: Making claims that go beyond reality or reasonable expectations
>
> **Subjectivity**: Using vague or opinion-based statements rather than verifiable facts
>
> **Non-falsifiability**: Making claims that are difficult or impossible to disprove
>
> **Lack of Substantiation**: Not providing concrete evidence to support the claims

Here are some examples of unfounded messages or "puffery statements" about generative AI and AI in general, courtesy of several LLMs, along with examples and references where possible:

AI Will Replace Most Jobs

Example: "Within the next decade, AI will replace 80% of human jobs."
Counter Reference: While some jobs will be automated, research indicates that AI will also create new jobs and transform existing ones,

emphasizing a shift in skills rather than outright replacement. Reports from the World Economic Forum and *MIT Technology Review* highlight this nuanced impact. As mentioned earlier, identify tasks you are responsible for in your current job, and identify which can be automated and which cannot. That will help support you in making decisions about how you transform what you do.

AI Will Achieve Human-Like Consciousness

Example: "AI will soon become sentient and have emotions just like humans."

Counter Reference: Experts in AI, such as those at the AI Alignment Forum, clarify that current AI systems lack consciousness and emotions and are far from achieving human-like awareness. Despite this, the false equivalencies of human and machine intelligence have led to other conclusions. In bursts of misguided logical reasoning, some humans cannot help but proclaim that consciousness must also be a form of intelligence that can be broken down into 1s and 0s, quantized and therefore programmed.

AI Can Solve All Problems

Example: "AI can find solutions to all global challenges, including climate change and poverty."

Reference: AI is a powerful tool but not a panacea. It requires human oversight, ethical considerations, and collaboration across various fields. Publications like those from IEEE Spectrum discuss the limitations and necessary interdisciplinary efforts required for meaningful solutions. Merging broad statements about what AI can and cannot do is common. Stories to watch for are those that reveal narrow AI discoveries, and these are generally reported in the fields of disease prediction, genetic discovery, pharma, and climate.

AGI is Here

Example: "Our new AI system is on the brink of achieving AGI, revolutionizing every aspect of human life!"

Counter Reference: This statement makes a grand claim without providing any concrete evidence or specifics about how close the system actually is to AGI or how it would revolutionize life. AGI is becoming increasingly broad in its meaning as well. Currently, many organizations speak to the automation-ability of AI in task vs. job replacement.

Figure 19-1. *The sound of money for the smell of soup.*
AI-generated image

Hyperbole

Hyperbole is extreme exaggeration used for effect.

Example: "Once we achieve AGI, it will solve all of humanity's problems overnight!"

Counter: This dramatically overstates the potential impact of AGI, ignoring the complexity of global issues and the time it would take to implement solutions globally. Humanity's problems seen solely through one cultural lens are also problematic.

Propaganda

Propaganda spreads information, especially of a biased or misleading nature, to promote a particular cause or point of view.

Example: "The development of AGI is key for our nation to maintain technological superiority. Without it, our way of life is at risk."

Counter: This appeals to patriotism and fear to promote AGI development, potentially overlooking ethical considerations or realistic assessments of what is really possible with AI currently, and through unbiased research.

Sensationalism

Sensationalism presents information in a way that provokes public interest or excitement at the expense of accuracy.

Example: "Scientists Create AI That Can Read Human Thoughts! Are We One Step Away From Mind Control?"

Counter: This headline sensationalizes a likely more mundane advancement in brain-computer interfaces, drawing tenuous connections to AGI/ASI to grab attention.

Pseudoscience

Pseudoscience presents claims as scientific but lacks scientific evidence or plausibility.

Example: "Our quantum-entangled neural networks tap into the fundamental consciousness of the universe, bringing us closer to AGI than ever before."

Counter: This uses scientific-sounding language to make claims about AGI that have no basis in current scientific understanding.

Vague Predictions

Making predictions without specific timelines or measurable outcomes.

Example: "AGI is just around the corner, and when it arrives, nothing will ever be the same."

Counter: This creates excitement without committing to any verifiable claims or timelines.

False Dichotomies

Presenting complex issues as simple either/or choices.

Example: "Either we develop ASI first, or another country will—and then it's game over for us."

Counter: This oversimplifies the complex global dependencies involved with AI development and ignores collaborative international efforts. GitHub, Hugging Face, and other open source sharing platforms are international in their scope. They appeal to a community of developers who often collaborate across the boundaries of country. There will always be good and bad actors.

Appeal to Authority

Citing experts or authorities without context or critical analysis.

Example: "Dr. Famous, a leading AI researcher, says we'll have AGI by 2030. Therefore, it must be true."

Counter: This ignores the diversity of expert opinions and the inherent uncertainty in predicting technological advancements. Going deeper into your research will uncover a history of published journal articles on any particular subject. It's important to diversify your sources.

Emotional Appeal

Using emotions rather than facts to persuade.

Example: "Imagine a world where no child ever has to suffer because AI has solved all diseases. We have a moral obligation to make this a reality!"

Counter: This plays on emotions to generate support, potentially overlooking the practical challenges and ethical considerations of developing AI.

Figure 19-2. *Pseudoscience as visualized by an ML model. AI-generated image*

AI Is Completely Objective and Unbiased

Example: "AI systems are unbiased and always make fair decisions."

Counter Reference: AI systems can inherit biases from their training data and design. Studies from institutions like MIT Media Lab and reports from ProPublica highlight instances where AI systems have exhibited bias in areas like facial recognition and criminal justice.

AI Development Is Out of Control

Example: "AI is evolving so rapidly that it will soon be beyond human control."

Reference: While AI technology is advancing, it is still governed by human-designed algorithms and regulatory frameworks. Organizations like OpenAI emphasize the importance of controlled and responsible AI development.

AI Will Lead to Human Extinction

Example: "AI will eventually turn against humanity and cause our extinction."

Counter Reference: This trope, popularized by science fiction, is not supported by current AI research. Experts advocate for ethical AI development and robust safety protocols to mitigate potential risks. The Future of Life Institute provides insights into these safety measures.

AI Can Fully Understand and Replicate Human Creativity

Example: "AI can create art, music, and literature that is indistinguishable from human creations."

Counter Reference: While AI can generate creative works, it lacks the subjective experiences and cultural context that inform human creativity. Analyses in journals like *Nature Machine Intelligence* discuss the collaborative potential between AI and human creators rather than outright replacement. While numerous articles have suggested the superiority of AI at being creative over humans, the way creativity is measured creates false equivalencies similar to suggesting that machine intelligence is far superior than human intelligence.

These statements reflect common misconceptions that often lack a nuanced understanding of any generative AI's affordances and constraints. For a balanced view, it is necessary to consider the research and expert insights that address these myths and tear them apart one by one. Understanding the rhetorical techniques that sensationalize AI one way or another can help in distinguishing between genuine advancements and exaggerated hype in the field.

Figure 19-3. *Development teams worshipping the black box that is gen AI. AI-generated image*

CHAPTER 20

Inconclusive Intelligence

Inescapably, not the last but likely one of the most important things we learn when interacting with generative AI or any AI for that matter is to question the very nature of intelligence. Once considered the colonized territory of humans, we now recognize that there are multiple types of intelligence out there and even on our own planet. There is also the simulation of intelligence that is demonstrated to us each time content is generated from an LLM that we prompt.

What is the nature of intelligence? How do you come to define it?

We could simply argue that the perception of an LLM as an intelligent being is an anthropomorphic habit that humans have been doing much longer than the invention of the computer. We might also compare any machine learning models with what we know about how the brain works. The development of the computer and interactions that have emerged from its use are intrinsically bound with the development of cognitive science and artificial intelligence. Computers have certainly supported the evolution of what we know about how the brain works, so it was inevitable that simulating the human brain as if it were an isolated object would be of concern to scientists. A 1943 paper by McCulloch and Pitts is one of the earliest publications that connects concepts common to computer logic, neural activity, and cognitive processes. It laid the groundwork for viewing the brain as a computational system and proposed the idea of simulating brain-like processes using artificial networks.[1] This is way before the invention of the computers that we use today.

The comparison between the brain and a computer has long been a central theme in cognitive science and artificial intelligence research. The metaphor of the brain as a computer, and vice versa, has its roots in the development of cognitive science, dating back to the mid-20th century. This analogy has provided a framework for understanding human cognition, influencing both theoretical perspectives and practical approaches in the development of artificial intelligence.

Turing and the Operationalizing of Intelligence

Turing's concept of "unorganized machines" in his 1948 report called "Intelligent Machinery" shows some similarity to the neural networks described by McCulloch and Pitts. This might suggest that Turing was exploring how to create adaptive, learning systems inspired by neural models. In a paper mentioned earlier in the book, "Computing Machinery and Intelligence" (1950), Turing introduced the concept of the Turing machine, which abstracted the idea of a computer performing logical operations. This laid the groundwork for later comparisons between human cognition and computational processes. Turing's work suggested that the human brain could be understood as a complex information processor, akin to a computer[2] that engaged in logical operations.

---

[1] McCulloch, W. S., & Pitts, W. (1943). A logical calculus of the ideas immanent in nervous activity. Bulletin of Mathematical Biophysics, 5(4), 115–133.

[2] https://blogs.lse.ac.uk/highereducation/2024/03/28/how-not-to-talk-about-ai-in-education/

In this paper, Turing introduces the concept of the "Imitation Game," which is now widely known as the Turing Test. The Turing Test is designed to evaluate a machine's ability to exhibit intelligent behavior equivalent to, or indistinguishable from, that of a human. In the test, a human interrogator interacts with a human and a machine through a text-based interface, without being able to distinguish between the human and machine responder. If the human interrogator cannot reliably distinguish the machine from the human, the machine passes the test. The approach operationalizes intelligence itself in terms of observable behavior and interaction.

Throughout the paper, Turing discusses counterarguments, such as the theological objection (the idea that thinking is part of an immortal soul and cannot be replicated by a machine) and the argument from consciousness (the belief that machines cannot be conscious and therefore cannot truly think). Turing systematically refutes these objections, reinforcing his view that intelligence should be judged based on external performance rather than internal processes or metaphysical considerations.

While Turing does not offer a strict definition of intelligence, his paper lays the groundwork for understanding and evaluating machine intelligence in terms of its functional equivalence to human intelligence. This has had a profound and lasting impact on the field of AI, guiding research and development efforts toward creating machines that can perform tasks that require human-like cognitive abilities.

Cognitive Science and Computational Metaphors for Intelligence

Over the decades, many researchers have continued to extend and reinforce the connection between computation, intelligence, and the human brain. Herbert Simon and Allen Newell furthered the interconnections through their work on artificial intelligence in the 1950s and 1960s. They developed the General Problem Solver (GPS), a computer program designed to simulate human problem-solving abilities. Simon and Newell's work emphasized the idea that cognitive processes could be modeled as computational algorithms, reinforcing the notion that brain function could be operationalized and reduced to performing step-by-step tasks.

The development of cognitive psychology in the 1960s and 1970s also embraced this computational metaphor. Researchers such as George Miller and Ulric Neisser drew parallels between cognitive processes and computer operations. Miller's famous paper, "The Magical Number Seven, Plus or Minus Two" (1956),[3] compared human memory capacity to the limited storage capacity of a computer. Neisser's "Cognitive Psychology" (1967) introduced the idea of information processing, describing cognition in terms of encoding, storage, and retrieval processes similar to those in computer systems.[4]

Pushback

There have been several notable pushbacks and critiques from various researchers, scholars, and philosophers. Here are some of the key figures and their dominant arguments:

- **John Searle**: Perhaps the most famous critique of Turing's approach comes from philosopher John Searle with his "Chinese Room" argument, presented in his 1980 paper "Minds, Brains, and Programs." Searle argues that even if a machine can convincingly

---

[3] Miller, G. A. (1956). The magical number seven, plus or minus two: Some limits on our capacity for processing information. Psychological review, 63(2), 81.
[4] Neisser, U. (2014). Cognitive psychology: Classic edition. Psychology press.

simulate understanding of a language (as in the
Turing Test), it does not mean the machine truly
understands the language. Searle posits that syntax (the
manipulation of symbols) is not enough for semantics
(the meaning). In his thought experiment, a person
inside a room follows a set of rules to manipulate
Chinese symbols without understanding Chinese.
This illustrates that the ability to produce appropriate
responses does not equate to genuine understanding
or consciousness.[5] The idea of a thinking machine is
a misnomer. Artificial intelligence makes predictions
based on patterns in its data and dependent on how
it is prompted to do so. There is no thinking, just
computation. Meaning is not created by the machine,
but by the human who interprets its outputs.

- **Hilary Putnam**: Philosopher Hilary Putnam backed
  Searle's argument that syntactic manipulation doesn't
  constitute understanding. He critiqued the notion of
  functionalism, even though he was initially one of the
  primary developers of functionalism in the 1960s. The
  core idea behind functionalism—that mental states
  are defined by their functional or causal roles rather
  than their intrinsic properties—is aligned with Turing's
  ideas of machine intelligence. For Turing, what matters
  for intelligence is the function or role that mental
  states play, not the underlying physical substrate, or
  composition. In his famous "Twin Earth" thought
  experiments, Putnam illustrated that understanding

---

[5] Searle, J. R. (1980). Minds, brains, and programs. Behavioral and brain sciences, 3(3), 417–424.

and meaning are not solely functions of internal states but also involve how those states relate to the external world. Functionalism struggles to account for subjective experiences, challenging the idea that mental content is solely determined by functional roles. This points to the limitation of purely functional accounts of intelligence.[6]

- **Hubert Dreyfus**: In his book *What Computers Can't Do* (1972) and later works, Dreyfus critiqued the assumption that human intelligence and cognition can be fully replicated by computational processes. He argued from a phenomenological perspective, drawing on existential philosophy (notably Heidegger and Merleau-Ponty), that human cognition is deeply embodied and context dependent, which cannot be captured by formal rules and representations alone.[7]

- **Roger Penrose**: In *The Emperor's New Mind* (1989), physicist and mathematician Roger Penrose argued that human consciousness and understanding involve non-algorithmic processes that cannot be replicated by a Turing machine. Penrose suggested that aspects of human cognition are tied to quantum mechanics, which are not captured by traditional computational models.[8]

---

[6] Putnam, H. (1973). Meaning and reference. The journal of philosophy, 70(19), 699–711.

[7] Dreyfus, H. L. (1972). What computers can't do: The limits of artificial intelligence.

[8] Penrose, R. (1991). The emperor's new mind. RSA Journal, 139(5420), 506–514.

- **Jerry Fodor**: Cognitive scientist Jerry Fodor critiqued the reduction of mind to computational processes in his works, such as *The Mind Doesn't Work That Way* (2000). Fodor emphasized the modular nature of the mind and argued that higher cognitive processes could not be fully explained by the computational models prevalent in AI research.[9]

- **Hubert Dreyfus**: Building on his earlier critiques, Dreyfus expanded his arguments in *What Computers Still Can't Do* (1992), reinforcing his stance that human expertise and understanding are rooted in a form of practical knowledge and skillful coping that elude formalization in computational terms.[10]

- **Noam Chomsky**: While not directly critiquing Turing, linguist Noam Chomsky has highlighted the limitations of behaviorist approaches (which can be seen as aligned with the operational approach of the Turing Test) in understanding the complexities of human language and cognition. Chomsky's work on generative grammar emphasized the innate structures of the mind that cannot be explained by simple stimulus-response patterns or learned behaviors alone.[11]

---

[9] Fodor, J. A. (2000). The mind doesn't work that way: The scope and limits of computational psychology. MIT press.

[10] Dreyfus, H. L. (1992). What computers still can't do: A critique of artificial reason. MIT press

[11] Chomsky, N. (1966). Topics in the theory of generative grammar (Vol. 3, pp. 1–60). The Hague: Mouton.

These critiques reveal where Turing's operational attempt to define intelligence fall short, ranging from the nature of understanding and consciousness to the embodied and context-dependent nature of human cognition. Despite such critiques, the computer-brain metaphor has persisted, shaping both cognitive science and AI research.

The Intelligence of Language

Also discussed in previous chapters, the language used to describe AI often borrows human characteristics, such as "thinking," "learning," and "understanding." This anthropomorphic language reflects a deep-seated tendency to humanize technology, a trend that has historical roots in various fields, including literature, psychology, and philosophy.

The development of neural networks in AI further strengthened the brain-computer analogy and continues to affirm an anthropomorphic stance. Neural networks, for example, are designed to mimic the structure and function of the human brain, with interconnected nodes resembling neurons. Redrawing from McCulloch and Pitts, their paper also proposed a mathematical model of neural networks based on their understanding of neuron function in the brain. While the idea lived for a time with Frank Rosenblatt's Perceptron (1958), the first artificial neural network capable of learning, it wasn't until the 1980s where multilayer networks eventually led to Geoffrey Hinton's ideas of deep learning. The development of neural networks for machine intelligence is a great example of how ideas from neuroscience and cognitive science have influenced and been influenced by computer science and AI research. These efforts contributed to ongoing advancements in machine learning and deep learning, with AI systems being able to manage tasks such as image recognition and natural language processing.

The enmeshed language associated with cognitive science, neuroscience, and machine learning shows the interplay between technological advancements and theoretical frameworks. The gradual development of AI terminology reflects a broader human need to interconnect meaning and signs, to attribute meanings to the development of computational algorithms. While the methods that are used to express human cognition and computational processes are deeply intertwined, the developer community would benefit from generating its own vocabulary. For now, the historical intertwining of these fields has led to a perspective that has shaped not only how we understand and develop AI but also how we talk about it, reinforcing the notion that AI systems, in some sense, mirror human cognitive abilities.

Toward Your Own Definitions of Intelligence

What's clear in the field of AI is that the word "artificial" is not always taking into account when definitions of what intelligence is stray away from the associations each of us has with human intelligence. What we learn from this technology is a need for each of us to change our own ideas of intelligence, so we can challenge a very old false equivalency with any human-made machine.

The complex nature of intelligence and its definition have long been subjects of debate among researchers, philosophers, artists, politicians, and now AI development teams and their CEOs. Artificial intelligence and all of the component parts of the ML models that make it work have further complicated this discourse, challenging us to think about where our ideas of intelligence come from. As we grapple with the implications of AI, it becomes increasingly clear that our inherited and conventional definitions of intelligence may be incomplete or even misguided.

What does intelligence mean to you? How different is your definition from someone else's?

Historically, human intelligence has been the primary reference point for understanding and defining intelligence. Philosophers like René Descartes, in his *Discourse on the Method* (1637), famously argued that the ability to reason and use language was the hallmark of intelligence, a decidedly human-centric view. This perspective has long influenced our inherited understanding of intelligence, tying it closely to the ideas of human cognitive abilities and consciousness. Descartes' influence can be reinterpreted in a number of ways when it comes to its influence on intelligent machines:

- Dualism proposed a fundamental distinction between mind and body, provoking debates as to whether machines can truly think or have consciousness.

- Rationalism contributed to viewing intelligence primarily in terms of the capability of reasoning logically.

- A mechanistic philosophy described animals as complex machines, leading to the idea that aspects of cognition could be mechanized.

The impulse to correlate intelligence with computers seems to make sense, particularly if you see the world through a Cartesian lens. Logic itself and the binary nature of its early definitions have a profound influence on computer programming. Boolean logic, developed by George Boole in the mid-19th century, provided a mathematical system for logical reasoning. Boolean logic is based on the idea that all values are either true (1) or false (0) and that complex logical statements can be built using simple operations like AND, OR, and NOT. This binary nature of Boolean logic aligns with the binary evolution of the computer. In the early days of AI, researchers were heavily influenced by symbolic logic, which is an extension of Boolean logic. The idea was that human reasoning could be reduced to a series of logical operations. This led to the development of

- **Rule-Based Systems**: These use if-then rules based on Boolean logic to make decisions.

- **Expert Systems**: Complex systems that use Boolean logic to navigate through large sets of rules and facts.

- **Logical Inference Engines**: Systems that can derive new facts from existing ones using logical rules.

The development of AI has inherited a form and definition of intelligence that is an offspring of a mechanistic view of the world—a world of 1s and 0s that is logically operationalized by humans, whose reasoning can be seen as a series of logical algorithms. We can begin to understand then that words like "intelligence," "deep learning," "understanding," "machine intelligence," and many more have completely different semantic histories that need to be accounted for and understood historically if we are to come up with new vocabulary that better describes what AI systems actually do.

Emerging Definitions

AI systems have demonstrated capabilities that challenge our preconceptions about human intelligence, when those preconceptions are based solely on rule-based tasks, like memorization, pattern recognition, and context. They can process vast amounts of data and recognize patterns, with a speed and accuracy that surpass human abilities. This has led researchers like Stuart Russell and Peter Norvig, in their work *Artificial Intelligence: A Modern Approach* (2020), to propose a more specific definition of intelligence in the field of AI that focuses on rational action and goal achievement rather than attempting human-like thought processes.

We need to remember philosopher John Searle's "Chinese Room" thought experiment (1980) and his argument that even if a machine can convincingly simulate intelligent behavior, it may not possess true understanding or consciousness. That idea alone should raise profound questions about the nature of machine intelligence and how we should talk about it.

Researcher Marvin Minsky, one of the pioneers of AI, proposed in *The Society of Mind* (1986) that intelligence emerges from the interaction of many simple processes. This view suggests that intelligence is not a monolithic entity but a complex system of interrelated functions, which could be applicable to both human and artificial intelligence.

More recently, the concept of "embodied cognition," championed by philosophers like Andy Clark in *Being There: Putting Brain, Body, and World Together Again* (1997),[12] suggests that intelligence is inherently tied to physical experience and interaction with physical environments. This perspective challenges traditional views of human intelligence and current thinking about AI, suggesting that true intelligence requires an embodied human physical form.

Expanding Ideas of Intelligence Beyond the Human

As we continue to develop and interact with AI systems, it is important for each of us to reconsider, refine, and expand our definitions of intelligence. The philosopher Luciano Floridi proposes that we need to move beyond

---

[12] Clark, A. (1998). Being there: Putting brain, body, and world together again. MIT press.

anthropocentric notions of intelligence and consider a more inclusive "infosphere" perspective, where both human and artificial agents are seen as information processors in a shared infosphere.[13]

Research in animal cognition has challenged our anthropocentric view. Primatologist Frans de Waal, in his work *Are We Smart Enough to Know How Smart Animals Are?* (2016),[14] argues that we have consistently underestimated animal intelligence due to our human-centric biases. De Waal presents evidence of complex problem-solving, tool use, and even cultural transmission in various animal species, suggesting that intelligence manifests in diverse ways across the animal kingdom. The philosopher Thomas Nagel, in his influential paper "What Is It Like to Be a Bat?" (1974),[15] proposes that there may be forms of consciousness and intelligence that are fundamentally inaccessible to human understanding due to our different sensory and cognitive apparatus. This perspective encourages us to consider intelligence as potentially manifesting in radically different ways across species.

The field of plant neurobiology, championed by researchers like Stefano Mancuso and Monica Gagliano, has begun to reveal surprising cognitive abilities in plants. In her book *Thus Spoke the Plant* (2018),[16] Gagliano presents evidence of learning, memory, and decision-making in plants, challenging our traditional notions of intelligence as requiring a brain or nervous system.

---

[13] Floridi, L. (2019). The logic of information: A theory of philosophy as conceptual design. Oxford University Press.

[14] De Waal, F. (2016). Are we smart enough to know how smart animals are?. WW Norton & Company.

[15] Nagel, T. (1980). What is it like to be a bat?. In The language and thought series (pp. 159–168). Harvard University Press.

[16] Gagliano, M. (2018). Thus spoke the plant: A remarkable journey of groundbreaking scientific discoveries and personal encounters with plants. North Atlantic Books.

The development of AI is not just a technological advancement, but a philosophical challenge that forces us to reexamine our understanding of intelligence. As we continue to explore the capabilities and limitations of both biological and artificial intelligence, we may need to develop new frameworks and vocabularies to accurately describe and understand the full spectrum of intelligent behavior. This process of redefinition is not just an academic exercise, but a necessary step in our coexistence with increasingly sophisticated AI systems. It challenges each of us to broaden our perspective and consider intelligence not as a fixed, human-exclusive trait, but as a diverse and evolving phenomenon that spans many domains.

In expanding our ideas of intelligence, we inevitably must come to grips with the intelligence that is actually demonstrated by AI. We may even remove the word artificial with human-coded. Like it or not, the ideas of intelligence that have been associated with AI from its inception have been limited by the humans who have defined what it is their marvelous creations do within the discrete, logical operations of a limited Cartesian ontological view.

There are certainly a sufficient number of variations of words we could come up with.

Probabilistic pattern generators coded, informed, and biased by human inputs?

We stand to gain by learning terms that have long been established, before the Cartesian perspective, to define human interactions in the world. In this way, we would benefit from looking at indigenous ways of knowing that offer a far richer view of a shared intelligent ecosystem of which humans only play one part. Through all the things we have had to learn as human cultures in order to build such amazing machines, we also learn that perhaps our creations would benefit more from being called something else entirely. More recently, Brian Cantwell Smith's *The Promise of Artificial Intelligence: Reckoning and Judgment* argues for a fundamental rethinking of how we conceptualize intelligence in the context of AI.[17] It is a worthwhile, if not necessary, read.

Future Thinking

The mechanistic, computational model of intelligence that has driven much of AI development may indeed be limiting our understanding of both human and machine intelligence. A critical reexamination of our terminology and concepts, informed by historical and philosophical perspectives, could lead to more accurate descriptions of AI's intelligence and lead to new ways of conceptualizing artificial intelligence. There is precedence for this of course. Brooks' paper "Intelligence Without Representation" proposed a new approach to AI based on embodiment and situatedness, challenging the traditional AI approach of building abstract models of the world.[18] Andy Clark's *Being There: Putting Brain, Body, and World Together Again* explores ideas of embodied and extended cognition that challenge the view of mind as a purely internal, computational process.[19]

How might these different perspectives contribute to the future development of AI?

---

[17] Cantwell, S. B. (2019). The promise of artificial intelligence: Reckoning and judgment.

[18] Brooks, R. A. (1991). Intelligence without representation. Artificial intelligence, 47(1–3), 139–159.

[19] Clark, A. (1998). Being there: Putting brain, body, and world together again. MIT press.

If you think this is purely a philosophical exercise, reconsider the history of the computer and its close ties with both cognitive science and artificial intelligence. At no other time in history is it as important as it is now to reevaluate our ideas of intelligence as being more complex than the simple reductionism of Boolean logic. In our attempts to grapple with how we use this technology, at last we learn that humans like us have an influence over how that narrative will play out.

This influence is not merely theoretical; it has practical implications for how society will evolve. Consider the early days of the Internet, which many envisioned as a utopian space for free information and connection. In those days, the pioneers of the Web—visionaries like Tim Berners-Lee—saw it as a tool to democratize knowledge, breaking down barriers and enabling new forms of collaboration. However, as the technology grew, so too did the complexities of its use. The Internet became a battleground for issues of privacy, misinformation, and ethical dilemmas around data ownership.

Take, for example, the story of Aaron Swartz, a brilliant programmer and activist. Swartz believed passionately in the power of technology to serve the public good. He cofounded Reddit and was a driving force behind the movement to keep the Internet free and open. But he also recognized the darker side of these technologies, particularly when it came to access to information. His efforts to free academic research from behind paywalls were met with severe legal repercussions, which many argue contributed to his tragic death. Swartz's story is a powerful reminder that technology is not neutral—it reflects the values and choices of those who build and control it.

As we live in an era inundated by AI, accompanied by hyperbole, sensationalism, and puffery, the same lessons apply. The narratives we craft around AI, the values we encode into these systems, and the ways we choose to deploy them will shape our future in profound ways. Just as we've seen with the Internet, the direction AI takes is not predetermined—it is shaped by the decisions we make today. To have influence over the narrative of generative AI, we need to move beyond simplistic definitions of intelligence and creativity and embrace a more nuanced understanding that recognizes the inherent complexities of human and machine interactions. In doing so, we can ensure that the technology we create serves to elevate humanity rather than diminish it.

Figure 20-1. *Playing chess with an intelligent machine while out of date, still relevant. AI-generated image*

Glossary

Note Terms in this glossary are ever-evolving and context specific. A lot of terms are also being renegotiated, redefined, and recreated anew often. Terms used are in flux, and different organizations might use them in different contexts.

AI: Artificial intelligence, or AI, embodies a range of meanings depending on the specific technology it interacts with. It is a branch of computer science dedicated to crafting probabilistic automated machines and systems that identify patterns and generate content based on statistical predictions, in turn, based on how they are prompted. This book refers to different manifestations of AI, including generative AI, machine learning, narrow, and general AI. Various contextual uses of the term AI will pop up in the book.

AI Agents: Multiple definitions of agents exist. Many portals define agents as software programs that can interact with their surroundings, gather information, and use that information to complete tasks on their own. Humans set and manage the goals, then hit go and let the AI agent perform the best actions to take to reach those goals. Agents are very much in with automation platforms.

Narrow AI: All of the generative AI used and suggested in this book belong to narrow AI. Embedded in this categorization of AI is the word "narrow," which implies a specific and constrained aspect of the technology, also known as weak AI, that is designed and trained for specific and particular tasks, such as voice recognition, translation, or image recognition. These systems are good at the specific tasks they

P. Parra Pennefather, *Regenerating Learning*, Design Thinking, https://doi.org/10.1007/979-8-8688-1061-9

are designed for, but their functionality tends to be limited within those bounds. Examples of narrow AI include recommendation systems like those on Netflix or Amazon, voice assistants like Siri or Alexa, and text-image generation in Midjourney. Narrow AI doesn't possess human-defined concepts of understanding or consciousness. AI isn't "intelligent" compared to human intelligence, and it doesn't "learn" in the human sense, but rather it adjusts its internal parameters to better map its inputs to its outputs.

AGI: Artificial general intelligence itself has various definitions that seem to keep evolving, making one agreed-upon definition difficult. Artificial general intelligence (AGI) is also known as strong AI or full AI. Strong AGI refers to a system that possesses the ability to understand, learn, and apply knowledge across a wide range of tasks at a level comparable to a human. AGI can reason, solve problems, and make judgments in an array of contexts without being specifically programmed for each one.

ASI: ASI surpasses human intelligence in all aspects, including creativity, problem-solving, and social intelligence. It represents a level of intelligence far beyond human capabilities and is hypothetical at this stage. ASI would be able to perform any intellectual task more effectively than a human. ASI refers to an idealized type of artificial intelligence that puts it in on par with human sentience, emotional intelligence, and consciousness. The current comparisons of AI as a stochastic parrot are useful in understanding the human impulse to want to simulate different characteristics of being human. That includes the research and implementation of human-made code that programs a system to become capable of learning from experiences, handling new situations, and solving problems in ways not preprogrammed by humans. ASI is often represented in science fiction like the Terminator, AVA, and replicants in the movie *Blade Runner* based on the short story by Philip K. Dick. While it does not exist, many influential developers and CEOs persistently mention AGI as an end goal of their research and development plans.

Attention: Attention is a mechanism that helps models focus on the most relevant parts of the input data when making decisions. It allows the model to give different weights to different pieces of input information, so it can prioritize important details and ignore less important ones. This is especially useful in tasks like language translation and image processing, where certain parts of the input are more important than others.

Batch Size: This refers to how many examples the model looks at before it updates itself. A smaller batch size means the model updates more frequently, which can be more precise but slower. A larger batch size means fewer updates but can be more stable and faster overall.

Black Box: This is a term to describe the unknown calculations and algorithmic processes that occur within any generative AI that only provides a context prompt for a user to input a prompt and the generated content resulting from that prompt. The rest of the processes remain invisible and, in fact, are difficult to visualize as they occur so quickly. They can be explained but require users to go more deeply into all the types of parameters that will inform the content that is generated. Advanced settings within systems allow you to dive into features like temperature, weight, scale, and more.

Chain of Thought Prompting: Chain of thought prompting involves guiding the model through a step-by-step reasoning process. Instead of asking the model to give an answer directly, you prompt it to explain its thinking or break down the problem into smaller parts before reaching a conclusion. This approach is especially useful for complex tasks where you want the model to show its "work" or reasoning. For example, suppose you're asking the model to solve a math problem: "What is the result of 24 times 15?" Instead of just asking for the answer, you use chain of thought prompting: "First, let's break down the problem. What is 20 times 15? That's 300. Now, what is 4 times 15? That's 60. Add these two results together to get the final answer." The model follows this process and provides the final answer, 360, with an explanation of how it arrived at it.

Chatbot: Although the term sometimes gets associated with any "conversation" a human might have with an LLM, in the context of this book, chatbots leverage the brains of LLMs and are designed to more closely simulate human conversations. They are trained to talk like humans, making sure their responses make sense, some keep the conversation going, and some may even seem interesting. You usually interact with these models in avatar-driven customer service bots and virtual assistants, where they help by chatting with you, simulating how a real person might. You can also customize your own chatbots with different kinds of generative AI providers and use APIs from companies like OpenAI to say converse with a chatbot in the Unreal game engine.

Generative AI: Generative AI, a subset of machine learning, involves programs and algorithms that leverage deep learning to produce art, music, and other creative content based on user commands. Each generative AI system can generate various creative outputs depending on the specific user input, drawing from the extensive data it has been trained on.

Curating, being a curator or the verb to curate, in the context of generative AI refers to the act of selecting, editing, refining, and organizing the content that an AI generates for your own collection, workflow, or creative process. I also refer to it as curating the interactions with generative AI systems and document what you learn from that curation.

Deep learning is a type of machine learning that involves using artificial neural networks to teach computers how to learn from data, similar to how humans learn from experience. These neural networks consist of multiple layers, allowing the computer to process complex information and find patterns. Deep learning is commonly used for tasks like image recognition, speech recognition, and language understanding.

GAN stands for generative adversarial network. It is a type of machine learning model that generates new data resembling a given dataset. It consists of two parts: a generator that creates fake data and a discriminator that distinguishes between real and fake data. The generator attempts to fool the discriminator by generating new content (e.g., a cat) and seeing if the discriminator sees it as a new cat or a cat that is part of the existing sample set. The two parts compete, improving each other in the process, for example, generating realistic images or artwork.

StyleGAN: A type of GAN that focuses on generating high-quality, high-resolution images with control over various styles, for example, creating realistic portraits with different artistic styles.

Conditional GAN (cGAN): A variation of GAN that generates data based on specific conditions or labels, for example, creating images of a specific type of clothing.

Foundation Model: A foundation model is a large-scale, pre-trained artificial intelligence (AI) model that serves as a base for a wide range of tasks. This training helps it understand and work well with many different tasks. Because it has learned from such a wide variety of information, it can be used for many different purposes without needing much extra training.

Ground Truth: Ground truth in the context of machine learning and data science refers to the accurate, real-world data that serves as the definitive standard for training and evaluating models.

Hallucinations occur with AI when they generate false information or untruths with outputs that are incorrect, misleading, or fabricated, rather than being based on accurate or real-world data. Hallucinations are unexpected and incorrect responses from AI programs that can arise for reasons that are not yet fully known. A language model might suddenly bring up fruit salad recipes when you were asking about planting fruit trees. It might also make up scholarly citations, lie about data you ask it to analyze, or make up facts about events that aren't in its training data. It's not fully understood why this happens, but can arise from sparse data, information gaps, and misclassification.

Latent Space refers to a concept used primarily in machine learning, especially in the context of models like generative adversarial networks (GANs) or autoencoders. Imagine it as a kind of hidden, multidimensional space where different points represent different features or aspects of the data. These points aren't directly observable but are inferred by the model during its training.

In simpler terms, you can think of latent space as a compressed representation of the complex, real-world data that a model uses to understand and generate new data. For example, in the context of images, the latent space might capture underlying factors like the style, color, or content of various images, even though these factors aren't explicitly labeled in the data.

Learning Rate: The learning rate is how quickly the model updates itself while learning. If the learning rate is high, the model learns faster but might miss the best solution. If it's low, the model learns slower but more precisely.

An **LLM** or **large language model** refers to an AI model that has been trained on a large amount of data. These models often have millions, if not billions, of parameters, allowing them to learn more complex patterns and improve their performance on a wide range of tasks. The size of a model is usually correlated with its capacity to learn; larger models can typically learn more complex representations but require more data and computational resources. Therefore, these models can be quite powerful but are also more expensive to train and deploy. ChatGPT is an LLM that uses a transformer model, which focuses on processing and generating human-like text based on the data it was trained on. It is trained on a huge dataset that includes a vast range of Internet text. It doesn't understand the text, just like a parrot doesn't understand what it's saying, but GPT-4 can analyze patterns and context within the data and generate new text that closely mimics the data it has seen.

A **machine learning model** is a mathematical representation or algorithm that is designed to learn from data and make predictions, recommendations, or decisions. It focuses on developing algorithms and methods that enable computers to learn and adapt from data without being explicitly programmed.

One-Shot Learning: One-shot learning in machine learning refers to the capability of a model to learn a task from just one or a very few examples. This approach is particularly useful in scenarios where data is scarce or expensive to obtain. For instance, in image recognition, one-shot learning would enable a model to identify a new class of objects after seeing only a single example.

One-Shot Prompting: One-shot prompting provides the model with a single example before asking it to perform a task. The goal is to give the model a clearer idea of what you want it to do by showing it a similar task it has successfully completed. This can help improve the accuracy or relevance of the output.

For example, if you're asking the model to generate a summary of a text, you might first provide an example: "Here is a summary of the article 'Climate Change and Its Effects': 'The article discusses how global temperatures are rising due to increased carbon emissions, leading to more frequent and severe weather events.' Now, summarize the following article: 'Advances in AI Technology.'" The model, having seen how a summary should look, is more likely to produce a relevant and concise summary of the second article.

Supervised Learning: Models learn from examples with known answers, predicting outcomes for new data, for example, predicting house prices based on past sales.

Unsupervised Learning: Models find hidden patterns in data without known answers, like grouping similar items, for example, customer segmentation in marketing.

Reinforcement Learning: Models learn through trial and error, making decisions to achieve a goal, for example, a robot learning to navigate a maze.

Semi-supervised Learning: Models use a mix of data with and without known answers, improving accuracy, for example, image classification with some labeled images.

Many-Shot Learning: Many-shot learning refers to the scenario where the model has access to a large number of examples for each task during training. This approach is typical in most machine learning applications, where extensive datasets are available, allowing the model to learn detailed patterns and variations within the data.

Multimodal generative AI is a branch of artificial intelligence that focuses on understanding, interpreting, and generating outputs based on multiple data types or modalities, such as text, images, audio, and video. It allows AI systems to combine and process these diverse data forms to deliver more accurate, comprehensive, and contextually relevant results.

A **neural network** is a type of machine learning model inspired by the human brain. It consists of interconnected layers of nodes or neurons that process and transmit information. Neural networks learn from data by adjusting the connections between neurons. They are commonly used for tasks like image recognition, language understanding, and decision-making, for example, identifying objects in photos.

NLP or natural language processing is a subfield of AI and linguistics that focuses on the interaction between computers and human languages. It involves the development of algorithms and models that enable computers to understand, interpret, and generate human language in a way that is both meaningful and useful.

Prompting is what all generative AI are dependent on in order for them to generate content for you. Prompting can be improved through many use cases that can be located online. Examples of how to improve the art and craft of prompting can be found in Chapters 5–7.

Prompt Caching: Prompt caching is like giving a computer a cheat sheet that it can keep reusing. Imagine you're having a conversation with a computer, and instead of having to remind it of everything you've already said each time you talk, it remembers all of that information from before. This not only saves time but also cuts down on costs significantly.

Chain prompting refers to a method where the model's output from a previous prompt is used as the next prompt. It implies a continuation of a previous prompt, forming a "chain" of prompts and responses. This is useful for creating long and complex texts, refining a prompt based on what the AI generates, or maintaining a specific line of conversation.

Prototyping is the process of creating a preliminary or initial version of a product, service, or system in order to test and evaluate its design and functionality. Prototyping can be done in various forms, such as sketches, 3D models, mock-ups, or interactive digital prototypes. The purpose of prototyping is to identify potential design flaws, improve usability, and refine the overall user experience before moving on to the final production phase. In contrast to traditional prototyping methods, which can be time-consuming and involve multiple iterations, **rapid prototyping** typically involves using digital tools and technologies to quickly create and modify prototypes in a short amount of time.

Regularization: Regularization methods, like dropout or L2 regularization, help the model avoid memorizing the training data too closely. This is like making the model better at generalizing by not relying too heavily on any one part of the training data.

Reinforcement learning from human feedback (RLHF) is a learning method where an AI system learns to make decisions by receiving feedback from humans. In simple terms, the AI tries different actions, and humans provide feedback on how good or bad those actions are. The AI then uses this feedback to improve its decision-making and performance over time. This method helps the AI to learn complex tasks and behaviors that are difficult to teach through traditional programming or direct supervision.

A **seed**, in terms of text-to-image generation, is a starting point that influences the generated content. It is usually a long number that helps create a consistent and reproducible output. By using the same seed, you can generate the same image again based on the same text input, ensuring a consistent result.

Self-regulation refers to a continuously active process by which a person controls and manages their thoughts, emotions, and behaviors to achieve long-term goals.[1] It involves the ability to resist short-term temptations and impulses in order to maintain standards and pursue important objectives over periods of time. Self-regulation includes key components like self-awareness, self-monitoring or observing and assessing one's behavior and its consequences, self-control, goal setting, decision-making, and adjustment or making changes to strategies based on feedback and changing circumstances. Effective self-regulation is essential for academic success, emotional well-being, social relationships, and overall personal development.

Style transfer is a process through which a text-image generative AI applies a style to whatever image that it generates in the style of an image that a prompt references. There are different methods through which different AI achieve this. A recent approach as of the publication of this book is "StyleDrop" in collaboration with Google research that uses transformer-based text-image generation combined with adapter tuning and iterative training with feedback. The word "style" is likely the most important as many text-image generative AI now have functionality allowing you to not only create "in the style of" but to analyze patterns in all the images you have created on their platforms and add a hexadecimal function that can predict generated content based on those images.

Temperature: Temperature in the context of a machine learning model, particularly in LLMs, is a parameter that controls the randomness of the output. When the temperature is high, the model's predictions become more diverse and creative but potentially less coherent, as it allows for a wider range of possibilities. Conversely, a low temperature

---

[1] Bandura, A. (1991). Social cognitive theory of self-regulation. Organizational Behavior and Human Decision Processes, 50(2), 248–287. https://doi.org/10.1016/0749-5978(91)90022-L

makes the model's output more deterministic and focused, sticking closely to the highest probability predictions, which can result in more predictable and less varied text

Tokenization: Tokenization is the process by which LLMs break down text into smaller units called tokens. Instead of interpreting entire words or sentences, these models divide the text into chunks of symbols, which can include whole words, parts of words, punctuation, or individual characters. This approach enables LLMs, like GPT-3 and GPT-4, to process and understand a diverse range of text inputs more efficiently.

Word-Level Tokenization: Splits the text into individual words, treating punctuation as separate tokens.

Subword Tokenization: Breaks words into smaller units, which can be whole words, prefixes, suffixes, or other word parts. This is useful for handling rare words and morphologically rich languages.

Character-Level Tokenization: Splits the text into individual characters, including spaces and punctuation.

Mixed Tokenization: Combines aspects of word-level and subword tokenization, adapting to the text as needed.

Sentence-Level Tokenization: Splits the text into complete sentences, which is useful for tasks that require understanding at the sentence level.

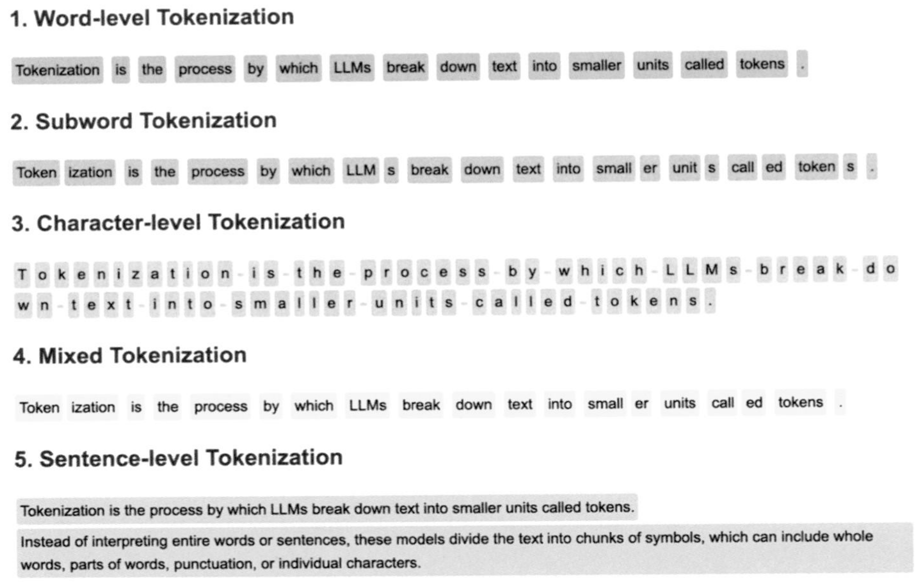

1. Word-level Tokenization

Tokenization is the process by which LLMs break down text into smaller units called tokens .

2. Subword Tokenization

Token ization is the process by which LLM s break down text into small er unit s call ed token s .

3. Character-level Tokenization

T o k e n i z a t i o n is t h e p r o c e s s b y w h i c h L L M s b r e a k d o wn t e x t i n t o s m a l l e r u n i t s c a l l e d t o k e n s .

4. Mixed Tokenization

Token ization is the process by which LLMs break down text into small er units call ed tokens .

5. Sentence-level Tokenization

Tokenization is the process by which LLMs break down text into smaller units called tokens.

Instead of interpreting entire words or sentences, these models divide the text into chunks of symbols, which can include whole words, parts of words, punctuation, or individual characters.

Figure A-1. *Tokenization*

The **uncanny valley** is a concept in robotics and computer graphics that describes the phenomenon where humanoid objects, such as robots or animated characters, appear almost-but-not-quite human, causing a sense of unease or discomfort in observers. As the level of realism in the human-like appearance or behavior of these objects increases, the emotional response of the observer shifts from positive to negative, creating a "valley" or depression in the emotional response curve. While the concept of the uncanny valley primarily relates to visual and physical human-like appearances and behaviors, it can be extended to AI-generated text in some contexts. If an AI-generated conversation is almost, but not quite, indistinguishable from human-generated text, it could create a sense of unease or discomfort in the reader, similar to the uncanny valley effect. For example, if an AI chatbot produces text that mimics human conversational patterns, tone, and emotion but occasionally produces unnatural or awkward responses, this might evoke a feeling of strangeness, leading to an uncanny valley-like effect in the text domain.

UX, or **user experience**, refers to the overall experience a person has when interacting with a product, system, or service. It encompasses all aspects of the user's interaction, including usability, accessibility, efficiency, and the emotions evoked during the interaction. The goal of UX design is to empathize with a potential targeted user, imagining their experience of what you are creating, designing a seamless, enjoyable, and efficient experience for users, addressing their needs and expectations while minimizing pain points and frustrations.

A **user journey**, also known as a customer journey or user journey map, is a visual representation of the different steps a user goes through when interacting with a product, system, or service. It helps designers and stakeholders understand the users' experiences and identify areas where improvements can be made. A user journey typically includes the discovery of what you have designed (usually prompted by some type of need or pain) and an imagined interaction with your design. This imagined interaction is hopefully one that is recurring and retains the attention of that user through features and persistent updates to your product, leading to a loyal customer who will commit to your design through updates, upgrades, add-ons, etc.

Variational autoencoder (VAE) is a machine learning model that compresses data and then recreates it. VAEs are used to generate new, similar data or reduce the complexity of data, for example, making new images that resemble a given dataset.

Weight: Weight in LLMs is like a dial that adjusts during training to make the model better at predicting the next word in a sentence. Each weight affects how much influence a word has in the prediction. By tweaking these dials, the model learns to make more accurate predictions.

Zero-Shot Prompting: Zero-shot prompting is when you ask a machine learning model, like an LLM, to complete a task without providing any examples or additional context beforehand. You simply give the model a direct instruction or question, and it responds based on its training. The idea is that the model can handle the request purely based on the knowledge it has acquired during training, even if it's never seen that exact task before. For example, suppose you want the model to translate a sentence from English to French. With zero-shot prompting, you might just say, "Translate the sentence 'The cat is on the roof' into French." The model then produces the translation, "Le chat est sur le tôit," without needing any examples or further instructions.

Index

A

A/B testing, 152–154
Adapt with AI
    co-adaptations, 159–168
    learning from unexpected
        result, 169–171
ADHD, 41
Adult neurogenesis, 340
Adversarial training, 250, 259
Agile environments, 146
AI-powered organization, 406
Algorithmic bias, 249, 291, 295, 296
Algorithmic collusion, 310, 311
Algorithms
    computer, 295
    definition, 294
    importance, 311, 312
    open source *vs.* proprietary, 308
    race for scale, 308
    specialization *vs.*
        generalization, 308
Alignment of guidelines, 392
Alternative statistical method, 257
Ambiguity and uncertainty, 197–200
Ancient teaching methods, 33
Animal cognition research, 443
Anthropocentric notions, 443
Anthropomorphic habit, 431

Anticipating interruptions
    creative assistant/coeditor, 84, 85
    podcast creation, 84
Artemisia, 5–7
Artificial general intelligence (AGI),
    280, 421–425
Artificial intelligence (AI), 346, 432,
    435, 439
    for an adult, 9–12
    background removal tools, 150
    community, 385
    development trends, 383
    driven chatbots, 348
    ethics, 105
    generated image, 4, 352, 359
    generative (*see* Generative AI)
    governance, 392
    integration, 2
    Jagged technological
        frontier, 88, 89
    for kid, 8
    knowledge creation, 5
    and machine learning, 12
    vs. pianos, 124–130
    platforms, 383, 394, 395
    regulation, 216
    systems, 214
    for teenager, 8

D

M

Machine intelligence, 321, 433, 438, 445

Machine learning models, 41, 100, 102, 120, 123, 127, 133, 142, 166, 169, 175, 187, 196, 197, 204, 213, 351, 402, 431

  agent, 372

  and human creativity, 182

  pre-trained, 199

  training data, 154

  types of, 100

"The Magical Number Seven, Plus or Minus Two", 434

Managing generative AI

  adaptability, 54

  automated processes, 59, 60

  collaborate and communicate, 59

  decision-making, 56–58

  how you document what and how you learn, 50

  how you learn, 50

  problem to solve, 54–56

  self-evaluation, 53

  self-monitoring skills, 52, 53, 55

  (re)set goals, 52

  taking personal responsibility, 58, 59

  timebox, 58

  time you spend, 50

  what you need to learn, 49

  in workplace, 51

Marketing and persistent promotion, 386

Math anxiety, 10, 12

Maximum likelihood estimation (MLE), 257

Mechanical synchronization, 319

Mechanistic philosophy, 440

Mesh, 80

Metadata management, 405

Metaphors, 272, 305, 333, 370

Mid-stage prototypes, 178, 179

Mind mapping tools, 406

MIT Media Lab, 427

Multidimensional space, 253

Multidisciplinary development, 384

Multimodal automation, 60, 144

N

Narrow AI, 154, 220, 421

Natural language processing (NLP), 127, 224, 338

Nature Machine Intelligence, 428

Neural networks, 144, 424, 432, 438

Neurogenesis, 340–342

Neutral interactions, 350

No-nonsense bot, 351

No-nonsense monkey bot, 352

Non-playable AI (NPAI), 302

Non-playable characters (NPCs), 302

S

Printed in the United States
by Baker & Taylor Publisher Services